PRIVATE CONSCIENCES
AND
PUBLIC REASONS

PRIVATE CONSCIENCES
AND
PUBLIC REASONS

KENT GREENAWALT

New York   Oxford
OXFORD UNIVERSITY PRESS
1995

Oxford University Press

Oxford   New York
Athens   Auckland   Bangkok   Bombay
Calcutta   Cape Town   Dar es Salaam   Delhi
Florence   Hong Kong   Istanbul   Karachi
Kuala Lumpur   Madras   Madrid   Melbourne
Mexico City   Nairobi   Paris   Singapore
Taipei   Tokyo   Toronto

and associated companies in
Berlin   Ibadan

Published by Oxford University Press, Inc.,
200 Madison Avenue, New York, New York 10016

Oxford is a registered trademark of Oxford University Press

Library of Congress Cataloging-in-Publication Data
Greenawalt, Kent, 1936–
Private consciences and public reasons / Kent Greenawalt.
p.   cm.
Includes bibliographical references and index.
ISBN 0-19-509418-2; 0-19-509419-0 (pbk.)
1. Religion and politics—United States.   2. Religion and state—
United States.   3. Liberty and conscience—United States.
4. United States—Religion.   I. Title.
BL65.P7G72   1995
323.44'2—dc20   94-11445

1 3 5 7 9 8 6 4 2

Printed in the United States of America
on acid-free paper

To Marija Kargotić Milić and
the memory of Milenko Milić

Their faith in a life together
made ethnic difference a
source of value, not conflict

Preface

When I wrote *Religious Convictions and Political Choice,* I thought I had nothing left to say about the use of religious and other broad philosophical positions for the resolution of political controversies in liberal democracies. I was initially hesitant to accept invitations to speak on aspects of that topic, but I found that when I did, my ideas developed. They also developed in response to the many thoughtful articles and books that have appeared in the seven years since the earlier manuscript was completed. Powerful systematic arguments have now been made for a broad political use of religious and similar premises, against such use of these premises, and for various intermediate positions. Many of these competing approaches have a powerful attraction for me and I rarely feel confident that any of them is definitely wrong. My own intermediate position has become richer and has shifted some over time, and I am more acutely aware of its relation to other issues in political philosophy than I was seven years ago.

This book confronts the arguments for various positions in much more depth than the previous book; it presents my own perspective in finer detail; and it draws connections with other central problems in political philosophy more explicitly. It stands by itself, and can be understood without reference to *Religious Convictions and Political Choice.*

The subject has had a sad personal aspect for me during these years. My late wife, Sanja, the child of a Bosnian Serb father and a Croatian mother, was decidedly against communism, but she was strongly Yugoslav. With the example of her own parents' powerful and happy union and their belief in the country of Yugoslavia, she did not consider the differences between Serbs and Croats to be major ones. She felt great pride at what Yugoslavs and the people of Sarajevo had accomplished with the 1984 Winter Olympics, recalling her university days when she skied at Jaherina, the site of many Olympic events. She died before a tragic chain of events brought wanton cruelty, devastation, and misery to Bosnia, and shattered the hopes and prospects of many people like herself. My sons have a strong identity with the peoples of the former Yugoslavia, born of ties with Sanja and her parents and of easy summers on the shores of the Adriatic Sea. They now bear the turmoil of that land as part of their heritage. It is with thoughts of these events that I have dedicated this book about how liberal democracy responds to cultural and religious diversity to my parents by marriage.

During the past years I have been exceptionally fortunate in the amount and quality of communication with those of differing perspectives. In conferences, seminars, and personal conversation and correspondence, I have talked with Larry Alexander, Robert Audi, Stephen Carter, Edward Foley, Franklin Gamwell, Charles Larmore, Sandy Levinson, Robin Lovin, William Marshall, Thomas Nagel, Michael Perry, John Rawls, Joseph Raz, David Richards, Maimon Schwarzschild, Steven Smith, David Smolin, Lawrence Solum, Jeremy Waldron, and Kenneth Winston. Among these, professors Audi, Foley, Larmore, Nagel, Perry, Rawls, Smith, and Smolin reviewed all or much of the manuscript, offering extremely helpful comments. Substantial differences of opinion among us remain, but I do not believe they are attributable to failures of understanding.

I have previously presented aspects of the subject of this book: the Seventh Annual Lecture of the Center for Church/State Studies, DePaul University, published as "Religious Convictions and Political Choice: Some Further Thoughts," 39 *DePaul Law Review* 1019 (1990); a lecture for the D.R. Sharpe Centennial Conference on Realism and Responsibility in Contemporary Ethics at the University of Chicago Divinity School, published as "Shortfalls of Realism, Shared Social Values, and Authority: The Problem of Political Coercion," 73 *Journal of Religion* 537 (1993); a paper for a conference on The Role of Religion in Public Debate in a Liberal Society at the University of San Diego School of Law, 30 San Diego Law Review 647 (1993); the J. M. Dawson Lectures on Church and State at Baylor University, published as "The Role of Religion in a Liberal Democracy: Dilemmas and Possible Resolutions," 35 *Journal of Church and State* 503 (1993); "The Participation of Religious Groups in Political Advocacy," 36 *Journal of Church and State* 143 (1994); "The Use of Religious Convictions by Legislators and Judges," 36 *Journal of Church and State* 541 (1994). (Related articles are "Religious Groups in Liberal Politics," 12 *Criminal Justice Ethics*, p. 3 (Summer/Fall 1993); and "On Public Reason," 69 *Chicago-Kent Law Review* 669 (1994).) The discussions that followed the oral presentations on these occasions often illuminated aspects of the topic that I had not yet perceived. I also learned a great deal from students in seminars in Political Advocacy and the Liberal State that I taught at Columbia Law School, and a similar seminar during a year I visited at New York University Law School. Elaine Pagels's comments on some of the chapters contributed much to their coherence and clarity.

When the project was close to completion, Andrzej Rapaczynski organized a group of scholars—including Akhil Amar, Mark Barenberg, Vince

Blasi, George Fletcher, Louis Henkin, Charles Larmore, Thomas Nagel, Joseph Raz, Alan Ryan Peter Strauss, and William Young—who read the manuscript, met twice for dinner, and conversed about the topic. I found out I still had a great deal to learn.

I also benefited from the incisive criticisms of Colin Bird, a doctoral student in political philosophy, whose thoughtful challenge to one chapter during a seminar led me to ask him to review the entire manuscript. Sam Mills provided very helpful research assistance. Galina Krasilovsky very ably reviewed the text and footnotes of the manuscript for errors, generously doing so on short notice. Susanne Vikoren, on even shorter notice, searched out items that had not previously been available; she later gave the page proofs a careful review. Without their help, and an exceptionally careful job of copy editing by Maura High, the manuscript would have more errors than I wish to contemplate. Sally Wrigley, with assistance from the Law School's faculty secretariat, kept typing successive versions of the manuscript, with variations of some sections for lectures and articles. She managed to keep everything together, with her usual good spirits.

I am very grateful for financial assistance that enabled me to devote summers substantially to work. These sources of support were the Columbia University Law School Alumni, Mildred and George Drapkin Faculty Research Fund, Stephen Friedman Fund, and the Columbia University School of Law Class of 1932 Law Research/Writing Fund. I have had the good fortune to be a Laurene Rockefeller fellow at the Princeton University Center for Human Values during my final week on the book.

My son, Robert, made helpful criticisms of parts of the manuscript; he and his brothers Sasha and Andrei have been the source of immeasurable support in the nearly six years since Sanja's death.

New York   K.G.
September 1994

Contents

PRIVATE CONSCIENCES
AND
PUBLIC REASONS

1

Introduction

The Fundamental Issues

As the twenty-first century approaches, people in the United States and Western Europe feel a deep unease about their cultures and their politics. Although, internationally, the idea of liberal democracy has triumphed over its only serious modern competitor among political visions, Marxist communism, the citizens of long-standing liberal democracies are far from sanguine about their own societies. At a practical level, racial and ethnic conflict (and domination), poverty and violence are proving distressingly intractable, and relations among men and women are unsettled and unsettling. Many people believe that something is missing at a more fundamental level. In cultures pervaded by a concern for material welfare and the pursuit of advantage for oneself and one's family, the sense of belonging to a community is weak. Those who are self-conscious enough to worry about the absence of community have sharply divergent diagnoses of the problem and have proposed different correctives. Some maintain that communities must be based on widely shared encompassing beliefs about the nature of humanity and about how people should live their lives. Some point to a "decline in spiritual values" as the cause of many social ills and look to the revitalization of religion in politics as the necessary medicine; others propose some nonreligious communitarian ideal around which people can unite in a more cohesive society. A radically opposed view is that we should welcome a wide diversity of ideas of the good life, that the best community is one whose unity is based on the recognition of difference, and that the immediate task is to work for increased tolerance and understanding. These various ideals of community carry corresponding ideals of what is fair within a society. Someone who believes that the state should support a particular vision of life may welcome measures that disadvantage those with competing views and that would seem unfair to a person who believes that the state should be neutral about such matters.

3

The topic of this book is one major subject of conflict in this general debate. What grounds are proper for people making political decisions and arguments within a liberal democracy? Should public reasons be more limited than all that properly counts in private conscience? Should officials, and even ordinary citizens, restrain themselves from relying in public politics on some grounds that appropriately influence them in their private lives and within their nonpublic associations? Do fairness, cohesiveness, and stability suggest that such self-restraint is desirable? Can someone engage in such self-restraint and remain true to his or her larger conceptions of how we should live? These are the critical inquiries of this book. Although constitutional principles bear on parts of the discussion, the book concerns applied political philosophy, not constitutional law.

The central issue is most strikingly posed in the United States by religious convictions that have political implications. Suppose Faith believes that an authoritative religious text indicates that human eating of meat is sinful: should Faith rely on her belief to support stringent regulation of factory farming and should she argue from that belief in the public political realm?[1]

We can quickly identify some positions. At one end of the spectrum is the view that Faith properly relies on whatever sources of moral and political insight she finds relevant. At the other extreme is the idea that citizens and officials in liberal democracies are (implicitly) committed to relying on common, nonreligious sources of guidance. The intermediate possibilities are many: Faith may rely on her religious beliefs if she is an ordinary citizen but not if she is an official; or, Faith may rely on her religious beliefs to reach a political decision, but she should not employ them in public political discussions; or, Faith may rely upon such religious beliefs for some political subjects, but not for others; or, Faith may rely upon some kinds of religious beliefs but not others; or, what Faith should do depends on some combination of the preceding considerations. Although this broad issue rarely receives careful public attention, the 1992 presidential campaign illustrated its importance. Then, some prominent Republicans claimed that positions they defended were called for in "God's country" and criticized Democrats for paying insufficient attention to God.

Because of the centrality of both religious belief and religious strife in Western history, the connection between politics and religious convictions is of special concern in liberal democracies. American constitutional principles guaranteeing religious liberty and forbidding any establishment of religion reflect this concern. These constitutional principles themselves underlie some arguments that religious grounds have no place in politics. Within liberal democracies, religious diversity is a fact; and many people suppose that reasoned argument cannot resolve some vital religious differences. Diversity and mutual inaccessibility are major bases for suggestions that religious beliefs should remain outside politics.

Proposed principles of restraint, however, are not restricted to religious beliefs. Restraint appropriate for religious beliefs may also apply to some other categories of belief. In recent political philosophy, the idea of divergent concepts of the good life has been prominent. Charles Larmore, for example, has written that "the central ideal of the modern liberal state" is that "the state should be neutral. . . . [It] should not seek to promote any particular conception of the good life because of its presumed *intrinsic* superiority—that is, because it is supposedly a *truer* conception."[2]

Larmore goes on to suggest that people making political decisions should not rely on controversial conceptions of the good life.[3] Those who talk about controversial ideas of the good life usually assume that religious beliefs make up a subcategory within that domain. This is *largely* accurate, because religious perspectives tell us how to live; but some religious beliefs *also* cover principles of social importance that reach beyond ordinary ideas of living well.[4] For example, if religious premises are used to conclude that an embryo is a person, and that therefore abortion is a grave moral wrong, the premises are directly used to establish something about moral justice and categorical obligation, not to take sides on how people should choose to live.

A broader category, into which almost all religious beliefs fall,[5] is "comprehensive views": overall perspectives that provide a (relatively) full account of moral responsibilities and fulfilling human lives. Although one might regard *any* comprehensive view as automatically religious, it causes less confusion and better clarifies distinctions to restrict the term "religious" in accord with common understanding. Roughly, what I take that understanding to be is that religion *typically* concerns a level of ultimate truth that is beyond, or deeper than, mundane human existence; the understanding also includes practices and organizations (such as the Ethical Culture Society) that largely replicate those of ordinary religions but do not make similar assumptions about ultimate truth.[6] If Allan is an atheist who believes in traditional Marxism or "greatest happiness utilitarianism" (that what is good is what promotes overall happiness), he accepts a nonreligious comprehensive view. A principle of restraint in politics might cover all comprehensive views, not only religious ones.

Finally, the critical feature of appropriate political grounds might be thought to be public accessibility. Perhaps people should refrain from relying upon all grounds that cannot be reasonably assessed by others, whether or not the grounds are religious, whether or not they are features of comprehensive views, and whether or not they are related to ideas of the good.

We have, then, at least four kinds of views about which the state might be neutral and which perhaps should not figure in political decision and argument: religious views, views about the good life, comprehensive views, and nonaccessible views. This complicates the analysis, but not unduly.

Basic Positions

My investigation of ideas of public reason and self-restraint engages complex arguments made by others. The overall theme of the book will be clearer if I briefly summarize my own positions, developed partly in response to proposals made during the last decade.

I assume that in a liberal democratic society neither officials nor citizens should seek legal prohibitions of actions simply because they are regarded as sins. Such prohibitions, as I argue in a previous book,[7] lie too close to imposing religious views themselves on people to be proper. Thus, someone should not urge that consenting homosexual acts be penalized solely because she believes they are sins in the eyes of God or will bring bad consequences in an afterlife. The decision on prohibition should depend on harms and benefits that are comprehensible in nonreligious terms in this life. Is this principle important at this stage of history? Rarely will anyone say an action is sinful despite its doing no damage in human terms. Nevertheless, the principle sets an important limit on appropriate justifications; and, by suggesting that arguments must be in terms of harms in the here and now, the principle can have practical effect. Its required reference to damages on this earth can significantly affect the weight of arguments for and against a prohibition.

The difficult problems arise when religious views and other wide views about a good life color one's evaluation of harms that *are comprehensible* in ordinary human terms. Here, I shall use the most stark and troubling example. Suppose Faith's view on abortion is informed by a religious judgment that from conception an embryo deserves the consideration due to a full human being. The harm done to an aborted fetus is then, for her, like the harm done to a newborn child that is killed—its possibilities for life are intentionally terminated. *That harm* is certainly comprehensible in nonreligious terms. Religious and similar judgments may also inform someone's sense of the magnitude of harms to animals, or the comparative harms and benefits of lowering the economic position of the poor somewhat to achieve gains for a larger middle class. This book is mainly about grounds used to identify and evaluate such harms.

One of my most important conclusions is that basic principles of liberal democracy do not themselves resolve whether citizens and officials should exercise self-restraint about the grounds they use to resolve such questions. Desirable standards of public reason depend on history and the present composition of a political society. I suggest that in the United States, we now have attitudes about grounds for political decision that reflect neither some rigid set of restraints nor a total absence of restraint. Yet, despite significant uncertainties and disagreements, we do have complex practices and expectations that make sense and serve us tolerably well. Trying to conceive a reasonable accommodation of robust religious liberty, fairness to minority groups, and stability in our pluralist society, I argue in favor of principles of restraint that correspond substantially with those that I claim now exist, ones that are much more nuanced than those commonly proposed by theorists.

I suggest that ordinary citizens should feel free to rely on convictions informed by religious and other similar views when they consider difficult political issues. Legislators and executives appropriately take into account citizen judgments that are formulated in this way. These officials should seek to resolve issues on the basis of public considerations (including the views of citizens), but they also may sometimes rely on their own religious or similar convictions. For judges, the demands of public reasons are more insistent, but in rare instances they also may look to more personal convictions.

I regard the problem of *public discourse* as significantly different from the problem of appropriate bases for judgment. Taking a position that has the unappealing feature of encouraging some discrepancy between actual bases of judgments and stated reasons, I urge that judicial opinions should always be cast in terms of reasons that are broadly public, and that narrow political discussion by public officials and by most "quasi-public" citizens, like newspaper editors and presidents of large corporations, should generally be carried on in terms of such reasons. However, religious groups appropriately do present positions that rely on religious premises.

I realize that this summary of my positions bristles with vague, undefined terms and with assertions that lack even the sketch of an argument. Most of my positive argumentation occurs in the last five chapters of this book, but what precedes those chapters elucidates the crucial concepts and elaborates the strengths and weaknesses of other views. The book as a whole presents, I hope, a clear explanation of many positions and a fairly persuasive defense of my own.

Related Concerns

Thoughtful views about my narrow subject require positions on an array of topics that lie at the core of political philosophy for liberal democracies. These broader topics inform the narrow issue of political self-restraint and are illuminated by it. Another purpose of the book is to explore these connections and thus to contribute modestly to the broader topics. I summarize those briefly here.

1. *The Idea of the Good Liberal Citizen and Loyalty to Liberal Government.* Discussions of self-restraint in politics tend to posit a "good liberal citizen" who tries to act in accord with the underlying premises of liberal democracy. The usefulness of such a concept is debatable. More particularly, the question arises how loyalty to a liberal structure of government should be understood. Does any set of responsibilities have claims on people that they will or should recognize, if the responsibilities do not fit with their own comprehensive positions? In what sense, if any, *should*

people be "good citizens" if their comprehensive convictions point toward contrary actions?

2. *The Degree of Autonomy of Liberal Political Theory.* Claims in favor of self-restraint in politics have typically assumed that a great deal can be said about a theory of liberal democracy that does not depend on acceptance of any religious or other comprehensive view.[8] Other authors have doubted the value of any political theory that does not rest on comprehensive views about human good and moral responsibility.[9] How far can a defensible liberal political theory be independent of comprehensive views in its development of general principles? How far can comprehensive views be excluded in the resolution of particular questions of social justice?

3. *The Liberal State and Ideas of the Good and Private Virtue.* The version of liberal theory that asserts that the state should be neutral among views of human good and some other controversial matters has come under recent attack from advocates of forms of political communitarianism, including a modern "civic republican" approach. They argue that a state should take positions on fundamental ethical questions about the good life; often, they also argue that the state cannot avoid taking such positions, that a goal of neutrality is impossible. The claim that a state should take positions on basic questions of human good and virtue fits comfortably with the position that political theory itself must emanate from comprehensive views. If one sought to find a comprehensive view around which most Americans (not most academics or intellectuals) might coalesce, that probably would be some broad Christian perspective. Wide adoption of a communitarian outlook might put religion closer to the center of political life than it has recently been (not a consequence most communitarians of the Left have in mind).

4. *The Range of Applicability of Principles of Self-Restraint.* Those proposing principles of restraint have generally treated liberal democracies as a class. However, this subject may call for much narrower tailoring. Conditions may vary enough so that principles for one place and time may not be appropriate for other places and times.

5. *Ingress and Egress and Federalism.* How much do appropriate principles depend on the ability of people to enter and leave a country? Perhaps less self-restraint in politics is called for when movement is relatively free. Within the United States, does our federal system provide some answer to worries that people in the minority may feel imposed upon or excluded?

6. *Various Functions of the State.* Principles of restraint are sometimes proposed for all the state's activities, sometimes only for its coercive actions. Is the appropriate range of grounds for decision narrowest when the state coerces behavior? Are principles of restraint otherwise applicable *also* appropriate for public schools? Can it be, for example, that teachers in public schools are not to take stances on controverted claims about the good life?

7. *Agreement about Concepts Contrasted with Agreement in Life*

about Practical Consequences. If one is thinking about the common commitments of liberal citizens, one may be able to come up with some list of basic concepts that are widely accepted—for example, that citizens should be regarded as free and equal and should enjoy freedom of speech and religion. But is such agreement genuine? Or does it represent endorsement of very different ideas that are somehow sheltered by vague concepts? Suggestions that citizens rely on common grounds of public reason to resolve political issues may be threatened by the reality that people often embrace different values when they adhere to the same concepts.

8. *Perfection and Reality.* How much concession, and in what domains and respects, should political theory make to social realities? A similar question arises about basic moral theory, but the considerations differ. Moral theories may use perfection as a standard of how we should behave: "Always act with the most love possible toward others," "Never use another person solely as a means," "Promote the greatest average happiness." A full moral theory will need to say something about how to come to terms with our failures to live up to such standards, but these perfectionist standards may be put forward as guides. Other moral theories purport to be more realistic, asserting that we should set moral standards that people can come close to achieving some of the time. Sometimes the two approaches are combined.[10] What differs about political theory is the question whether, in considering the *organization of the state* and *principles of justice,* there is *any point* in starting with what people ideally would be like. Perhaps in political theory the real makes more incessant demands. This broader question bears on what principles of self-restraint, if any, might be recommended.

9. *Intuition and Reason.* In many religious convictions and other nonaccessible views, personal inspiration or intuition plays an important part. Principles of self-restraint may call for reliance on some public criteria of reason. The possibility of excluding some intuitions raises the question of how far reason can be distinguished from personal intuition and the related question of how far intuition is a basis for rational judgment in various areas.

10. *Culture and Politics.* For most people, religious and other comprehensive views are not *just* personal, they are appropriate subjects of discussion with others, including broad discussion within the culture.[11] From this starting point, a principle of self-restraint *for politics* must depend on some "separation" of that realm from other public realms. Is such a separation feasible enough to make a principle of self-restraint viable?

These are tremendous questions about political philosophy and broader philosophies of life. I certainly do not aim to resolve any of them in a systematic way but my concentration on the main subject of this book helps one to understand the dimensions of these wider issues.

The Structure of the Book

The book aims to develop an increasingly rich understanding of the possible principles of self-restraint and possible notions of public reason, before drawing major conclusions in the last five chapters. Chapter 2, which contains an allegory about plans of settlement for a new planet, plays an important role in supporting the thesis that appropriate principles may be different for different liberal democracies. The chapter's major lesson is that which plans make the most sense depends in part on which sorts of groups will settle together. The chapter provides a modest stock of illustrations from which I draw in the remainder of the book. Chapters 3 and 4 help set out the heart of the problem about personal moralities and public reasons. They focus on bases of judgment for ethical and political decisions. Chapter 3 indicates that officials and citizens appropriately rely upon what I loosely term realist reasons, shared social reasons, and authority reasons. Both chapters suggest that in their own personal lives people also rely on intuitions or reasons drawn from experience, even when they recognize that a reasonable outsider would give less weight to the basis for the reasons than they do. Chapter 3 concentrates on nonreligious reasons of this sort; chapter 4 on reasons drawn from religious experience. The two chapters raise the question of whether reliance on reasons that are "nonaccessible" in this way to other citizens should underlie decision and justification in politics.

Chapters 5 through 10 present and analyze various positions about self-restraint in politics. In chapter 5, I state two simple arguments for no restraint and indicate their weaknesses. I then go on to propose some needed qualifications to any principle of no restraint, qualifications that clear the ground for the major problems with which the book deals. The next five chapters examine the proposals and arguments of other scholars. Chapter 6 deals with self-restraint for religious grounds, a principle proposed in various forms by Robert Audi, Edward Foley, and William Marshall. Chapter 7 shifts to restraint for nonaccessible grounds, as suggested by Thomas Nagel, and restraint for controversial ideas of the good or comprehensive views, as urged by Charles Larmore and Lawrence Solum. In chapter 8, I look at Franklin Gamwell's idea that natural claims about religion belong in the political process and Michael Perry's recommendation of an ecumenical dialogue that would include accessible references to religious understandings. Chapter 9 considers various arguments for no restraint, including those urged by David Smolin, an evangelical Christian. Chapter 10 takes up the complex position of John Rawls. He recommends self-restraint with respect to comprehensive views when one deals with constitutional essentials but he allows greater latitude for ordinary political issues. In the course of these chapters, I engage in critical analysis, but I do not draw my own final conclusions until all these views are set forth and examined.

In the last five chapters, I develop a position that is influenced by the strengths and weaknesses of the proposals of others. Chapter 11 deals with broad theoretical questions about how one should approach the subject. Chapter 12 uses two personal experiences to contrast restraint in judgment with restraint in discussion. Chapters 13 and 14 contain major concrete suggestions for appropriate principles in the United States at this time. Chapter 13 focuses on the judiciary; chapter 14 on legislators and ordinary citizens. Chapter 15 covers the activities of religious organizations. Both chapters 14 and 15 draw from empirical information about past and present practices. I treat this information as highly relevant, in light of my view that one cannot move from general ideas of liberal democracy to specific recommendations about self-restraint without looking at the history and culture of particular societies. In all these chapters, I am making judgments about the appropriate scope of religious freedom and of fairness to others, as well as about the conditions of stability, in a widely diverse society. The discussion invites the reader to measure his or her own judgments against my own.

2

Settling Sretna Bosna

The following allegory highlights possibilities to which I refer in the rest of the book. It helps to distinguish liberal democracy from other forms of government. More significantly, it helps to distinguish what may be fundamental to all liberal democracies from features of just government within some liberal democracies. The allegory is artificial in the relatively narrow, and decidedly Western, nature of the groups it discusses; these kinds of groups are more familiar to me and are more relevant at present for political practices within the United States and most other liberal democracies.

The Setting

In the year 2094, citizens of Earth need to settle a planet of a remote sun. Government leaders estimate that a hundred thousand people will be required to establish a self-sustaining colony that will last at least twenty years. It may be advantageous to have the settlement last much longer. Easy electronic communication between the planet and Earth will exist, but few physical contacts will be feasible. The plan is that one very large spaceship will travel back and forth each year to carry people from one planet to the other.

Rather than itself establishing qualifications for settlers and the government institutions and principles of justice under which they will live, the Agency for Planetary Settlement has decided to accept proposals from nongovernmental groups. Each proposal must explain the kinds of people who will settle the new planet, the basic principles by which they will be governed, and the extent to which the prospective settlers are committed to those principles. The agency has offered to supply executive and judicial officials for the new planet if that is desired. Proposals are to indicate how things will change over time, if relevant changes are contemplated. Agency

12

officials have offered to confer with groups over the terms of proposals, but the agency will not dictate conditions of government. It will choose one of the proposals as it stands, or, if it deems no proposal minimally adequate, it will declare this experiment for establishing terms of colonization a failure. What the agency decides is subject to review by the chief executive of Earth and to possible interference by Parliament.

The idea behind this plan belongs Draga Lubić, the deputy administrator for new settlements. She is a citizen of the United States. One pair of her great-great-grandparents emigrated to the United States in 1994 from Sarajevo, having lost family members and their home during the devastation in Bosnia-Herzegovina that followed the splintering of the country known as Yugoslavia. Draga's great-great-grandmother was a Moslem who had grown up in Mostar; her great-great-grandfather had grown up in Banja Luka with a Serbian father and a Croatian mother (a common union in Bosnia during the decades leading up to 1992). Draga has a vivid sense of the appalling violence between neighbors and one-time friends that struck parts of the former Yugoslavia beginning in 1991. An intense student of political philosophy, she believes an ideal state would approximate government by consent as closely as possible. That vision underlay her plan to have the people who wished to settle the new colony propose the terms of their life together. Draga believed that this course might enhance the chances of a just and peaceful social order. With a sense of hope that many colleagues thought was hardly borne out by historical events, Draga named the uninhabited planet Sretna Bosna (Happy Bosnia).

Given considerable prosperity and tolerance on Earth in 2094, no one had to emigrate to satisfy basic material needs or escape persecution. Since material conditions on Sretna Bosna would be fairly harsh for at least three years, the attractions of settlement were almost entirely nonmaterial. The only "pressure" on people to join a settling force were those of family, close friends, and cobelievers. Some people were understandably loath to be left behind if those nearest and dearest to them were journeying to settle.

On the deadline of November 3, 2093, the agency received five proposals; these were given to Draga for review. On December 19, the holiday of Saint Nicholas, which had remained the saint's day of Draga's family through the generations, she submitted the report of her office to the administrator, her supervisor.

The Report of the Office of New Settlements

This report consists of a brief summary of each of the five proposals we have received followed by a recommendation for action.

The Proposals

The Mother Mercy Proposal. This proposal has been made by the leadership of a worldwide movement whose members believe that a woman born as Gloria Sun is the embodiment of the Holy Spirit. Mother Mercy, as she is now called, has absolute authority within the movement, which numbers over four million. Mother Mercy preaches a strict communal life in which all property is shared and sexual intercourse is solely for the purpose of procreation between partners chosen by church officials. Responsibilities within Mercyite communities, including the raising of children, are shared by adult members. Members spend many nonworking hours in meditation and serious reading; they are not allowed to watch television or go to movies. Participation in ordinary sports is forbidden, but daily exercises are required to benefit body and mind.

The Mercyite movement has appealed to people disturbed by the growing materiality of life in the twenty-first century. Nevertheless, maintaining strict discipline is not easy, since members are constantly exposed to more relaxed ways of life. Problems have arisen with recalcitrant children and with state prescription of much of the teaching content in Mercyite schools. The movement sees settlement of a new, remote colony as providing an opportunity to carry out its tenets with less compromise and distraction.

According to the proposal, all settlers would be established members of the movement, active for at least the preceding year. The leader of the government would initially be a man named Flowing Grace, a cousin of Mother Mercy. He, and any successors, would be subject to the authority of Mother Mercy and her successors. Sretna Bosna would be governed entirely on movement principles. Officials would endorse and promote them, and schools would teach them. All political and legal decisions would be made in accord with the standards of Mother Mercy. No religious services of any other kind would be allowed, nor would any expressed challenges to the truth of Mercyite principles.

The proposal recognizes that some people might "fall away" from the movement. These people would be allowed to leave the planet on the yearly spaceship to Earth. Children who were not persuaded of the truth of the movement would be allowed to emigrate to Earth when they reach the age of sixteen.

The New Lanark II Proposal. In many respects, this proposal resembles that of the Mother Mercy movement. All the settlers would be members of this rigorously atheist, socialist, and communitarian movement. The basic principles of virtuous personal life and of social life have been laid out by a theorist named Robert Owen III, who himself would lead the settlement. The new planet would provide an opportunity for followers of Owen to carry out his principles of industrial socialism on a scale that has not been possible on Earth. Although social life would be highly communal, government would be strictly hierarchical, with absolute authority in the leader. The main difference in political organization between this movement and that of Mother Mercy is that all citizens would vote each year to determine if they wanted the leader's authority to continue. If they did not, they would then vote for a new leader, according to a specified procedure. Religious practices would not be allowed on Sretna Bosna, and any public criticism of the leader or of principles of industrial socialism would be forbidden. Again, the only "out" for those who became disenchanted with the movement would be return to Earth.

The "Short Episcopalian" Proposal. This proposal gets its nickname because it is indeed not very long and is sponsored by an Episcopalian-Anglican group that seeks to make religion a much more vital aspect of culture than it has been for many years. Seventy thousand members of this group want to settle on Sretna Bosna *if* the planet's government will have a distinctly Episcopalian caste. The entire spectrum of Episcopalian belief, ranging from theologically liberal and modernist to conservative and strongly biblical, is well represented among the proposed settlers, so the Episcopalian character of government would not be rigid. It would, however, include a formally established church: that is, Episcopalianism would be the formal religion of the government and would be supported by it.

Realizing that it was unable to supply a hundred thousand people, the Episcopalian settlement movement invited applications from other groups and individuals. The Episcopalians decided early that it would be best not to include just one other major group, but rather a number of small groups and some unaffiliated individuals. Groups and individuals applied for various reasons. Among the groups were Amish wishing to establish small agrarian communities that would have virtually no contact with the government; members of Simplicity in Art and Music, all of whom are devoted to recapturing centuries-forgotten techniques in music and the fine arts and most of whom are indifferent to formal religion; and devout Orthodox Jews who plan to work in ordinary society but live in small, highly religious communities with schools of their own. All these groups are willing to live in a larger democratic society with an Episcopalian coloring.

Since the Episcopalians were happily surprised at the large number of people interested in joining them, they did not have to engage in genuine negotiations over the terms of their proposal. Nevertheless, wishing to be fair to the other prospective citizens, to create a peaceable society, and to win agency acceptance of their proposal, the Episcopalians did discuss with other groups what would be appropriate terms of government.

The proposed form of government is democratic, with most standard written constitutional guarantees of liberal democracies. There is, of course, no provision for nonestablishment of religion or separation of church and state. Political officials will be elected by normal democratic procedures; so Episcopalian dominance of the government may not continue over time. Since part of the effort of the Episcopalians is to create a society with an Episcopalian character, officials, both in legal interpretation and in political debate, will appropriately refer to relevant religious understandings. Episcopalian understandings are not given priority directly in the constitution; but all groups realize that for the near future these understandings, though varied in themselves, are likely to dominate official life.

The Diverse "Fervent Believers" Proposal. This proposal emanates from medium-sized groups, whose members are no less fervent in their beliefs than the followers of Mother Mercy and Robert Owen. None of these groups alone has enough members who want to make the trip to settle, but each group has twenty-five thousand people who are willing to do so even though they will make up only a minority in Sretna Bosna. We need not describe the particular beliefs of these groups in detail. Suffice it to say that in their views of ideal governance, two communitarian groups, one religious and one atheist, do not differ much from the followers of Mother Mercy and Robert Owen. A third group is made up of former Roman Catholics who think the church has strayed much too far toward modernism. For example, they strongly reject the acceptance of noncelibate and women priests that occurred earlier in this century. Unlike the first two groups, they do believe in forms of religious and political liberty as matters of principle. They think an ideal government would be based on traditional Roman Catholic principles, teaching the true faith and grounding ordinary legislation on it. Nevertheless, they would permit other religious practices and even open criticism of their Catholicism, as well as ordinary political debate and a government selected by democratic procedures.

The fourth group believes that a fulfilling life must be agrarian and within nuclear families. This group contains a few committed atheists and religious believers; most members are agnostics. The members think that an ideal government would strongly support family agrarianism and would forbid both industrialization and heavily mechanized farming. Like the traditional Catholics, however, the agrarians would allow open political discussion, selection of officials by democratic processes, and liberty of religious practices.

The members of all four of these groups are, typically, quite certain they understand the truths that matter for personal and social existence. Consequently, they are highly skeptical they have much to learn from different points of view. Each group, however, strongly believes in reaching outsiders to convert them. The faith of the two religious groups includes an instruction to proselytize to save the souls of nonbelievers. With the atheist and agrarian groups, the aim is to spread a message that will be richly fulfilling for all who accept it. Members of all the groups sense a kind of unity in human life that leaves them unsatisfied if others have failed to understand what they do; further, the members realize that their own ability to carry out their ideals for themselves and their children will be enhanced if more people come to see life as they do.

All groups want open religious and political discussion in Sretna Bosna, the Catholics and agrarians because they believe in it in principle;

the religious and atheist communitarians because members of each group know they cannot dominate political life and regard open discussion as preferable to any other alternative. The attitude of these two groups differs in one respect. If the religious group somehow acquired political power, it would feel comfortable about suppressing competing views, even if it constituted only a minority of the population. The atheists believe they should suppress other outlooks only upon first becoming an overwhelming majority.

In any event, given circumstances as they may be on the new planet, each group wants the chance to reach the rest of the population; but each fears it may somehow be ganged up on by a combination of the other groups and also fears that, over time, by dint of a high birth rate or emigration from Earth, one of the other groups may actually become a majority of the population. Given the beliefs of the various groups, members of each worry that if any other group achieves majority status, it will place its stamp on the entire planet.

Members of each group are united in their wish to extract from the others powerful commitments that will protect them. Since all wish these commitments to carry through time, they have included major features of what will be a written constitution. It has guarantees of liberty of speech and religion, of standard legal processes, of private property, and of specific democratic institutions, including proportional representation. All groups view proportional representation as a way to prevent their future exclusion from the legislature. The two communitarian groups accept the guarantee of private property, because they will be able to establish subcommunities in which property is shared. They expect most of their own members to live within these subcommunities. All groups expect the planet's economy to involve substantial interchange between members of various groups. Group leaders expect that over time the result will be some citizens who have divided loyalties or are committed to none of the groups. They hope that such people can live in harmony with the various fervent believers on Sretna Bosna.

The leaders know from history that various constitutional guarantees can be interpreted in different ways. They are aware that during most of the last half of the twentieth century the American guarantee of nonestablishment of religion was read to bar both voluntary class prayer in public schools and substantial aid to private religious schools. They also know that many critics, including some Supreme Court justices, took contrary positions. Discussion among the groups quickly showed that they had rather different ideas about the proper scope of the constitutional guarantees. The leaders considered drafting highly detailed constitutional provisions to close gaps they could see. But they were aware that no language could close all gaps, and on many important points they doubted they could achieve agreement. They agreed, instead, that constitutional interpretation would be according to publicly agreed principles, not the principles of any particular group. Concerned about how far fervent believers of any group could accomplish this, absent an established political culture on Sretna Bosna, they propose for an initial twenty years to take advantage of the agency's offer to supply judicial and executive officials from Earth. In that way, they believe that administration and interpretation can be carried out as far as possible in terms of shared political values. After twenty years, they propose that citizens of Sretna Bosna will take over these positions; but part of the oath of officials will remain "I promise to interpret and administer the constitution and laws of Sretna Bosna in accord with generally shared political values."

Although the groups welcome a culture in which all religious and social positions may be discussed, the leaders fear that disputes over political issues could become highly divisive. Realizing that the political community may be fragile, they want to encourage a political culture in which reliance is on what citizens share rather than on what divides them. They agree that not only officials enlisted from Earth, but also legislators elected on Sretna Bosna and those citizens taking an active role in public political debate, should rely as much as they can on the basic principles of governance to which the groups have consented. They also agree that political debate should be carried out in terms of these shared principles; in particular, no claims of a positively religious, atheist, or agnostic sort should be advanced in the public political process. It is not that someone who utters a claim of this sort will be committing a crime, but such argument will be considered unfaithful to the founding agreement, and, if it plays a very great role in the legislative process, resulting legislation may be regarded as violating constitutional principles of religious liberty and separation of church and state.

The Egalitarian Liberal Coalition Proposal. The fifth proposal was by groups sharing three attitudes in common: distress over enduring racial and ethnic prejudice and hostility, a sense that—short of radical communitarianism—people should have roughly equal chances to realize their talents, and a commitment to a genuinely decent life for all people. Most of these groups have worked together to achieve racial and ethnic justice. They have become discouraged about the intractability of social stereotypes and the way these poison the social atmosphere on Earth. The groups hope that, with members who are committed to racial and ethnic equality and harmony and who genuinely desire to live in an interracial and interethnic community, they will be able to build a society on Sretna Bosna that is nearly free of harmful social attitudes.

The prospective settlers have widely diverse racial, ethnic, and religious backgrounds. One group is an interdenominational organization of liberal Protestants. All its members regard their religion seriously, and understand the commitment to equality largely in terms of the Christian message that God loves all people infinitely and enjoins us to treat all people as sisters and brothers. A second group is made up of liberal Roman Catholics; within their church they tend to be relatively antihierarchical and open to union with other Christian traditions. A third religious group comes from a splinter Baptist denomination; its members are conservative theologically, believing strongly in the unique correctness of a Christian faith based on the authority of scripture. Unitarians make up a fourth group; they range from people whose religious views are close to those of liberal Protestants, except in the way the nature of Jesus is conceptualized, to those who disbelieve in any traditional God and accept a kind of pantheism. A fifth group is drawn from a long-standing interracial civil rights organization. Its members have varying religious beliefs, but all regard equality and harmony in this world as extremely important. The sixth group is the Society of John Stuart Mill. Members think Mill's philosophy should guide our personal and social lives. Virtually all are atheists or agnostics about religious claims; they believe that Mill took a similar view although he was hesitant to express it publicly. In the spirit of Mill, they do not believe they have arrived at any final truths, and they are strongly committed to an open society.

Members of these various groups have cooperated with each other on many practical projects. They have developed a large degree of mutual respect, and most members of each group feel they have learned a great deal from members of the other groups. Almost all those who wish to settle believe they could live happily in a society whose politics were dominated by any of the other groups or by any combination of the other groups. This is partly because relatively little separates the liberal political philosophy of all the groups, and partly because each group trusts in the reason and fairness of the members of other groups.

All favor a liberal democracy, with constitutional guarantees that people will enjoy liberty of speech and religion and also equality of opportunity and at least a minimum level of welfare. The groups agree that the state should be substantially separate from religious activities and should not sponsor religion or antireligion. They also share the following understanding about how political activity should be carried out: citizens and legislators should feel free to rely on any sources of truth they think are relevant and to express that reliance publicly as the basis for their positions. Judicial and executive officials should aim to rely on shared sources of value, but when these leave them uncertain as to what they are to do, these officials too may rely on particular sources of understanding that derive from their own religious or philosophic views.

Within most of the groups, members feel unsure enough about religious truth to welcome full public dialogue about religious subjects. Political discussion provides an important opportunity to understand political commitments of faith and deeper theological premises. People fear that if an effort is made to remove explicit religious (and Millian) perspectives from discourse about particular political issues, this opportunity to learn from each other will be lost; and they worry that attempts to divorce religious understanding from political positions would be very difficult. The prospective settlers recognize a slight risk that decisions will be made on unshared grounds, but believe that the multiplicity of social groups makes that unlikely and that, in any event, substantive results will probably be acceptable.

The reasoning of most splinter Baptists is somewhat different. They are more certain of the truth and human completeness of their religious understanding, so they think they have less to learn from members of other groups about that subject than those whose religious views are themselves more tentative. The Baptists, however, have a stronger sense of the importance of proselytizing. They regard joint political activity as a valuable occasion to state their convictions to others. Since they do not fear the political results of decisions based on differing premises, they also favor wide acceptance of religious perspectives in political deliberation. Thus, the proposal states that citizens and legislators should feel under no constraint to eschew reliance on religiously, or antireligiously, based premises, so long as people respect religious liberty and nonestablishment.

Evaluation and Recommendation

We have chosen the Egalitarian Liberal Coalition proposal for settlement, though our decision was not easy.

First, we commend all of the groups involved for their thoughtful proposals. Each has attempted to develop government structures and approaches to justice that are fair within its own full understandings of the meaning of human existence and of fulfilling life.

Our rejection of the proposals of the Mother Mercy and Robert Owen groups is straightforward. We cannot be sure that every government should always refrain from enforcing some particular religious truth. But *we are* an agency of the government of Earth, a place of wide religious diversity committed to basic democracy. We are aware that in some subdivisions of Earth areas remain in which political life has a distinctive religious coloring, and religious liberty is less than complete. We need not argue here that that is undesirable. As an agency for the whole planet, we may not represent or promote one particular religious outlook. Given viable alternatives, Sretna Bosna should not be settled by a religious or antireligious group that would implant its outlook on all political life. Mother Mercy has urged us that granting settlement rights to her group would merely establish genuine freedom of religion for a widely unpopular group. Small communities of those who have like religious views may well be appropriate, but a whole planet without religious and political liberty is different. The progress of religious movements is dotted with schisms, heresies, and apostasies. We cannot believe that the unity of the Mercyite settlers would maintain itself fully over time. The more time that elapses, with children who have made no informed commitment growing toward maturity, the greater this problem would be. Allowing the disaffected once a year to return to Earth is not a satisfactory solution. Since the group would be so strongly communal in raising children, the particular tragedy of nuclear family breakups would be avoided, but the severing of close ties would be painful nonetheless. This would generate heavy pressure on those tending toward disaffection to stay within or reenter the fold.

The basic problems with the Owenites are similar. We can no more endorse a government of strong antireligion than one that propagates a particular religious faith. Further, Owen's peculiar brand of socialism is not one that reflects dominant attitudes on Earth. Given the history of the dissolution and breakup of idealistic voluntary socialist communities on Earth, and the harsh conditions that will face settlers on Sretna Bosna, we consider the problem of likely disaffection to be severe. The combination of exit to Earth and a yearly vote on the absolute leader, taken in an absence of free political discourse, is insufficient to meet this threat.

Unlike the Mercyites and Owenites, who do not propose anything approximating liberal democracy (now the dominant form of government on Earth though not the form within each of its territories), the Short Episcopalian proposal does adopt almost all the features of the main liberal democracies. We take these features as including indirect democratic governance, equality of citizens, freedom of expression and religious exercise, respect for the dignity and autonomy of all people, and the rule of law.[1] Whether a religious establishment is consonant with liberal democracy is widely debated, but so many liberal democracies in history have had at least weak establishments, we are disinclined to say that an Episcopalian Sretna Bosna would fail to be a liberal democracy.

Nonetheless, we are worried by a preferred position for that church and for Episcopalian ways of understanding social issues. The groups that will join in settlement are highly diverse. They may reasonably suppose that they can thrive as well or better under benign Episcopalian rule than in their present political conditions. But once they are firmly in place in Sretna Bosna, they may begin to chafe at the dominance of Episcopalian perspectives. Again, we worry that this problem may increase over time. The dominance of the Episcopalians may recede somewhat, and divisions among them may increase. Alliances may be made between some Episcopalians and members of other groups, with members of still other groups feeling excluded. Perhaps the Episcopalian character of political life will diminish over time, but it is also possible that the Episcopalian understandings brought to bear in political debate and in interpretation may increasingly seem to create a second class of citizens that is intolerable.

We faced a genuinely difficult choice between the proposals of the Diverse Fervent Believers and the Egalitarian Liberal Coalition. Each will maintain all the main requisites of liberal democracy; and since each promises an environment in which citizens of different views may live comfortably, the problem of disaffection from the original settling groups is minimized.

Two features of the Liberal Coalition counted in its favor. The nature of the groups involved, especially their present congeniality and openness, promises more harmony over time. And the aim of racial and ethnic equality is so urgent on Earth, an "experiment" with that as a chief objective is of great public importance. We, of course, do not want to minimize the value of what the groups of Fervent Believers wish to do, but, as a government not itself committed to religious truth, we cannot endorse any of their particular religious perspectives, and putting those aside, we do not perceive their objectives as being as important for the welfare of Earth as racial and ethnic justice and harmony.

The Fervent Believers, aware of the Liberal Coalition proposal, have suggested that their own more extreme divorce of religious concerns from government and their aspiration to have political decisions based on shared values best exemplify liberal democratic ideals of free and equal citizens. We have paused over this claim, and we confess to some division among us. *This* is not the place for a treatise on liberal democracy, so we will be relatively brief. Most of us agreed that for groups like the Fervent Believers, the political principles they propose are both wiser and more liberal than alternatives. Given their fundamental convictions, open political reliance on religious, antireligious, and other particular perspectives would be bound to make political life a sectarian battlefield. Given the certainty with which members of each group regard their insights into truth, the respective education from diverse perspectives would not be great. We think the dangers of serious divisiveness are real and would not be eliminated by proportional representation, so the proposal is eminently sensible in making political life depend as far as possible on shared values.

We were divided on the subject of whether the Liberal Coalition would have done better to adopt similar principles. Some of us thought they would have, but nevertheless supported their proposal because their relative unity prepares them for harsh life on the new planet. Most of us thought their own principles were appropriate for their circumstances. We did not think reliance on religious grounds for political decisions necessarily amounted to religious imposition or a subtle denial of religious liberty. We recognize that this is debatable, and that the line between what is imposition and what is not is elusive. We also recognize that over time the nature of beliefs held by citizens of Sretna Bosna may change, that, for example, people may be attracted to less tolerant religions, and that open reliance on religious and antireligious grounds may take on a sharp edge that the proposal does not anticipate. But this danger strikes us as much less portentous than the problems of disaffection under the social life contemplated by some other proposals. Given the positive advantages of open reliance on "complete" views emphasized by the Liberal Coalition, we think the dangers are worth running. We therefore recommend approval of the proposal of the Liberal Coalition.

3

Accessible and Nonaccessible Grounds
of Political Decision

What exactly are the problems concerning political decision and advocacy that the proposals for settlement of Sretna Bosna illustrate? As a start, the proposals help to distinguish various kinds of grounds for ethical and political decisions. This chapter concentrates on accessible and inaccessible bases for decisions. Chapter 4 treats bases that rest on religious or on other comprehensive views. These chapters help provide a foundation for the analysis of possible principles of restraint that occupies the remainder of the book.

Reasons for Objecting to Grounds of Political Decisions

Why might one person challenge the grounds on which someone else makes political decisions? The most obvious reason is that the grounds are simply in error for all purposes, flowing from a faulty methodology or a misguided substantive premise. If most people were told that Astra makes political judgments on the basis of the position of stars, they would respond that astrology gives no true guidance in any respect, that Astra's method is defective. If Wally's decisions in politics rest on the assumption that every white person is inherently superior to every member of other racial group, people would conclude that this premise is substantively faulty, however Wally may have arrived at it.

The second reason why grounds for decisions are considered inappropriate is more interesting. Suppose Cal said, "I am voting to prohibit the televising of all sports events because they waste people's time." Many would object that whether television wastes their time is finally their own business. As a private citizen Cal can encourage people to engage in useful pursuits, but his reason is not an appropriate one to employ political coer-

23

cion. His employing of this ground in this context will, if successful, violate a moral right to liberty or autonomy of fellow citizens.[1] Use of some other grounds of decision may impair rights of equality. I shall lump these objections based on moral rights together as fairness objections. The basic idea underlying such objections is that in relations among people, or citizens, respect for integrity and equality precludes using some bases for decision that might otherwise be appropriate. The objections claim that reliance on particular grounds involves a lack of due respect (for reasons that are explicated differently by different moral and political theories).

The third reason for rejecting someone's grounds for decision looks to consequences. For example, one of the agency worries about the Short Episcopalian proposal was that a pluralist society would not remain harmonious if political decisions were based on Episcopalian understandings. One kind of harmful consequence is people's feelings that they are being denied liberty and equality; so fairness reasons are usually closely linked to consequential worries about *perceived unfairness.* Consequential objections based on harmony, stability, and progress are more distinctive; these will be my main focus among consequential concerns.

We, thus, have three kinds of reasons for rejecting grounds for political decisions: intrinsic inadequacy, unfairness and danger to social harmony, stability, or progress. These reasons may be drawn from different underlying sources; they may arise from encompassing views about human existence and morality or from some narrower political conception that does not rest on any particular comprehensive view. For example, Ruth might reject Cal's ground that people will waste their time watching sports because that ground does not fit with her full Protestant conception of human autonomy or because it is at odds with an idea of liberal democratic premises that is understood without reference to any particular comprehensive view.

In this chapter, I introduce the idea that for political life, grounds that are accessible to fellow citizens may be distinguishable from those that are not. As later chapters develop, someone may offer unfairness or consequential reasons for a claim that people should not rely on inaccessible grounds to make political judgments or to defend those judgments publicly. In considering which grounds may be inaccessible and possibly inappropriate for political decisions, I focus especially on feelings, attitudes, and insights developed mainly in response to personal experience. Before I discuss those grounds, however, I consider three kinds of grounds that seem to be appropriately used in politics: what I term realist, shared social, and authority grounds. These grounds lay claim to greater objectivity and accessibility than at least some grounds that are based on individual experience.

The basic problem I am considering can be put in this crude form. If some ethical views seem to come down to idiosyncratic personal expressions of attitudes or emotions, if they have no objective basis that can be established, should they provide any ground for coercing others? It may be fine for people to act on such personal bases in their own behavior, just as they act on all sorts of individual preferences, but should people band together to coerce strangers to do what happens to feel right to them? At first glance, this seems distinctly unjust and illiberal.

This problem of political philosophy is genuine only if some moral and political judgments do have a more solid or widely comprehensible basis than others. If *all* such judgments were undiluted expressions of divergent personal feelings, and this were broadly recognized, the apparent problem would dissolve. If legislators adopted a law that forbade homosexual acts and someone complained that the law was based only on the subjective distaste of most citizens for such behavior, the response, then, would be that the complaint itself rests only on a subjective distaste for such laws. Unless some basis exists for saying that one ethical attitude or argument is *really* better than another, no basis exists for believing that principles of political philosophy that limit government are *really* better than those that do not.[2]

The serious question of political philosophy exists if certain moral and political judgments have bases that are in some sense more objective than other bases. Suppose that some moral judgments are really true or have been accepted by virtually everyone. One such judgment is that ordinary killing is wrong. Coercion to support these judgments is defensible on a basis that goes beyond mere attitudes or feelings. What then is the status of coercion that *is* based only, or mainly, on attitudes and feelings? Is that indefensible? A belief that some moral and political judgments rest on more objective bases casts into doubt the legitimacy of those that do not. I begin with the bases for moral and political judgment whose credentials seem most solid within a liberal democracy.

Judgments Based on Realist Premises and Reasoning That Are Broadly Accessible

A Realist View That Moral Claims Assert a Truth and That There Is a Truth of the Matter, Contrasted with Mere Tastes

Without offering any general account of what makes a moral or political judgment a realist one,[3] I shall explain how I understand that idea for these purposes. As a general philosophic position, moral realism most importantly consists in the belief that moral claims assert some truth and that there is, indeed, some truth of the matter that does not depend (finally) on what people in a particular time and place happen to think is moral.[4]

Moral realism can most easily be understood by drawing a contrast with simple matters of mere taste. Evelyn says, "Apple pie tastes better than blueberry pie." We probably suppose there is no truth of the matter as to whether apple pie or blueberry pie *really* tastes better; it is only a question of individual preference.[5] We might guess that Evelyn knows this, that when she says, "Apple pie tastes better," she really means only that apple pie tastes better to her. She would not think Addison was *wrong* if he said, "Blueberry pie tastes better than apple pie," because he would mean that blueberry pie tastes better to him.

Suppose Evelyn says, instead, "Lying is wrong, even when it saves serious embarrassment," and Addison responds, "No, saving serious embarrassment is a good enough reason to lie." Evelyn and Addison probably believe they are disagreeing about something, that one is right and the other wrong. They believe there is a truth about whether lies to save embarrassment, and particular lies to save particular embarrassments, are morally wrong. Ordinary moral usage passes the first hurdle of moral realism: moral claims do assert some truth.[6]

Ordinary moral usage might be misconceived, however, for a variety of reasons. People might be mistaken in thinking there is any truth of the matter. I shall not discuss the explanations why people might believe moral claims have a status they do not, but I want to clarify the logical possibility. Suppose Evelyn believes that her predecessor Eve ate an apple offered by a serpent, that the apple has a special significance for human beings, that, unless someone's taste is inherently defective or corrupted by a malign culture, apples will taste better than any other fruit, that this superiority is built into the structure of physical reality, and extends to pies. *Our* best judgment is that Evelyn is wrong in believing that apples have any inherent taste superiority. It is not that we think she happens to be mistaken about apples in comparison with blueberries, we think she is wrong in believing that comparative taste among such fruits is a matter of true or false.[7] The view that acknowledges that moral claims include claims of truth but says that these claims are misconceived treats moral claims similarly, as mistakes like Evelyn's claim about the superior taste of apples. Under a realist view, moral claims do not suffer from this sort of mistake.

The Relevant Realist View as Including General Accessibility of Grounds of Judgment

Realism thus asserts that moral claims are subject to predicates of truth and falsity, that they are objectively correct or incorrect. This alone is not *enough* for the problem we are considering. The truth or falsity must be available to some degree to common human understanding. It may be that the truth now can adequately be assessed only by people with a particular training or cultural background, but the supposition is that these people possess reasons capable (at least eventually) of persuading others who now lack their training or background.[8] The realism that counts here does not include a view that God reveals moral truth to a selected few who have no common ground with other people to persuade them of the truth they have learned. Nor does it include other views that people see a truth they cannot justify to others in some way.

As one position concerning the nature of moral judgment, realism is a competitor with other positions. However, realism may explain the grounding of some moral judgments while not explaining the grounding of others. People who think realist arguments of the required kind provide full support for some of their moral beliefs, substantial partial support for others, and perhaps little or no support for still others will think that such realist reasons explain part of the entirety of their moral beliefs.

From now on, I shall generally talk about accessible realist reasons and arguments. These reasons that are accessible in some sense to common human understanding support a conclusion that a moral stance is correct. They include some value claims as well as ordinary factual assertions that are relevant to moral conclusions.

If accessible realist reasons apply to morality, that is, questions about the good life and about how we should act toward others, they also apply to the structure of political institutions. A person might believe that all or some sound judgments about what a government should be like can be supported by realist reasons. If, for example, one believes that placing a very high value on human freedom can be justified on accessible realist grounds, one will also think that such grounds show that a totalitarian state is undesirable.

I believe a great many moral and political judgments can be justified on accessible realist grounds: "Other things being equal, happiness is better than pain, love is better than hate, health is better than illness"; "Other things being equal, people should act to promote health, happiness, and love, rather than illness, pain, and hate." If we understand what it is to be a human being, it seems nearly impossible to resist these judgments, and someone who did disagree would seem not to be of sound mind. These judgments, at least, we would expect to transcend culture. If we found a society in which the apparently gratuitous infliction of pain was thought desirable, we would expect to discover some belief that this infliction of pain conferred some social or personal benefit. One can move from the moral judgments about happiness, health, and love to *some* judgments about political orders, for example, that unrestricted governance by sadists is undesirable.

Could there be reasons to exclude some claims of accessible realist grounds from decisions about political coercion? It may seem that in an open society where the search for truth is valued, all such realist claims must be appropriate for political evaluation and decision. However, reliance on some realist claims in some contexts may seem unfair or undesirable. Some valid grounds may be overridden in context. Even if Cal produces strong realist arguments for why watching sports on television is unproductive and does not contribute to human flourishing, an overarching right to liberty may make that an inappropriate basis to forbid coverage. Are there more general principles for excluding claims that offer accessible realist arguments? One basis for excluding some realist claims despite their actual or supposed accessibility to common understanding might be that they are now rejected by most members of the society to which one belongs. I consider some more complex variations on this possibility in connection with religious beliefs in the next chapter.

Judgments Based on Shared Social Grounds

Making political judgments on grounds that are commonly shared is often appropriate, even if these grounds extend beyond what can be justified directly on accessible realist bases. This would be most clear if *everyone* had freely agreed that political decisions could be based on particular premises. Someone who ended up being coerced on those premises could hardly complain. No such explicit agreement is achieved in modern liberal societies, but a broad consensus does exist about some matters.

One widely shared assumption is that the government should treat people equally, or show them equal concern. Does this shared assumption represent genuine agreement about values? A skeptic might say that wide acceptance of the formula about equality is delusive, that no real consensus about values exists because people differ so greatly in their ideas about what equal treatment or equal concern implies. The skeptic is right that actual consensus about relevant values is less than what consensus about the formula intimates; nevertheless, most people believe that some sorts of inequalities are unacceptable. Hilary Putnam has suggested that the minimal content of the idea of equality in Western culture is

> (I) There is something about human beings, some aspect which is of incomparable moral significance, with respect to which all human beings are equal, no matter how unequal they may be in talents, achievements, social contribution, etc.
>
> (II) Even those who are least talented, or whose achievements are the least, or whose contribution to society is the least, are deserving of respect.
>
> (III) Everyone's happiness or suffering is of equal prima facie moral importance.[9]

Many governments throughout history have been built on the premise that some human beings just count more than do others, that their lives are intrinsically more important. Indeed, the original United States Constitution embodied the assumption that black slaves (or perhaps blacks in general) counted less (or could be held within states to count less) than white members of society. Any such premise is at odds with the principle of equal treatment. Whatever his intuitive feelings might be, someone would be out of step with this consensus if he argued for a political decision favoring whites because they are simply more important than blacks.

Coercing people on the basis of widely shared principles that they happen to reject is not so obviously appropriate as coercing them on the basis of principles to which they have agreed. Nevertheless, it is *ordinarily* appropriate. Part of the reason for this involves relations between realist and shared social principles. In actual life, disentangling realist arguments from arguments based on shared social principles is largely impossible. People in any society lack the self-transcendence to understand which arguments are grounded only in shared assumptions and which are grounded in the nature of things and are true, independent of what people at that time and place happen to think is right. Most of what is accepted by consensus will seem to be true on realist grounds. This is most apparent with factual assessments; people tend to think that the methods for determining facts dominant in their culture are the best human beings can do to approximate "correct" methods. People also typically think that most cultural values, such as the principle of equality, can be sustained by realist reasons. Everyone's evaluation of realist arguments is influenced by culture, as well as by more individual factors. For human beings, there is no "seeing the realist arguments in terms of their real force." It would be a counsel of impracticality to say, "Rely only on accessible realist grounds, but do not rely on shared social grounds," because people usually lack the ability to distinguish between them.

Suppose that valid realist arguments could be sharply separated from arguments based on shared social premises. It would still be appropriate to rely on reasons that have nearly universal acceptance. If a premise is needed for social action and realist arguments do not tell against a widely accepted premise, relying on that premise rather than on an alternative that lacks acceptance makes sense.

How far explicit, self-conscious reliance on shared premises is warranted depends a bit on the perceived potentialities of realist argument. Reliance on shared premises, even when the premises do not seem grounded in realist reasons, will seem more often appropriate if the conclusions of accessible realist reasoning appear modest. The more that realist reasons leave open, the more will need to be filled by something else, and when something else *is needed,* widely shared premises have a strong claim to priority. Not only is using them usually fair, it will yield a society that is more stable and less dissatisfied. If the law is seriously out of line with values most people hold, frustration and disaffection result. Thus, underlying realist reasons themselves support reliance on shared social principles.

What I have said about reliance on shared social values is, however, subject to the conditions under which those values have developed. Suppose a consensus results from structural injustice. Perhaps a century ago almost everyone believed that women should be denied many opportunities available to men, but these views were a consequence of unjust male domination. If someone can provide reasons indicating that the basis for particular shared values is unjust domination, she has a powerful argument against their use.[10]

Another possibility is that values have developed because of practices, say in child rearing, that are not unjust but are misguided in terms of human fulfillment.[11] When someone grasps the causal relation between practices and values, he may see that the values are at odds with deeper values that are justified on realist grounds or are also part of the culture. If social values can be identified as a product of stunted development, their claim to be relied upon is gravely weakened. Any explicit argument based on shared social values must be ready to meet challenges that the values have illegitimate or unhealthy roots.

My aim in discussing realist and shared social grounds is not to develop a systematic exposition of differences between them. Since both accessible realist and shared reasons are generally appropriate bases for political coercion, major conclusions about that problem would be unaffected if the two kinds of reasons are connected in ways I have failed to identify or are wholly indistinguishable in practice.

Hypothetically Fair Conditions and Discourse Ethics

I shall say a few words about categorization of certain moral and political arguments based on hypothetically fair conditions or discourse ethics. In the most prominent argument about hypothetical conditions, John Rawls constructs an original position of ignorance;[12] the choices that artificially conceived persons[13] in the original position would make out of self-interest in constructing social institutions are the choices that are just in liberal democracies. The force of the original position analysis and the underlying conditions of the original position itself are said by Rawls to rest on the basic premise of liberal democracy as "a system of fair social cooperation between free and equal persons."[14] In contrast to what many readers originally assumed when *A Theory of Justice* was published, Rawls does not claim that this premise of liberal democracy is necessarily superior to premises that may underlie other political regimes. For Rawls, the conclusions drawn about justice are ones that may rest on an overlapping consensus about political values within liberal democracies. For someone who is otherwise a Rawlsian but who thinks that liberal democracy is objectively superior to other forms of government, the development of the argument will be in the realm of realism.[15]

The status of discourse or dialogue ethics depends on the particular claims made. For proponents of these views, undominated dialogue is connected to what we should do morally and politically.[16] I do not want here to explore these rich and complex theories, but to indicate how various kinds of claims would fall out for the conceptual structure this chapter employs. Absent some claim about what is really right or good,[17] discourse ethics would not be consonant with realism. Absent belief that people within a community will come to similar judgments, such a view would not rely on shared social values.[18] However, the tenet that we discover truth more in conversation and intersubjective deliberation than in individual abstract thought can by itself fit with either realism or shared values, or both. Suppose it is claimed that what is *right* is what people *would agree to* in hypothetically perfect conditions of dialogue. *If* the assumption is that human beings in general *under ideal conditions* of dialogue would reach particular conclusions, this seems a realist argument in favor of the conclusions. It appeals to the notion that what human beings would agree to after discussion in perfect conditions must really be right to do.[19] A claim that emphasizes what real people would agree to in actual conditions of dialogue seems more closely focused on shared values. What actual people would agree to certainly depends on the culture in which they live, so such a perspective on dialogue seems to recommend deep conversation with fellow citizens as a method for eliciting underlying convictions. Dialogic theories that maintain claims about what is moral or just may look toward realism or shared values or both.

Authority

Officials who apply laws must pay attention to authority. Often they are supposed to do what someone with higher authority has instructed, and even when they have a wide range of choice, they are not supposed to violate rules laid down by higher authorities. Thus, in systems with written constitutions, legislators, as well as judges and executive officials, lie under constraints of authority. They are not to violate specific constitutional prohibitions, and they are supposed to act in harmony with constitutional purposes. Here I shall merely sketch the complicated subject of legal authority, mentioning straightforward applications, discretionary exercises, and difficult interpretations.

Straightforward Applications

A tax auditor, Olive, must determine how much tax Martin owes. Martin's circumstances are simple. Congress has set increasing rates for ordinary income, providing some credits, exemptions, and deductions. Olive's responsibility is to make the required calculations and assess Martin that tax. The conventions of our system of law do not grant Olive the power to reject the instructions of legislatures and executive superiors.[20] From the law's point of view, Olive should charge Martin according to the acts of Congress. From this perspective, Olive need not worry whether Martin's tax rate conforms with justice as measured by standards of realism and shared social values. Olive may be able to figure out what the law "requires" of her without looking directly to realist and shared social reasons.

However, Olive can disobey the law. Whether she should is a moral question. In 1850 some simple legal cases required the return of fugitive slaves. But a minor official might have decided to let slaves go free, rather than keeping them in custody for their return. Even as to the tax assessment, Olive may ask herself whether, overall as a human being, she should charge the legally required amount.

Three strong moral bases support her performing her prescribed duties. The first is the benefits of authority. Government is needed for decent human life. Government requires chains of authority. Representative bodies are able to make effective decisions on which people can rely only if executive officials carry out the decisions. This argument for hierarchies of authority is realist. Second, within relatively stable societies in which citizens accept the form of government, there is a consensus that officials should perform duties. With some exceptions, performance of prescribed duties is what people want and expect officials to do. Finally, an official who enters an office has explicitly or implicitly promised to perform the duties that go with the office. Realist and shared value arguments about moral duties will include some obligation to keep promises.

Olive, thus, has substantial moral reasons to perform her legal duties; but if what she is required to do is *bad enough*, she may, from the complete moral perspective, properly disobey. When Olive charges Martin the prescribed tax, she implicitly decides that what she is required to do is not so wrong from the moral point of view that she should refuse to comply with her legal duty. But she does not need to decide whether the legislature's choices are the best among available alternatives or instead somewhat unjust or unwise. An official will often properly apply a legislative standard that she does not think fits as well as some possible alternative with realist and shared social reasons.

Discretion

Very often officials have discretion under the law. To stick with our tax example, prosecutors have discretion to decide which violators to prosecute. Only a small minority are actually charged. How should the prosecutors make the judgments whom to charge? The law may contain some direct standards for how the authority is to be exercised. Other aspects of the law may also point in the direction of who should be prosecuted. The scales of theft and other property offenses, for example, suggest that someone who has intentionally cheated on taxes to the tune of $10,000 warrants prosecution more than someone who has cheated on only $200 of tax liability. In exercising discretion, officials frequently need to reach beyond the law and make their own moral and political judgments;[21] what I have said about realism and shared social values is relevant to how they should do this.

Interpretation

Judges and other officials sometimes must interpret the law, deciding what it means. In form, at least, this judgment is about what the law requires (or should be said to require), not a judgment within a legally permitted discretionary range. Thus, a judge might have to decide if a statute that prohibits intentional killing covers a doctor who assists suicides by providing a mechanical device that a person may employ to take his or her life.

Most of those who write about legal interpretation agree that judges must make judgments that combine reliance on authoritative materials in the law with some kind of independent sense of what is right and good. One way of conceptualizing the process is that the judge figures out how far the law settles things and then, if necessary, fills in from nonlegal sources, such as community morality and independent views about justice and utility. In this view, the judge fills in gaps in the law with legislative judgments of his or her own.[22] The other way of looking at the process is that the judge brings to bear independent views on morals and politics in interpreting all the relevant legal materials. The independent views merge with assessment of the law in an overall consideration of what the law requires.[23] Perhaps the second account more accurately captures the ordinary psychology of most judging, although judges sometimes consciously do suppose that the law leaves them free to decide one way or the other. In any event, these niceties of legal theory do not resolve what bases judges should use to make the independent judgments of morals and politics. Accessible realist reasons and shared values are obvious sources.

Responses to Life's Situations

I now turn to a basis for ethical judgment whose appropriateness for politics is more questionable. Some people believe that ethical judgments are developed largely in personal response to life's circumstances, that personal experience yields beliefs and attitudes about what we should do. This general perspective can emphasize various aspects of personal experience, such as dialogue or action; it can be secular or religious. The religious form is a major focus in the next chapter. As with realism, an approach that emphasizes personal responses to life's events can make a general claim about the nature of ethical judgment or a less grand assertion that many of our ethical judgments are primarily supported by personal experience. I shall concentrate on the latter standpoint, inquiring about the status of judgments largely grounded in personal experience.

In analyzing what we may broadly call responsive ethical judgments, I first draw a threefold distinction among experience that a person thinks is applicable for most people, experience the person thinks is individual, and experience that the person thinks reveals some objective truth, but that in some crucial respect is inaccessible to many other people. I then turn from nonmoral judgments to ethical judgments. Finally, I consider in a preliminary way the relevance of these possibilities for political coercion, its actual justification and public arguments for it.

I have personalized much of what follows. Personal reflection has seemed the best way to clarify distinctions, and it well suggests how fragile these may be in application. Dealing with my own actual beliefs provides a more severe test of the defensibility of claims than would examples of hypothetical beliefs held by hypothetical people.

Generalizable Responses, Personalized Responses, and Responses That Seem Generalizable in a Sense but Not Accessible

If anyone asked me for my three most joyful experiences, I could respond easily. They were the moments of birth of my three children, shared with my wife Sanja in the delivery room. Other parents who have been present and conscious at their children's births speak of similar feelings. I am confident that being at the birth of a much wanted, healthy child is a profoundly moving and joyful event for almost anyone, and that for couples who love each other, the joy is enhanced because it is shared. Have I learned these truths from having the experience or from talking with others? Dialogue has strengthened my belief in the universality of what I felt, but only my own experience has illumined the power of the feeling. That experience is also an element in my confidence about what others will feel. I would have quite a different sense if I had heard the same observations by others but never had the experience myself. As it is, I would be comfortable making my own experience part of the relevant basis for some hospital policy, because I am so sure that this experience is replicable, is one almost everyone else (at least in this culture) would have.

I have reached a stage in my career when I like to sit down and write. Earlier I found setting pencil to paper very difficult; I preferred teaching and, believe it or not, committee work. Many people, even many academics, do not enjoy writing. Some people believe the preference for detached reflection and written expression is odd. They may be right. Even if I knew a great deal about a twenty- or thirty-year-old who found writing painful, I could not predict how he or she would feel years later. I believe my own experience is personal to me, not generalizable to others.

I take some pleasure in some popular music, but I find the music of Mozart, Bach, and Schubert to be more deeply enjoyable, and I believe it is better music. With the help of a musicologist, I *might* be able to explain this view, but I would not expect to make much of a dent on someone who dislikes classical music. That person would probably view supposedly objective claims that classical music is superior as the babble of artificial refinement. Having noted a newspaper report a few years ago that the three FM stations in New York City that devote all or much of their time to playing classical music received a total audience share of about 5 percent, and having witnessed the subsequent demise of one of those stations, I believe most people would not find arguments in favor of classical music to be persuasive. No particular objective events, like playing more classical music for them, would probably change their minds. Given their predispositions, they really are not open to the line of understanding or perception that I continue to find powerful.

Ethical Sense as a Response to Experience

This threefold categorization applies to ethical obligations we feel. Some experiences leading to ethical feelings seem fairly generalizable. My sense of what matters in life has been altered by Sanja's illness and death. I slip back into old attitudes, but my reflective understanding is that many things to which we devote our energies, most particularly evidences of status and material prosperity,[24] are less important than our attachments to them.[25] I do not suppose this experience can be generalized in quite the same simple form as my joy at my sons' births, but I do believe that when most people face desperate illnesses and deaths of those they deeply love they feel the comparative insignificance of much our culture values. To a large degree, I think this impact of such experiences is replicable, and its content is not so hard to explain: next to life and death, small matters of prestige or material enjoyment really do seem shallow. From some experiences we believe the glimpse of meaning that we attain is true and is one that most others would have as well.

At the other extreme are personalized ethical feelings. Because I had some seizures six years ago, I now feel some responsibility to respond to solicitations for epilepsy foundations. Although the experience of modest obligation I have had is one that some other people also have, I do not believe there is any general ethical obligation to respond to such foundations or to charities for illnesses one has happened to suffer.[26]

Another variation of personalized ethical responses involves *emotional feelings* about the obligations others have that are out of line with one's reflective beliefs. At stages of my life my "honesty" in personal relations extended well into the domain of tactlessness. Once I realized that bluntness is not always a cardinal virtue, I still sometimes *felt* emotionally that people should be frank beyond what I *thought* was appropriate. At this point, I regarded my own intuitive sense as unsupported by generalizable experiences or general reasons. I then took my own feelings as personal, not really applicable to others.

The intermediate category, the difficult category, is experience that we believe teaches us something objective, something that is generalizable, but which we understand is in some important sense not accessible to others. I have said that my time with Sanja up to her death made me feel the triviality of much striving; it also made me feel, to put it simplistically, the overwhelming value of caring and love. I believe that this part of my insight is no less true than the other, so I believe it is generalizable to others in the sense of being relevant for them. But I am much less confident that it is generalizable in another sense. The pain of suffering and loss present a large temptation to withdraw, to decide that caring for others is a recipe for more suffering and loss and that a self-contained existence is the best that we human beings can do to survive life's arbitrary inflictions. Within myself, this tendency competes powerfully with a wish to be engaged. Why has that not seemed to me the dominant lesson? Why do I believe that caring *is* morally better than withdrawal? Mostly because Sanja was an extraordinarily loving person, and remained so until her death, because her love opened me and my sons to the value of caring, and because their love and the love of other family and of friends surrounded me in this most difficult time.[27] I think modest changes in circumstances might have made the counsel of withdrawal dominant, and I suppose that for some people it does dominate. I do not think any simple set of external circumstances will produce in others what I felt and what I feel I understand. Nor do I think I have any decisive argument why caring is better[28] than a self-contained life of withdrawal for the person who is capable of the latter and believes it is preferable. So, I feel that I am in the possession of true ethical insight, based largely on experience, but that I lack the bases to show its truth.

Use of Insights from Experience as a Basis for Political Judgment: Some Preliminary Conclusions

How should the reasons from personal experience that lead to ethical views figure in political and legal decision and discourse? Judgments or feelings that one clearly recognizes as individual, that one thinks have no generalizability, should not underlie political coercion. If I believe many others do not share my ethical feelings, and I have no sense that they should, obviously I should not endeavor to coerce or pressure them into doing what happens to feel right to me.[29]

The inappropriateness of relying on such personalized judgments is most obvious for decisions within the law. Part of the ideal of the rule of law is uniform and nonarbitrary decision under legal standards. That ideal, of course, is often not achieved even when standards are available, and it is incapable of achievement when officials have discretion or must exercise difficult interpretive judgments. If officials rely on accessible realist and shared social reasons, there remains at least some hope that similar situations will be dealt with similarly. However far it may stray from the actual bases for decisions, officials hold up a model that reasons for decision are generalizable. If officials candidly acknowledged that they relied on personal feelings not backed by generalizable reasons, the dependence of outcome on who happens to judge would be built into the very process of justification. Of course, we know that outcome often does depend on the personal attitudes of judges, but their striving is for a less idiosyncratic justice.

I can imagine at least two arguments in favor of outright personalization of legal justification. One is that explicit reliance on personal feelings would only express what takes place anyway, and would be a healthy corrective to the deceit and illusion that now characterize legal decision. My response to this is that explicit reliance on personal feelings for justification of legal decisions would increase the personalization that now exists and would move the system away from the desirable striving for nonarbitrary justice.

The second argument is more subtle. It asserts that the ideal of the bureaucratic, utilitarian state impoverishes values and, in particular, suppresses diversity and otherness. A richer understanding of human beings demands recognition of their broad diversity. If officials themselves made judgments that were more explicitly personalized, this would counteract the baleful tendencies of rational bureaucracy and contribute to a more sympathetic, humane society.

This argument is a direct attack on the ideal of a uniform law. The issues it raises are deep and troubling. Almost certainly, however, the best way to recognize diversity and otherness is for the law and most officials to acknowledge and promote them, not for officials to respond to problems mainly in light of their own individual characteristics.[30] In practice, the sense of citizens that diversity and otherness are valued will not best be achieved by having officials act upon personal feelings. Most officials, especially higher officials, come from dominant groups in society. Their feelings will not usually be specially sympathetic to the oppressed and powerless. Allowing the officials to give fuller expression to their own individuality might lead to poorer treatment of those who are genuinely out of the mainstream.

Rule of law considerations are not so central to *making* laws. As long as laws are applied with relative consistency, the ideal of a uniform law could be preserved even if legislators relied heavily on their own personal feelings or those of their constituents. But an important argument against such reliance remains. If I am going to coerce others, I should have reasons that I think are fairly applicable to them. Simply satisfying my own personal feelings about a subject is not sufficient in a society that accepts basic notions of liberty and equality. The freedom of people to decide what to do with their lives should not be subject to the whims of others, even a majority, about what happens to feel right.

This conclusion needs some qualification. In some situations all realize that satisfaction of subjective preferences is what is at stake, and some uniform plan is needed; in that event, coercion of some on behalf of the subjective feelings of others is required. Suppose a university must decide whether to alter its calendar to begin the fall semester before Labor Day. There are some "objective" reasons each way, but all acknowledge that the subjective preferences of faculty and students are what mainly counts. Since the calendar needs to be uniform, the minority will end up being coerced. In such circumstances, voting one's subjective preferences is proper. And if one's subjective preferences happen to include personalized ethical feelings, these may appropriately influence one's position. But this is different from coercing other people to do something because one *feels* it is obligatory, when one perceives neither genuine reasons why others should regard the action as obligatory nor any need for coordinated action. That is what should not be done.

My conclusions are different for the ethical insights that people have that come from personal responses to events, dialogue, or action, when the people think their insights are replicable for most others in similar circumstances and are defensible. If experience is believed to be a basis from which one can generalize about what most other people do feel, or would feel, it is an aspect of using accessible realist or shared social reasons. Our own experience is sometimes the primary means by which we grasp realist truths or the implications of shared social premises. Almost all learning combines personal experience with rational reflection. For some matters one of these looms much larger than the other. Basing judgments about compelling other people partly on experiences that some of them have not had is common and inevitable. If we believe that similar external events would cause roughly similar reactions in most people, we cling to an accessible, replicable means for discovering the insight on which we rely.[31] If we think that the insight and the ways of learning it transcend cultural variations, then a claim that we have learned through experience will fit within a broadly realist approach. If, instead, we think the insight is deeply conditioned by our particular culture, a claim may have more to do with shared values, or something so deeply rooted in the culture that people do not self-consciously consider it. In either event, reliance on what one has grasped from experience would seem appropriate, if one further condition is met.

The insight should be defensible. If the claimed significance of the experience is not just feeling but ethical insight, it may be important to suggest why the insight is genuine, why it does not reflect a typical aberrational reaction of those who happen to have been struck by some good or ill fortune. Of course, if one has full-dress rational arguments for the ethical insight, one need not rely on the experience directly at all (though the experience may have initially led one to the arguments). What I have in mind, rather, is some account that is less than a full rational argument for the ethical insight but that suggests why the insight may have merit rather than being a kind of reflex emotional reaction to unusual circumstances. (If people who are seriously injured by paint cans falling on their heads feel painters are less reliable than other people, the rest of us doubt that these experiences have produced true insight about this question.) Some account of why an ethical insight is defensible provides the strongest basis for relying on insight from experience when one is deciding upon political coercion.

The most troublesome questions about reliance for political coercion are raised by the intermediate category. One believes one's personal experience has yielded an objective ethical truth that applies to all people, *but* thinks both that the force of this insight cannot be fully persuasive for others and that no series of external events will assure that others have the same insight. I postpone discussion of these questions until I have considered religious and other comprehensive grounds for decision in the next chapter.

4

Religious Grounds and Grounds Based on Other Comprehensive Perspectives

Religious Convictions, Comprehensive Views, and Nonaccessible Bases

This chapter continues my exploration of grounds that might be inappropriate bases for political decision and discourse. My main focus is on religious convictions, but I also discuss other comprehensive views. I indicate how religious grounds relate to nonaccessible grounds; I briefly suggest some reasons why grounds connected to religious or other comprehensive views might be thought inappropriate bases for political decisions even when proponents believe these grounds are accessible all the way down; and I develop the idea of nonaccessible grounds drawn from personal experience that happens to be religious.

As I said in the introductory chapter, not all comprehensive views are religious. As I shall use the term, religious bases for decision are connected to theistic belief or other belief about a realm of ultimate value beyond, or deeper than, ordinary human experience, or to forms of life or institutions understood to be religious, such as Buddhism or the Ethical Culture Society.[1] If Jerry says, "I favor a legal ban on homosexual acts because God has indicated in Holy Scripture that human societies should abhor such behavior," he offers a religiously grounded basis for his position. Comprehensive views include overarching philosophies of life, whether religious or not.[2] Thus, maximum happiness utilitarianism, standard Marxism, and Millian liberalism are nonreligious comprehensive views. What I mean by "not generally accessible" has been largely explained in the last chapter: the believer lacks bases to show others the truth of what he believes. A simple religious example would be Caroline's saying, "Last night, I had an overwhelming experience, and I realize that Jesus Christ is Lord."

A great many people, including large numbers who hold traditional

39

religious beliefs, think that the most fundamental religious convictions fall within this broad category of nonaccessible beliefs. According to this understanding, persons who hold religious convictions do so substantially on the basis of experience that is not fully accessible to others. This does not mean that reason plays no part in the development of religious convictions. Possible religious understandings may be measured against various tests of reasonableness. But something more is involved: a choice or judgment based on personal experience that goes beyond what reason can establish.

Since "nonaccessibility" may connote some sort of "unintelligibility," I want to stress that the experience need not be unintelligible. Others may have a considerable sense of the nature of that experience; what matters crucially is that they are not in a position to evaluate and credit the insights drawn from the experience. Some notable Christians have claimed that true understanding flows from a special grace that God does not bestow on everyone. On this view, people lacking such grace are not equipped to recognize what those specially blessed can see. When I was in college, a "leap of faith" theology had wide currency. Owing much to Kierkegaard, this Christian analogue to secular existentialism claimed that only by committing oneself to Christian belief and life could one grasp their validity. The truths that one person learns by making a leap of faith are not fully accessible to others who have not made a similar leap; and generally accessible reasons alone are not powerful enough to induce a leap of faith. I do not mean to suggest that the convictions of most Christians or of all "true" Christians rest heavily on such personal experience; but that sort of belief presents certain issues about nonaccessibility in their most stark form.

A position that is relevantly similar places less emphasis on individual personal experience and more on finding oneself within a tradition. A person is born and raised in a particular religious tradition; she believes that she is fortunate to be within the tradition whose religious understanding most closely approximates truth; but she does not think any generally accessible arguments are sufficient to persuade those outside the tradition of the validity of its understanding. I believe that many Jews have this attitude about their religious tradition. When I subsequently discuss religious convictions whose bases are not generally accessible, I concentrate on the position that emphasizes personal experience, but what I say largely applies as well to convictions that are tradition-based in the way I have just described.

Many religious people *do not* think that their fundamental convictions are less than fully accessible; they suppose these convictions can be established on grounds that are subject to general rational evaluation. The kinds of possibly accessible grounds for belief differ significantly. I shall mention three.

The first ground of belief is philosophic arguments for God, or for a God with particular characteristics. Some philosophers have thought, for example, that the ability of human beings to conceive of an omnipotent God, or the purposive nature of the universe, or the capacity of human beings to engage in moral practices establishes (or points toward) the existence of God.

A second ground for belief is particular evidence in the stream of human history. Certain events are thought to have taken place that cannot be explained in ordinary natural and human terms; these events indicate the existence of God, and further indicate much about God's nature and will. Thus, Hope may believe that persons claiming to be inspired by God have prophesied historical events they could not have foreseen without divine inspiration, that people have prayed to God for extremely improbable events that have then taken place, that persons invoking God's assistance have been able to perform miracles, such as healing or the raising of the dead, and that other miraculous occurrences, such as the parting of the Red Sea, the resurrection of Jesus, and appearances of Mary, the mother of Jesus, show God's power and nature. These extraordinary occurrences within history are closely connected to teaching about God. Jesus, the same person who performed miracles, also told us much about God. Hope believes we can thus identify certain revelations about God as highly authoritative.

Hope's grounds for belief are accessible, of course, only if the claims of prophecy and miraculous intervention rest on a historical record that carries weight on its own terms. If no ordinary historical evidence existed for these occurrences, other bases, probably a nonaccessible faith, would have to support Hope's understandings. If independent historical evidence does exist for critical events described in the writings collected as the Bible, then an accessible basis exists for believing in the truth of historical assertions in the Bible and *further* for believing in its religious claims. To take the most central events in the Gospels, independent historical evidence exists that Jesus was crucified and that Christians believed fairly early in his resurrection. Many modern Christians believe that given the discouragement among the followers of Jesus reported before the crucifixion, belief in the resurrection would not have arisen unless something truly extraordinary had happened after his crucifixion. Some Christians believe that the Romans, faced with resurrection claims, would have shown the body of Jesus if it remained in the tomb. These are the sorts of theses that rest miraculous biblical claims on grounds that are generally accessible.

A third ground of belief is what we may call the fruits of conviction. If people with a certain set of religious beliefs lead lives that are deemed specially fulfilling even by those who do not share their beliefs, this constitutes evidence that the practice of life according to these beliefs is good for people. That, of course, does not establish by itself that the beliefs are true,[3] but many people may think there is a kind of natural move from understanding that practice according to beliefs is fulfilling to a conclusion that the beliefs are true.[4] The connection will seem especially appealing if people see no evident explanation at the human level why practice according to this set of beliefs should be regarded as particularly fulfilling.[5] A somewhat similar ground for belief might be the wisdom displayed by a religious community over time. Someone who believed that for many centuries the Roman Catholic Church had displayed great sensitivity to human needs and to justice might claim that this is evidence that in some sense the church has been divinely inspired.

I have made these points crudely; actual claims are richer and more complicated. For many Christians, some of these accessible arguments may carry weight without being regarded as sufficient by themselves to induce belief in a reasonable person who begins as a skeptic. Even if they think the accessible reasons are sufficient to induce belief, Christians often suppose that full Christian convictions require experience of a more personal kind. What I have said, however, is enough to indicate that many religious people do not concede that their religious convictions, in their entirety or in crucial elements, lie outside the domain of accessible arguments.

A skeptic might respond that these religious people are misguided, that only nonaccessible forms of experience can genuinely support religious belief. We must examine this response carefully to see why it cannot lead us to place all religious claims conveniently within a broad category of claims resting on nonaccessible bases, a category to be used for a possible principle of political self-restraint.

What is the position of the skeptic who claims that religious belief inevitably rests on grounds that are not accessible to those who begin without such belief? The challenge to philosophic arguments for God is likely to differ importantly from the challenge to historical evidence.[6] Consider the argument that a purposive universe shows a purposive creator. Many people find the universe to be without purpose; as they see it, the instances of purpose that exist *among creatures* yield no indication about the nature of the universe overall or whether it was created. These people find the teleological or purposive argument for God to be totally unconvincing as an argument.

A skeptical response to the argument about the resurrection of Jesus is different. If convincing evidence existed that Jesus really died, according to all relevant modern medical criteria, and that his body actually came to life again, and that he then walked, and spoke, and ate like a normal human being for a space of time, I do not think many people would deny that this would be *some* indication of the likelihood of a supernatural power with the ability to intervene in nature and alter the natural course of events, and further would be *some* indication that Jesus bore a special relationship with this supernatural power. I do not say all this would be irrefutable proof of a supernatural power—some natural explanation might indicate that random movements of subatomic particles make the regeneration of human life an occasional occurrence—only that this evidence would constitute significant data in favor of a supernatural power. Most people who find the claims about the resurrection of Jesus to be unconvincing do not believe credible historical evidence exists for it.[7]

How would a principle of "no reliance on nonaccessible grounds" apply to the original arguments for the existence of God, given these two sorts of rejections of the arguments? The claim rooted in history is simplest. Suppose the skeptic says that historical evidence for the resurrection of Jesus is so unpersuasive that people can believe the evidence only if they already believe in the resurrection. In other words, the skeptic says, faith precedes belief in evidence of the resurrection, not the reverse. Would this kind of rejection be a sufficient basis by itself to bar someone's reliance on the historical argument for the resurrection in politics? The answer is no. Calling for self-restraint because the *listener* does not find claimed evidence to be persuasive would make a joke of the principle that grounds for decision or argument should be accessible. This is why. People often find the arguments of others to be unpersuasive. When they do, they frequently suppose that the others could believe in these arguments only because they have predispositions not related to the actual force of the arguments. The truth is that we all believe in the arguments we do for various complex psychological and social reasons. Many elements other than the force of the arguments we sincerely make figure in causing us to develop and maintain beliefs. If that alone were enough reason to disqualify arguments, we would then have to disqualify virtually all arguments for everything.[8] Instead, the main response to accessible arguments must usually be to address them directly on their own terms. Unless a special principle of exclusion applies to religious arguments or arguments based on comprehensive views, the skeptic must meet the historical argument for the resurrection of Jesus, taking it as a weak (in his view) accessible argument, not claiming it falls outside the range of accessible arguments altogether.

The status of the purpose (teleological) argument for God is more complicated. The skeptic may perceive the substance of the argument as having no force whatsoever. This suggests that the argument is not accessible to him, because no further factual data or philosophic analysis remains to be considered. For him, this fails to be an accessible argument for God because it is nonsense or based on confusion. The person who propounds the argument, however, thinks it does have force, which a sensitive, intelligent, open-minded person would recognize. As the skeptic looks for psychological or cultural reasons why the proponent accepts the argument, the proponent looks for similar reasons why the skeptic's mind is so closed. There turn out to be some arguments that nonbelievers think are not accessible and that proponents think are accessible.

For *such* arguments, it would matter how a political principle excluding nonaccessible arguments were understood. If the principle excluded only arguments that the proponents understand are not accessible, then proponents would properly continue to make some arguments that skeptics do not find accessible. Suppose, instead, the principle is that arguments are to be avoided unless they are generally understood to be accessible. (For this purpose, an argument could be generally understood to be accessible even if it can actually be grasped only by highly trained people.) In this event, the skeptic may be able to persuade proponents that some arguments that they believe are really accessible do not meet this threshold.

Even this latter approach, however, would not exclude the claim that historical evidence supports the resurrection of Jesus and many other accessible claims in favor of particular religious beliefs.

We are now in a position to see clearly that however the line of accessibility is drawn, the categories of religious and nonaccessible grounds overlap, as shown in figure 4.1.

If a political principle were directed against all, and only, nonaccessible grounds, it would not exclude some arguments for moral and political conclusions that proceed from religious premises.

The picture becomes even more complex if we include all "comprehensive" philosophic views, a category that includes all fundamental religious conceptions and some nonreligious perspectives.[9] In a subsequent chapter, I shall say more about accessibility and most nonreligious comprehensive views in liberal societies. Here I shall indicate only that for various nonreligious comprehensive views, as for religious positions, there will be accessible arguments, nonaccessible arguments, and arguments whose status will appear different to proponents and skeptics. (A similar conclusion would hold for "controversial ideas of the good," a category that overlaps to a large degree with comprehensive views.) What emerges are the relationships depicted in figure 4.2.

These figures make clear that a simple principle of exclusion of inaccessible grounds will not reach all grounds derived from religious convictions or other comprehensive views. There can, of course, be other arguments for excluding these bases, and subsequent chapters explore those arguments in some depth. Here, I shall briefly mention three commonly related reasons why one might conclude that some kinds of claims believed to be accessible by the persons who make them should not be employed in the political process.

Figure 4.1. Relation of Religious and Nonaccessible Grounds

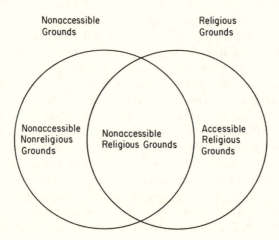

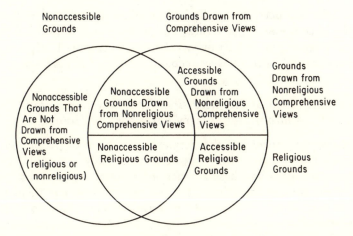

Figure 4.2. Relation of Religious Grounds, Grounds Drawn from Comprehensive Views, and Nonaccessible Grounds

The first reason for exclusion is an interpretation of history. Reliance on certain *kinds* of grounds may have proved very harmful in the past. People might infer that their society will be more stable and less contentious if certain accessible arguments are foresworn.

The second reason is a problem about accessibility in practice. Imagine that Patricia thinks a chain of reasoning about prophecies, miracles, and demonstrably effective prayer shows that scripture carries authority and is literally true, *yet* she also recognizes that many people in society, including many Christians, do not think that this chain of argument holds up at all. These other people may even understand that Patricia's argument is a realist one but assign it a radically different degree of plausibility than she does; both sides may recognize they have little left to say on the subject. Patricia might sensibly decide that her realist analysis is so distant from what many people understand to have force that it should not be relied upon to coerce others.

The final reason for not relying on kinds of realist arguments might be perception of a high error factor. Suppose we recognize that people have believed certain types of arguments in the past and later virtually all of these arguments have seemed erroneous. When it comes to these types of arguments, people now disagree sharply over which have force. Rather than bringing this radical disagreement into the political process, we might dispense with reliance on such arguments. Even people who are quite confident of the truth of their convictions and the realist reasons that support them might be willing to forego reliance on their own beliefs in return for a similar forbearance by others.

We can begin to see why some people think that explicitly religious arguments should be outside the forum of political discussion, even when these arguments are honestly formulated in realist terms. A history of religious conflict and persecution, limited practical accessibility, and the error factor might combine to make these undesirable bases of political decision.

What I explore in the rest of this chapter is the idea of religious convictions that the holders themselves recognize are *not fully accessible.*

The Basic Idea of Nonaccessible Religious Convictions That Appropriately Carry Force for the Holder

The last chapter considered the perplexing problem of people relying on convictions whose bases, they know, are not fully accessible to others. As we saw, saying what these convictions amount to, and why they may appropriately have greater force for the person who has them than for others, is not so easy. This problem arises strikingly for some religious convictions.

The Book of Acts carries the following account of the start of the conversion of Saul:

> As he neared Damascus on his journey, suddenly a light from heaven flashed around him. He fell to the ground and heard a voice say to him, "Saul, Saul, why do you persecute me?"
>
> "Who are you, Lord?" Saul asked.
>
> "I am Jesus, whom you are persecuting," he replied. "Now get up and go into the city, and you will be told what you must do." [10]

According to the account, when Saul stood up, he could not see, and was led by the hand to Damascus. There, Ananias placed his hands on Saul and said he was sent by Jesus "so that you may see again and be filled with the Holy Spirit." Saul could see again and was baptized.

If we treat this as a roughly accurate account of Saul's subjective experience, we can ask what force Saul should give to his experience and what force an outsider, Rachel, should give it. The question of crediting what Saul says arises first. Since he is telling the truth of his memory, Saul knows that he is sincere; Rachel may wonder if Saul is lying or shading the truth. Neither can be sure Saul's memory is accurate, but Saul will reasonably have more confidence in his own memory than will Rachel. Also, the serious difficulty of giving an adequate description of complex experiences may make it very hard for Saul to find words to convey what he has seen and heard. But sincerity, memory, and incapacity to describe hardly go to the heart of the matter. We know that people have conversion experiences with some frequency in our culture. They tend not to be as striking as Saul's, but we do not usually doubt either the sincerity or the memory of those who report them, and their reports of experiences are at least roughly comprehensible for many listeners. These reports are *publicly intelligible* to a large degree. [11]

Once Saul and Rachel accept the *experience* on the road to Damascus as having occurred, the question of what it means remains. It might be a genuine intercession in Saul's life by God; but it could be the natural product of some acute physical condition or extreme emotional stress,[12] not involving any authentic insight into religious truth. A reasonable Saul as well as a reasonable Rachel will need to consider these possibilities. (In one sense, Saul's experiences together have some special force for both of them. Saul's temporary blindness and apparent cure by someone who claimed to be sent by Jesus makes his more than a freestanding conversion experience.)[13] Saul feels the experience is genuine in the sense that it reflects true divine intervention in his life, but Rachel is likely to be more skeptical; Saul's conversion is not her conversion.

Should Saul give no more credit to his experience than would a reasonable Rachel? We do occasionally have experiences that we know are not very reliable. We feel *sure* the next throw of the die will be "five" or that our favorite team will win a big game. Past experience has taught us that our intuitions on such matters are not reliable; in our reflective judgment we are aware that the chance that the die will come up "five" is only one in six and that our team may lose. Conceivably this is how Saul should view his own experience, giving it no more credit than would a reasonable outsider who was able to know Saul's sincerity, memory capabilities, and emotional state as well as Saul. (Of course, some outsiders might grasp a person's emotional state better than he does.) But Saul has no objective odds against which to compare his experience. And the experience, in a sense, presses on Saul for a decisive interpretation. He cannot comfortably say as might Rachel, "People have all sorts of experiences, for all sorts of inexplicable reasons. I can't know which to credit, and I can't worry too much about it."

When experiences relate to such "deep" subjects, normal persons assign much more force to their own experiences than to the experiences of others who they think are sincerely reporting with accurate memory what they have perceived. Here precisely is the gap that conversion experiences and leaps of faith create, the gap that characterizes many religious feelings and other deep intuitions. The insights an experience suggests have much more weight for the person who has done the experiencing than for other people. That person does not suppose the experiences are replicable for other people under similar sets of external circumstances; he does not reasonably think the basic convictions about truth that rest on his experiences can be conveyed with anything close to equal power for those who listen to him.

The existence of such a category has been vigorously challenged. One challenge takes the form of skepticism whether the kind of experiences I describe differ in quality from other experiences on which people rely.[14] One striking comparison is the following: "Suppose Sally, alone in a remote location, saw creatures emerging from a flying saucer that had landed; the creatures and the flying saucer then left without a trace." The relation of Sally to other people in respect to this experience may be thought to be essentially similar to that of a person who has had a conversion experience. I do not agree. It is true that Sally will have a hard time convincing other people, and she will reasonably understand why they are skeptical. Nevertheless, Sally's basic difficulties involve convincing others that she is not lying, that her memory is sound, and that she exercised ordinary perceptive capacities in ordinary conditions of observation at the time of the event. Sally believes that other people of ordinary perception would have seen what she did if they had been there. Saul's circumstance is different. Others on the road to Damascus did not see what he perceived, and he does not suppose that identical external circumstances would produce the same perception in others. In this sense, he does not believe the experience is replicable. Of course, if everything, including the characteristics of the person involved *and* God's will were identical, the experience of someone else might be the same; but that is not replicability according to ordinary human standards for a broad range of human beings. Thus, I claim that Sally's perception is, in principle, replicable in a manner that Saul's is not,[15] even if she faces great difficulties persuading others that she observed what she did.

A different challenge acknowledges that people do in fact rely on experiences that are personal in the manner of conversion experiences, but asserts that such experiences are not *rationally* indicative of truth for the persons who have had them to a degree beyond their force for an outsider (who does not doubt the honesty, memory, and perceptive capacities of the person claiming the experience). On this view, grounds for truth are completely interpersonal. In a rational inquiry into truth, a person who has had a conversion experience should not assign it more force than would a fully informed outsider aware of the experience.

As far as this challenge is concerned, it is important not to get too entangled in phraseology, or the complexities of rational epistemology. The critical practical question is whether the person who has had the experience appropriately gives it extra weight in deciding what will count as true for his own life. On this question, we can initially say that it is *natural* for people to live in this way. They do give special force to such personal experiences, and their doing so is not a product of some particular cultural setting. One might say that such experiences are relevant to a rational individual evaluation of what is true;[16] or that it is rational for people to live in this way, even if the experience should carry no extra force for their rational evaluation of what is true; or that it is psychologically healthy and *not irrational* for people to live in this way. These three characterizations differ significantly, but all acknowledge the reasonableness of assigning extra force to the insights gleaned from one's own experience.

Some people may deny that individuals *should* give their experiences extra force in deciding what will count as true in their own lives. Ronald Replogle has taken this view. He recommends an "epistemic equality" that is better realized in the *formation* than in the *application* of our moral beliefs."[17] According to Replogle,

> the fact that an intuition is ours should add nothing to its probative value in our deliberation. An intuition's probative value . . . is a function of its

persistence in the moral calculation of a deliberating person. Yet epistemic equality dictates that its probative value not vary according to the identity of the person experiencing it. . . . Experience varies among persons, but not the methods of drawing sound inferences from experience. Reasons are by their nature impersonal in that any reason one has for believing a moral proposition must count as a reason for any other potential believer confronted with the same evidence.

On the interpretation I am pursuing, one who aspires to reflective equilibrium has every reason to treat other people's equally strong intuitions as having the same evidentiary weight as his own. Indeed, the failure to do so is a mark of irrationality.[18]

Recognizing that religious conversion experiences are "the least congenial example for my thesis," Replogle goes on to claim that Saul's conversion experience should "have *the same value* for other nonbelievers" as it should have for Saul.[19] If Replogle is correct that *for all purposes* those having experiences and those knowing about them should assign them the same weight, it would follow that a person should not assign extra weight to *his own* experience in political judgment and argument.

Replogle's thesis is a competitor to any view that a person who has a strong intuitive experience appropriately gives it more weight in his personal life than would a reasonable outsider. I would like to begin by modestly reformulating the language of his claim. Replogle calls the failure to give the same evidentiary weight to other people's equally strong intuitions a "mark of irrationality." Since this failure is natural and nearly universal, I think it would be clearer to claim that giving the same weight would be a mark of the highest or fullest rationality, not that a failure to do so is a mark of irrationality.

In considering the recommendation of "epistemic equality," we need to distinguish between two kinds of situations: situations in which the person who has a strong experience has, *after* the experience, a coherent explanation of why he has had the experience and others have not, and situations in which the "experiencer" has no such explanation. After his experience, Saul, now Paul, believes that God's grace has caused his experience and that that kind of grace is not given to everyone. Others believe their religious experiences result from some initial leap of faith that others are not inclined to make. These coherent explanations provide an overall perspective why the person with the experience should give it great weight, while the reasonable outsider might not. In such circumstances, it is not clear why the person who has had the experience should rationally reduce its weight in his own life to that a reasonable outsider would give, or why the reasonable outsider should increase the weight given the experience to that given by the person who has had it. For these situations, "epistemic equality" seems uncompelling, or needs to be understood in some qualified way.

Suppose the person with the experience has no such coherent explanation. He feels strongly, say, that higher animals deserve great consideration, but has no explanation why he has those feelings and others do not.

It is for these situations that "epistemic equality" seems most persuasive; but there remain two problems. The first is that disentangling one's intuition from one's reasoning is difficult, if not impossible. Many "intuitions" are flashes based on not wholly conscious reasoning (as "intuitive solutions" to mathematical puzzles reflect). In Replogle's view, people are to reason for themselves; they appropriately do not give equal weight to reasoning of other people (that is unconvincing to them). If someone discounts heavily his own moral intuitions, he will probably be discounting some reasoning of which he is not fully aware. (One might say in response to this problem either that such personal unconscious reasoning should also be discounted or that the separation of intuition from reason, though not complete, is sufficient to recommend epistemic equality for intuition.)

The second problem is the incredible difficulty for human beings of affording their own moral or religious intuitions no more weight than would a reasonable outsider. Given all the intuitions in the world, or within a single culture, a reasonable outsider gives extremely little weight to *my* intuition or *my* conversion experience. The effect of Replogle's recommendation would be that everybody would be giving their own intuitions and conversion experiences infinitesimally little importance.[20] The result could be a striking incompatibility between what people *felt* on some extremely important subjects (based on their intense experiences) and the rational assignment of the likelihood of truth by which they would try to live.[21]

I believe that trying to live in this way would be disorienting and psychologically unhealthy, that it is much better for people to give extra weight in their own personal lives to their own deep experiences. Thus, I conclude that people should not try to carry out Replogle's principle of epistemic equality in all of their lives. A category of personal, nonreplicable experience does exist, and reliance on such experience is natural and appropriate in people's private lives, whatever the precise status of such experience for the rational assessment of truth.

If giving extra force to one's own experiences of this sort[22] is appropriate in personal ethical decisions, the question about their use for political decisions remains. That is explored in subsequent chapters.

5

Simple Arguments for No Restraint: Some Answers and Necessary Qualifications

This chapter and the next five examine arguments for and against various principles of self-restraint in politics. Since citizens of liberal democracies enjoy wide freedom of choice and expression, inquiry sensibly begins with two simple arguments against self-restraint. Here I state those arguments, indicate some of their limits and weaknesses, and propose qualifications that yield some minimal principles of self-restraint. The possibility of more robust principles of self-restraint is what is seriously controversial, and it occupies the remainder of the book. In this chapter, I consider "authority reasons" as restraints on some official bases for decisions and then turn to decisions not heavily constrained by authority. I suggest that public officers and, to a lesser extent in some respects, ordinary citizens have responsibilities not to rely on reasons that look to violently overthrowing the government, promoting unconstitutional consequences, or undermining fundamental liberal democratic premises. I recognize that people may have comprehensive views that for them override the reasons underlying such principles of self-restraint; but I claim that thinking in terms of the broad responsibilities of officials and citizens is nonetheless useful. In the last part of the chapter, I address specifically religious reasons for decisions. Claiming that "imposition reasons" differ from other sorts of reasons, I argue that imposition reasons are indeed barred by the principles of self-restraint I have discussed, but that other religious reasons are not. The status of these other religious reasons constitutes a primary problem for the remaining chapters.

The Simple Arguments for No Restraint

Citizens in a liberal democracy are free to vote and advocate as they choose. Indeed, these liberties are fundamental aspects of our form of government, and if citizens enjoy them, they should also regard themselves as free to rely upon whatever grounds seem apt, and to make public arguments in those terms. Further, an implicit assumption of democratic government is that outcomes will be best if they reflect the feelings of most citizens. This aspiration will come closer to achievement if citizens regard themselves as free to rely upon all they care about, rather than some restricted subset of what matters to them. These are the simple arguments against restraint.

These arguments do not establish on some purely conceptual basis that principles of self-restraint *must* be antagonistic to the idea of liberal democracy. People could be free, in the sense of not being subject to constraint by others, to vote and advocate on whatever grounds they choose and still be under some moral or political duty to restrain themselves. I am "free" to pay no attention to adult children of mine, but I would be violating a moral duty if I did so. Citizens may have various moral and political duties whose fulfillment cannot be imposed by others. The assertion that outcomes will be best if they reflect the feelings of most citizens is subject to a somewhat similar reservation. If certain outcomes violate rights of fellow citizens because they are based on impermissible reasons, then these outcomes are not desirable in a liberal democracy, even though the feelings of a majority support them. No simple argument from individual freedom or majoritarian outcomes somehow conclusively establishes that proposed principles of self-restraint are indefensible.

What reference to freedom and majoritarianism *does show* is that people should be able to rely on all of what matters to them *unless* a substantial reason emerges why they should not. The burden of persuasion rests on those who argue for self-restraint, those who argue that people should eschew using grounds they believe are valid. I now proceed to consider certain minimal respects in which officials and citizens do lie under principles of restraint.

Official Duties, Authority Reasons, and Constraint

The most obvious situations in which some members of liberal democracies lie under constraints concerning the decisions they reach are when officials have duties to comply with authority. As I argue in chapter 3, executive officials and judges are supposed to act as the law or superior officials instruct them, and legislators are not supposed to violate the Constitution.[1]

What is the relationship between the reasons that are approved by the authoritative materials or human superiors and other possible reasons? The first level at which to examine this problem is within the domain of the official's authority. Using the example of a tax official, Olive, who found that the tax code clearly dictated a particular assessment, I said in chapter 3 that her official duty was to charge the prescribed amount. If Olive happens to think a provision is unjust or that circumstances call for a lighter tax, her official duties require her to disregard her sense that the taxpayer really should be charged less. The "authority reasons" displace the power of other reasons Olive might have for making a decision.[2]

At a second level, Olive must decide whether as a complete human being she should perform her official duty. For *this decision*, as chapter 3 shows, reasons external to the instructions of official authority will be crucial. Olive will naturally employ her own "comprehensive" view (religious or other) to decide how to act. If Olive has a full comprehensive view, and is rigorously self-reflective, she will think that, taking everything into account, she should do what the comprehensive view calls for. If she is a greatest happiness utilitarian, she will think she should act to promote the greatest happiness; if she is a religious believer who believes everyone should try to do God's will, she will think she should do what seems to be God's will. Since most comprehensive views place value on keeping promises and fulfilling expectations and Olive has promised to perform her official duty and is expected by others to do so, Olive's comprehensive view will almost certainly include reasons for performing her official duty. Indeed, this is *so common* among comprehensive views that, without referring to any particular comprehensive view, one can say, "It is important for Olive to keep her promise to do her official duty."

For various reasons, Olive may not match her official duty against her comprehensive view in the straightforward way I have so far supposed. Many distinctive comprehensive views say little directly about common situations of choice. Thinking she should do God's will, Olive may suppose that on rare occasions God's manifested will calls upon her to violate official duties, but that God's will usually is that we carry out settled social responsibilities. Olive might conclude that in deciding whether to do her official duty, her religious understanding ordinarily guides her to use standards that are shared and are independent of her own religious beliefs.[3] Another possibility is that Olive's comprehensive view will be inadequate, failing to address at all subjects that a full comprehensive view would cover.[4] Or, she may not have considered the implications of her comprehensive view. (Not wishing to subject themselves to personal hardship, people tend to suppress implications that would require a choice between moral duty and self-interest. Since refusing to perform official duties usually does not enhance one's career, someone may be laggard in thinking much about that choice.) Finally, Olive may feel that the requirements of official duty *somehow outweigh* the implications of her comprehensive position, although she cannot logically defend that position.

Olive's comprehensive view may, of course, include giving weight to official duties to an extent that predominates over considerations that would otherwise predominate and determine a different course. In that event, her comprehensive view incorporates reasons to perform her official duty. Here I mean more—that after all is considered, Olive thinks her comprehensive view suggests a decision different from her official duty. It follows that she should think she should do what her comprehensive view suggests, since that is overriding. But people are not always logical.[5] Olive may somehow stubbornly feel she should do what her official duty dictates, anyway.

These complications about how comprehensive views relate to official duty do not obscure the two major points of this section. Discourse about official duty and about the reasons that duty makes relevant can often be carried on independent of particular comprehensive positions. These reasons of authority and the decisions they recommend are sometimes opposed to the implications of various comprehensive views.

General Limits on Appropriate Reasons for Legislators and Citizens

Do any principles of self-restraint in politics reach beyond the constraints of authority? Much of the practical relevance of this question is contained in the more specific question whether such principles apply to legislators and citizens who are considering proposed laws or electoral choices. In these decisions, neither group has official duties to perform particular acts, as might a judge. Against the possibility that institutions of liberal democracy carry *no* implications for how legislators or citizens should act politically, leaving them free to act on behalf of any values or interests, I claim that both legislators and citizens have roles that foreclose some reasons for acting. I first address the clearer case of legislators.

Legislators

Legislators represent the public. They are usually supposed to act to achieve what is good for the population at large or in their district, not narrowly to promote their own self-interest. More importantly for our purposes, legislators in the United States typically take an oath to uphold the Constitution and laws. The oath is not a promise to resist all constitutional change, but it is, at a minimum, an undertaking to comply with basic legal mechanisms for accomplishing change. A legislator participating in violent revolution to overthrow liberal democracy in favor of an absolutist theocracy would not be acting in accord with his oath. The "role" of legislator does not countenance engaging in violence to overthrow liberal democracy. It follows that a legislator also should not support ordinary legislation because he believes that will indirectly promote violent overthrow.[6]

Constitutional provisions further limit appropriate legislative objectives. A legislator may openly seek to amend the Constitution, but since he is bound by it in his ordinary legislative activities, he should not vote for a bill that he understands is unconstitutional.[7] Similarly, he should not promote a bill *because*, though not directly violating the Constitution, it will undermine enforcement of constitutional rights. In these respects, the legislator is restrained from relying on reasons that violate the Constitution.

Is there a further limit concerning basic essentials of liberal democracy? To take an extreme case, suppose a legislator seeks by peaceful constitutional amendment to reintroduce slavery or allow only one form of religious worship. He is attempting by legal means to overthrow the basic requisites of liberal democracy;[8] he fails to support the Constitution and laws of the country if he seeks to undermine its fundamental political premises. Legislators are constrained not to do this, even by legal means.

Citizens

Does an ordinary citizen have responsibilities similar to those of a legislator? This is a harder question. Although traditional social contract theory asserts that citizens have in some way consented to a liberal government and are obligated not to undermine it, no theory of actual consent is plausible for the general body of citizens or residents. They have given no explicit consent. Proposals that voting, acceptance of public benefits, or remaining in residence amount to implied consent are unpersuasive, because ordinary requisites of implied consent are lacking.[9]

People, however, can have roles to which they have not consented. Adult children are thought to have family responsibilities toward infirm parents to which they may never have agreed. We can imagine a liberal democracy as an ongoing enterprise in which citizens have at least the minimal responsibility not to undermine the enterprise. That would be sufficient to speak of the role of a citizen.

Should we conceive of liberal democracy in this way? An alternative is to consider citizens as having no basic responsibilities, free to manipulate the system as best they can, although subject to the state's coercion if they violate laws. On this view, each citizen could properly regard himself or herself as a "bad person" (or "bad man" in Oliver Wendell Holmes's terminology)[10] as far as the political system is concerned, connected to it by relations of fear and advantage instead of relations of responsibility and duty.

Liberal democratic societies certainly aspire to something more. A rhetoric of citizen responsibility is widely accepted. At a minimum, citizens who themselves are fairly treated by the system are believed to have a political responsibility not to undermine the system by violent revolution. Such a responsibility is supported by shared social values, and also, I believe, by deeper realist grounds concerning justice and social stability. It follows from this responsibility that citizens should not vote for candidates and advocate the adoption of laws because they believe these will promote violent overthrow of liberal democracy.

Is there also a constraint, paralleling that for legislators, against promoting unconstitutional actions or undermining the basic essentials of liberal democracy? Here, political history matters. We can imagine countries with fragile, even jerry-built, institutions of liberal democracy, where it would be implausible to think that citizens have an obligation to sustain the constitution that happens to exist at one point in time. Further, if even the wisdom of basic fundamentals of liberal democracy is itself a subject of wide controversy, one cannot regard all citizens as having a responsibility to maintain those fundamentals (unless, of course, people in general have a responsibility to promote liberal democracy because it is the best form of government). On the other hand, in a country with a long-standing, relatively stable, liberal democracy, thinking of one role of citizens as not to undermine the basic requisites of that system makes sense. This difference illustrates a theme to which I will return: the application of much political theory needs be tied to the history and culture of particular societies.

The Significance and Force of a Principle of Self-Restraint

Before I turn to self-restraint and religious reasons, I focus on the *significance* and *force* of any principle of self-restraint, an issue posed most sharply by the responsibilities of citizens. (The voluntary assumption of office, and oaths, provide extra reasons why legislators should perform their responsibilities.) Is there any point in conceiving the responsibilities of citizens of liberal democracies? How far do these conceptions indicate reasons of force for actual people?

Imagine a citizen, Victoria, whose own comprehensive view envisions a government that may only be achieved by violent overthrow of the present system. Why should Victoria be disturbed by overstepping a restraint on how "liberal citizens" are supposed to act? Here we face directly a troublesome question, which I posed in chapter 1: Does talk about a "good liberal citizen" have any value?

To urge Victoria that her role of citizen minimally includes not promoting violent overthrow of the system is to propose what she may owe fellow citizens as a matter of fairness. Others are restraining themselves in ways that benefit her; she should at least play by the rules. Moreover, actions that deviate from the minimal responsibilities of good citizens can be severely destabilizing; when people don't play by the understood rules of the game, the harms tend to spread well beyond the immediate incidents. If Victoria is thoughtful, she will consider whether her comprehensive view makes room for these factors, and, if it does not, whether that view itself is defensible. Nevertheless, Victoria's comprehensive view may lead her to believe some other form of government is so far preferable to liberal democracy that temporary unfairness and extensive bloodshed are warranted. She may also think liberal democracy is itself so grossly unfair or immoral that the possible unfairness of violent overthrow is not very important. Thus, any model of how "good liberal citizens" should act may have only limited persuasiveness for those whose comprehensive views lead powerfully in contrary directions. Others cannot conclude that people like Victoria are wrong (all things considered) to violate responsibilities as "good citizens," without concluding that she is wrong in her comprehensive view or the implication she draws from it. However, even when those disinclined to fulfill their responsibilities consider models of citizenship to be hardly relevant, thought about the responsibilities of citizens can assist other members of society to identify certain activities as outside the range of actions that a good citizen undertakes.

Religious Grounds and Basic Premises of Liberal Democracy

I have thus far suggested that legislators, and, more arguably, citizens have failed to fulfill appropriate roles in liberal democracies if their grounds for political behavior are promoting violent overthrow of liberal democracy, promoting constitutional violations, or undermining basic premises of liberal democracy. How far do these conclusions carry us for possible self-restraint about religious grounds? Here great care is needed.

Practices of Religious Imposition and Imposition Reasons

In the remainder of the chapter I claim that basic premises of liberal democracy definitely preclude practices of religious imposition *and* reliance on what I call imposition reasons, but I argue that some reliances on religious grounds neither generate impositions nor amount to imposition reasons. Whether self-restraint is appropriate for these latter religious grounds is a critical subject of later chapters.

A substantial degree of religious liberty is a basic requisite of liberal democracy. Many think the government should not encourage any particular faith or religion in general; others disagree. Almost everyone concurs that the government should not actively suppress religions or sharply discourage the exercise of particular faiths.[11] To take a concrete example: although most people in the United States are Christians, forbidding or actively discouraging the practice of the Jewish religion would be antithetical to existing premises of our political order. Legislation that imposed a special fee for the practice of Judaism would offend a widespread sense of what is just and it would violate constitutional rights, not only as those rights are presently construed, but also as they would be construed by people who would allow many more connections between government and religion than has the modern Supreme Court. A fee to practice a particular religion would be a religious imposition at odds with premises of liberal democracy. Such a fee would by its objective operation constitute an imposition, independent of the motives of those who adopted and administered it.

What I call an imposition *reason* can be illustrated with respect to classroom prayer in public schools. People disagree whether such prayer itself constitutes an imposition on those whose beliefs do not correspond with the prayers. Many people are critical of the Supreme Court decision barring such prayer[12] and do not think modest state support of religious practice violates basic premises of liberal democracy. Supporters of school prayer tend to say that so long as students need not participate and can be excused from the classroom, the pressure on nonbelievers is not very great and is acceptable. Suppose that Herman is a local school board official who is supporting a constitutional amendment to permit organized classroom prayer. It happens that Herman is extremely hostile to the Jewish religion and *wants* the school environment to embarrass Jewish children into abandoning their faith. Herman assumes that in his dominantly Christian community most school prayers will be explicitly Christian, and he believes that school prayer will actually put tremendous pressure on nonbelieving children. That, indeed, is his main but unexpressed reason for supporting school prayer. His reason is an imposition reason. Whether or not school prayer objectively amounts to an imposition, Herman's reason for supporting it is an aim to impose that itself conflicts with basic premises of liberal democracy.

Other Nonimposition Religious Reasons

Imagine, instead, that the issue is whether factory farming will be regulated in a way to assure a decent life for animals that will be slaughtered. Frances thinks that animals deserve substantial consideration from human beings, and she favors the regulation. Her underlying grounds are religious; she thinks the Bible calls for human concern for animals. She has no wish that the factory farming law affect anyone's religious belief or practice; she wants only to protect animals. She relies on a religious ground that I shall call a nonimposition reason.

Is this distinction defensible? Or is every reliance on a religious basis an imposition? It might be said that if Frances's ground is prevailing, the government compels "nonbelievers to conform to a standard of conduct inspired in large measure by religious belief" and that this imposes "a kind of compelled religion."[13] It might be said, further, that the regulation would tacitly approve Frances's religious views and disapprove those that support a contrary position.[14] These are genuine worries to which I return in the next chapter. Here, I shall say only that the "endorsement" of Frances's religion is very weak if all that is involved is a decision to protect animals that rests for many people on that religious perspective. Neither "disapproval" of religious views supporting a contrary position nor the impingement on the behavior of those holding that view is greater than would be the case if purely secular reasons supported the regulation. Each time the government adopts a coercive law that is deemed obnoxious according to some religious views, it constrains those who hold those views and implicitly "disapproves" the views.[15] Thus, a law requiring racial integration implicitly disapproves a religious view that God wants racial segregation and constrains the behavior of those who hold this view. Of course, "imposition" can mean different things to different people, and this challenge does show that any reliance on religious grounds can be considered in some weak sense to be against other religious views. However, it need not involve imposition in the sense I am using it, that is, of seriously discouraging, or aiming to discourage, the holding of other religious views or the practice of those religions.

The attitudes behind the Liberal Coalition proposal in chapter 2 strongly suggest that not every reliance on a religious reason is necessarily an imposition. Remember that the groups there felt comfortable about having members of other groups employing religious grounds across a wide range of political subjects; and no group sought to limit the religious freedom of the others. No group would feel its religious liberty was being imposed upon if it happened to be the loser in a decision about regulation of factory farming.

A rather different, but related, response to my distinction between religious grounds that impose and those that do not is one that seeks to connect reasons behind legislative decisions to legislative preambles in the following way:

> We can imagine legislators putting into a preamble their religious grounds for protecting animals; in principle, a majority of legislators voting on those grounds and stating them in deliberation is not different; in principle, *some* legislators doing that is not different from the majority doing so; in principle, their voting but not stating their reasons is not different; in principle, citizens seeking legislation on that basis is not different from legislators doing so.[16]

By constructing this chain from reasons stated in the legislation itself, someone could claim that the use of religious reasons in the political process itself constitutes a violation of basic premises of liberal democracy. I shall examine this argument more fully in the next chapter, but here I note two important aspects. If a serious problem exists, it is mainly one of "establishing" dominant religious views, not of imposing upon or restricting those with other views. Of course, many people believe that establishment in and of itself constitutes a kind of imposition, but it is not imposition in the sense I have suggested. And, as noted in chapter 2, many liberal democracies do have some form of established religion. Moreover, given the typical nature of preambles, carrying the reasoning in one so far back as to explain the religious source of belief why animal life is valued would be highly unusual. That would probably occur only if legislators had some religious objective, beyond justifying their choice to protect animals. Thus, a significant break does exist between preamble statements and religiously grounded explanations of votes on the floor of the legislature. Whatever may be true of preambles, voting and explaining on religious grounds need not involve an imposition.

Imposition and the Claims of Liberal Democracy

For imposition practices and reasons, the question arises (as it did with Victoria) why a legislator or citizen should feel constrained to observe basic premises of liberal democracy. Suppose Herman wants to have the U.S. Constitution amended to provide explicit favoritism for the Christian religion and someone says he is not acting in accord with basic liberal democratic premises, or with the present theory of governance in this country, or with the country's political traditions. Herman may contend that what he proposes is consistent with the basic premises of liberal democracy, but he may instead simply state that disregard of the true religion shows the poverty of liberalism. Probably he will assert some support in the country's political traditions, but he might acknowledge that the country has drifted into premises of governance that should now be rejected. Although arguments that his view is out of step might cause Herman to reexamine the political implications of his own religious perspective, he may, at the end of the day, conclude that liberal democracy itself countenances legal shifts away from features of liberal democracy, and that he should act according to his own religious view, which recommends such a shift. In these circumstances, categorization of Herman's activities may indeed matter more for those committed in some broad way to the country's liberal democratic premises than it does for Herman. Although I shall not say a great deal more about it, this problem, of how legislators or citizens may be subject to a principle of self-restraint that does not accord with their own comprehensive views, lurks in the background of much of the subsequent discussion.

The Possibility of Restraint That Extends beyond No Imposition

I have suggested that much reliance on religious grounds does not amount to religious imposition.[17] Does it follow that such reliance is appropriate? Not necessarily.

In the proposal of the Fervent Believers of chapter 2, we saw reasons why people establishing a liberal democracy might self-consciously agree to eschew religious bases for political positions. Members of those groups wanted to protect against decisions based on fundamental premises radically different from their own. If explicit agreement about restraint is possible, it is also possible that a society could over time develop some similar principle of self-restraint as a loose premise of political life. Yet another possibility is that such a principle, although not *yet* a premise of political life, would fit better with other basic premises and realities of that life than would the absence of restraint. Arguments for various principles that reach beyond imposition reasons will occupy us in the chapters that follow.

Impositions and Nonimpositions of Other Views

In this chapter, I have concentrated on impositions, imposition reasons, and reasons that do not amount to impositions, as these relate to religion. One could carry out a similar exercise in respect to other views: comprehensive views, like utilitarianism, and narrower political principles such as gender equality before the law. I have not attempted that exercise here because there is serious disagreement how far the government properly supports and discourages nonreligious principles. The idea that it *should* give some support to fundamental principles *of liberal democracy* itself is not controversial; but people differ over how much it should support these political principles and over whether it should give any direct support to more extensive ideas about the good life. The rest of this book provides a sense of which views I think are properly supported by government, and to what degree support is appropriate. Here I need say only that for any views the government should not directly support or discourage, the divide between impositions and imposition reasons, on the one hand, and nonimposition reliance on the views, on the other, will be significant, as it is in respect to religious views.

6

Restraint as to Religious Grounds: Separation of Church and State

Relying on Religious Premises

The first possible principle of self-restraint in politics that I consider is that people should not rely on religious grounds or make arguments in those terms. The history of religious conflict in Western Europe and the growth of toleration and liberal democracy out of that conflict inform all the principles of restraint that people now propose, but many principles are not cast directly in terms of religious bases of judgment. I here address the idea that officials and citizens should refrain from relying on religious grounds in particular. The claim is that such reliance is contrary to fundamental premises of separation of church and state and religious liberty, or is particularly threatening to social life.

Before exploring the arguments for such a principle of restraint, I need first to explain what amounts to reliance on a religious ground. This involves brief comment on religious grounds as opposed to other grounds; reliance at the time of decision as contrasted with mere causal influence; religious support for chains of common reason; and reliance on religious premises as compared with reliance on religiously influenced culture and religious symbols.

A principle that one should not employ religious premises in political decision and argument would obviously cover the following excerpt from an imaginary speech given by a legislator, Leslie, against the regulation of factory farming: "The Book of Genesis clearly states that animals are for the benefit of human beings. Factory farming benefits human beings; God has told us that we need not worry about effects on animals." Even when a ground for judgment lacks explicit religious content, it can involve reliance on religion if a religious basis underlies it or motivates it. Thus, if someone opposing legally permitted suicide says, "No one has a right to take his own life," this is a religious ground if the speaker believes the ground can only be supported by belief in God. As presented by the speaker, the ground is religious *even if* adequate nonreligious reasons could support it. An argument is also religious if the speaker is trying implicitly to promote religious objectives.[1]

A principle barring reliance on religious grounds would permit reliance on intuitive judgments that are unconnected to religious premises. It would also permit reliance on most *non*religious comprehensive views. Suppose Kathy claims that human reason supports a Kantian approach to morality, whether or not God exists. Her reliance on Kantian morality would not count as religious. Certain comprehensive views, however, are *anti*religious, resting heavily on the rejection of religious premises.[2] Suppose a person relied on grounds that *derived from* atheist beliefs; for example, Lester might say we can be indifferent to animal welfare because neither God nor an afterlife exists. If separation of church and state and religious liberty mean that the government is not to assert a religious truth, the state is supposed to be neutral between positive religious views and antireligious views. The government's promoting antireligion would violate basic principles regarding religion.[3] Since there would be an obvious inequity if Lester was free to invoke antireligious grounds but Leslie was not free to invoke religious grounds, I shall assume that a principle of restraint against reliance on religious grounds would also bar reliance on antireligious grounds.[4]

A principle of restraint *would allow* reliance on some grounds one had initially "discovered" through religious involvement. Imagine that Leslie had grown up indifferent to the plight of the poor and that religious involvement led her to concern for them. As a legislator, she examines all the nonreligious arguments for and against welfare cuts and is persuaded that the cuts would be wrong, quite apart from any religious premises. She may recognize that she would never have arrived at the position she now supports had it not been for her religious involvement, but she sincerely believes her present position is correct independent of religious beliefs.[5] This sort of influence does not amount to reliance on religious grounds.

Although reliance on religious premises might seem to contrast with reliance on common nonreligious reason, the two can intertwine in subtle ways. Suppose Leslie *believes* that common, "natural" reasons support her position that early abortion is wrong, but she does not understand why the "natural" arguments are compelling, relying instead on assurances of the Roman Catholic Church to that effect. Leslie's position rests on religious premises despite her honest belief that common reasons support it. Another way that religious premises can be interwoven with common reason is in setting the question to be addressed. Suppose Leslie's religious assumption that God ensouls human beings at a single moment in time leads her to look for one point of critical importance for valuing the fetus and to reject the idea that the consideration owed the fetus grows slowly over time. Her ultimate conclusion on the subject will rest partly on religious premises even if she uses naturalist reasoning to determine the exact point at which the fetus should be protected.

More troublesome questions of categorization involve cultural traditions and symbols from religious sources. There is no doubt that our culture, and perhaps almost every human culture, has been deeply influenced by religious beliefs and practices. When people seek to fulfill cultural traditions, these will be powerfully tinctured by religious influences. Further, many of the most evocative symbols and stories in the culture will have religious roots. Does nonreliance on religious premises entail disregarding deep cultural assumptions and symbols with religious origins? I assume not. Thus, if Leslie opposed cuts in welfare, she would not necessarily be relying on religious premises if she explained her position as follows: "Should we care for the poor? Our deepest traditions have always included the idea that we should do unto others as we would have done unto us. We cannot be true to ourselves and those traditions if we fail to care adequately for the poor and needy." Here Leslie refers directly to a principle that is found in the Bible but has a broader significance. The traditions to which she refers are partly religious. But if she does not rest her argument on the truth of any religious premises and invokes cultural traditions for their own sake, *not because* they are partly religious, she is not relying on religious grounds.[6]

Restraint Implied by Principles of Church-State Separation

With these clarifications in mind, we are ready to consider the position that religious premises should not be relied upon in the political process. A version of this position has been advocated with precision and care by Robert Audi in a series of articles.[7] According to Audi,

> [I]n a free and democratic society, people who want to preserve religious and other liberties should not argue for or advocate laws or policies that restrict human conduct unless they offer (or at least have) adequate secular (nonreligious) reasons to support the law or policy in question (where an adequate reason for a law or policy is a proposition whose truth is sufficient to justify it). . . . [A] secular reason is, roughly, one whose normative force . . . does not (evidentially) depend on the existence of God . . . or on theological considerations.[8]

Audi leaves open whether his "principle of secular rationale" applies to all laws and policies, but it does apply to laws that restrict conduct.[9]

Audi further urges that people should not construct secular rationalizations when they are really persuaded by religious considerations, and they should not present to others as being sufficient any reasons they find less than persuasive. He argues for a "principle of secular motivation," which provides that "one should not advocate or promote any legal or public policy restrictions on human conduct unless one not only has and is willing to offer, but is also *motivated by,* adequate secular reason."[10]

That is a stronger requirement than the one imposed by Audi's principle of secular rationale, as is apparent from the illustration of a Roman Catholic who has a weak grasp of the natural arguments for giving the fetus (embryo) full moral status upon conception, but believes on the authority of the church that these arguments are valid. If she presents the natural arguments as a basis for restricting abortions, she may satisfy Audi's principle of secular rationale by offering possibly adequate secular reasons that she regards as adequate.[11] But she is not now motivated by the force of those reasons, since she has attempted no independent assessment of the reasons and is unsure what she would conclude if she were to disregard church authority. Thus, she fails the test of secular motivation. To comply with it, she must try to determine whether, apart from the church's authority, she thinks the natural arguments are persuasive.[12]

The "principle of secular resolution," Audi's third related principle, requires that political issues be finally resolved along secular lines; decisions should be fully warranted by secular considerations.[13] These three principles apply to private citizens as well as public officials. Audi believes that if secular reasons, by themselves, are inconclusive about whether behavior should be restricted, then the behavior should be left free.

In Audi's view, the principles of secular rationale and motivation do not preclude *some* argument for political positions in terms of religious reasons, "though this has its dangers."[14] Audi explains that people employ religious arguments in expressive, communicative, persuasive, evidential, and heuristic roles; and he suggests that despite his principles of restriction, "religious arguments can, in certain ways, be quite properly used in all [these] roles."[15] I agree with Audi that people faithfully following his three principles should be able to indicate additional religious reasons for a position to set forth their feelings (expressive) or indicate where they are "coming from" (communicative).[16] The other uses seem more questionable. Audi's idea apparently is that everyone would try to find adequate secular grounds for positions, but would also employ supplementary religious arguments in order to persuade (persuasive),[17] to offer support for a view or course of action (evidential), and to stimulate the discovery of truth (heuristic), for example, by raising the question of what God would command. In theory, one can imagine people employing secular reasons to decide whether to support state use of coercion and engaging in further discourse to explore their religious perspectives and their implications; but for real human beings wide discussion of religious implications is almost certainly bound to affect evaluation of nonreligious reasons far more than whatever extra enlightenment the religious discussion provides to the secular merit of secular reasons. Audi is aware that too much religious discussion might work counter to the effective operation of his "secular" principles, but his published work does not indicate *how* severe he thinks the tension is in practical contexts or the kinds of circumstances in which people who think they fulfill the demands of the secular principles should restrain themselves from using religious arguments.[18]

Audi presents his three secular principles as ones that are implied by basic ideas of separation of church and state and religious liberty; he thinks his principles are appropriate for liberal democracy and are aspects of our constitutional order. If it is wrong for the state to take a position on religious truth and to interfere with religious exercise, then it is wrong for the state to impose upon some people on the bases of other people's religious beliefs. (Audi also contends that reliance on religious grounds is offensive to the liberal principle of autonomy that people should not be coerced without grounds that they would accept if fully rational and adequately informed.)[19]

Similar conclusions based on the desirability of disentangling politics from religion are reached by Edward Foley[20] and William Marshall.[21] Foley builds on the constitutional principles found in major Supreme Court cases that the government should not favor or endorse religion over irreligion.[22] Assuming that a direct statement of religious reasons in a preamble to a statute would violate the establishment clause of the First Amendment, Foley argues that legislators offering justifications for their votes on religious grounds does not differ significantly.[23] Legislators are constrained by establishment clause values not to make religious arguments, and Foley claims that citizens are similarly situated from the perspective of political philosophy. Foley suggests that people can have virtually identical social philosophies despite radically different views about the meaning of the universe (he uses followers of Paul Tillich and Albert Camus as examples); thus, it is possible for them to resolve practical social problems without interjecting their religious perspectives into debate.[24] The "secular politics" that he envisages favors neither religion nor irreligion, because it removes that subject from the field of discussion.[25] In a society such as ours in which positive religious views dominate, the employment of arguments from religion and irreligion will effectively discriminate against the irreligious in a manner at odds with the value of "no establishment."[26]

Marshall supports what he takes as "the general perception that religion and religious conviction are purely private matters that have no role or place in the nation's political process."[27] Marshall's underlying justification for this principle of constraint is an account of the "dark side of religion" that I will develop in the next section. Foley and Marshall both focus on political discourse, rather then unexpressed bases for decision, and it is unclear whether they would be as restrictive as Audi is on personal grounds of decision that are not ventilated in the public square. Both are more restrictive than Audi on religious argument in public political discourse.

Does Church-State Separation Require Restraint as to Religious Bases?

How compelling is the argument from church-state separation to a politics based on secular grounds? If we disregarded political history and asked what practices regarding religious premises would best suit separation and the free exercise of religion, we would probably not come up with exclusions as rigorous as those proposed by Audi and Foley. Their argument starts from the assumption that the United States should be committed to a relatively full separation of church and state, that the government should not support religion or profess a religious truth. In chapter 9 we will examine the views of some writers who dissent, but here I take the separationist assumption (which I share) as a starting point.

The most basic defense of separation of church and state is that it is conducive to religious liberty; religious liberty is considered *more fundamental* than nonestablishment of religion. Religious liberty entails being able to act on one's beliefs as well as to hold the beliefs and to engage in worship. People are properly guided by their own religious beliefs in nonpolitical ethical decisions, including what donations to give, what causes to pursue, what associations to form, even which actions of others to accept as proper and which to criticize.[28] If people are told that, at least in the absence of adequate secular reasons, they should not rely on religious beliefs to vote for candidates who will protect animals, this is a serious constraint on the free exercise of their religion. As a modern statement of the Presbyterian Church (U.S.A.) puts it, "[I]t is a limitation and denial of faith not to seek its expression in both a personal and a public manner, in such ways as will not only influence but transform the social order. Faith demands engagement in the secular order and involvement in the political realm."[29] Constitutional lawyers are well familiar with the idea that in many circumstances a tension exists between the fullest implementation of the free exercise of religion and the fullest implementation of nonestablishment. The possibility of self-restraint presents one such circumstance.[30] The most expansive idea of "no establishment" may call for eschewing religious grounds in political decisions, but that program would significantly curtail religious liberty. Professor Audi obviously thinks that because the state's coercion will be used against people, the development of a philosophy of political action calls for nonestablishment concerns to prevail over the fullest liberty of choice for those making decisions;[31] but I see no neat way to establish that.

It might, of course, be claimed that political choices are in the public domain, whereas the exercise of religion is in the private domain.[32] Thus, restraint on political choice would not limit free exercise in the domain where it really matters. Challenges to the public-private distinction common in political liberalism have been a staple of much recent critical and feminist writing in political philosophy and constitutional law. Even if, as I believe, some such distinction is appropriate, its boundaries are not imposed by a natural order of categories, they are subject to considered choice. People throughout history have been moved to achieve in political life objectives recommended by their religious understandings. Telling them that crucial aspects of this behavior are improper is to suggest the curtailing of significant activity that flows from their religious beliefs. That is a sacrifice that could be justified only by strong reasons. A simplistic division of public from private does not itself amount to a strong reason.

As I suggested in the last chapter, many uses of religious grounds by legislators and citizens do not involve imposition against religious liberty in any ordinary sense, and they do not involve the state in staking out a position on religious truth. If *some people* support a factory-farming regulation on religious grounds, the government is not asserting the truth of their religious claims against those of competitors. In pluralist societies no single dominant religious approach is likely to underlie such regulations. This reality drives a large wedge between the legislature's publicly adopting a religious rationale in a preamble and normal reliance on religious convictions by citizens and even by legislators. Normal reliance by people on various grounds will not lead to any single religious rationale that explains legislation.

In the unusual instances when one dominant view underlies a statute, the problem of imposition and state promotion of religion is more serious. Nevertheless, an important difference still exists between the state symbolically saying, "We are promoting a particular religion or religious outlook" and its saying,

> We have this practical problem that needs resolution—how animals are to be treated. Legislation on this properly follows the views of most citizens (even though coercion of other citizens is involved). To that minimal extent, the state may come down on the side of one religious view rather than others, but we are not promoting the truth of any religious view or trying to discourage belief in any religious view; we are just settling this particular problem about how people should behave.

This approach is certainly plausible for legislators who *are deferring* to the views of most citizens on protecting animals; it is plausible even for legislators who are relying on their own religious views. From this standpoint, *putting* the religious grounding in a preamble would not be proper, since that would place the formal endorsement of the state behind a particular religious form of reasoning to protect animals. Such an endorsement is not given if all that happens are individuals' expressions of why they think legislation is warranted.[33] Thus, even when a dominant religious opinion lies behind legislation, nonestablishment values do not yield a clear principle of restraint.

In any event, whatever may be true about such examples taken in isolation, the great majority of instances in our pluralist society remain ones in which no single dominant religious view controls. General principles of self-restraint for such societies are properly developed for what will usually occur, not for rare instances.

The proposal of the Liberal Coalition in chapter 2, developed by groups with great mutual trust and an interest in learning from each other on religious subjects, indicates that citizens who are creating a liberal democracy with a general principle of nonestablishment of religion might choose to have free play for religiously based justifications among legislators and citizens in ordinary political life.[34] Thus a rigorous "secular rationale" principle is compelled neither by simple logic nor by intelligent judgment in all circumstances.

If rigorous (self-imposed) restrictions on the employment of religious grounds are not warranted by abstract argument alone, perhaps they will find support in political history or other disciplines of social science. One conceivable point of relevance from history is that principles of restraint are rooted in American traditions. For most of this country's history, however, political life has been influenced at least as much by religion as it is now. Until recently, people have never asserted that all reliance on religious premises is improper. Whatever notions of nonestablishment have been essential, they have not included as an explicit feature any principles as sweeping as Audi's or Foley's.

The relevance of political history that could favor Audi and Foley is more complex. Given the dangers of imposition and social divisiveness that history shows accompany religious disagreement, we might draw the lesson that political life is more stable, and that pluralist societies are fairer and more harmonious, in accord with how far religion is excluded from politics. On this view, Audi's principles can be defended as the most sensible understanding of separation of church and state and religious liberty, given actual conditions in liberal democracies or the United States.[35] The political history of the country might be seen as *moving toward* Audi's or Foley's principles, which would be the final and desirable culmination of earlier developments.

Marshall develops support for principles of restraint from literature and social science.[36] He discusses at length the allegorical story of The Grand Inquisitor, told by the atheist Ivan to his religiously devout brother, Alyosha, in Dostoevsky's *Brothers Karamazov*. In the story the Grand Inquisitor rejects Jesus, who has reappeared, because his message of human freedom will disturb the church's successful efforts to make people happy; those efforts are founded, the Grand Inquisitor says, on miracle, mystery, and authority. The lesson in Marshall's view is that

> [r]eligion and humanity have a potentially dangerous symbiotic relationship. Humanity needs religion to alleviate its spiritual and moral anxiety. Humanity wants to be led, to be told that it is right, and to be relieved of the burden of its own conscience. In order to respond to these needs and anxieties, religion must proclaim its infallibility and universality. It must be dogmatic and authoritarian; for if it were to express self-doubt, it would no longer possess the claim to certainty that makes it attractive.[37]

Marshall claims that a substantial literature in social science indicates that the story of the Grand Inquisitor "accurately captures what may be termed the 'dark side' of religion and religious belief—the side of religion that is inherently intolerant and persecutory."[38] People desperately search for meaning, partly because they fear that their lives are meaningless. Religious belief is a protection against existential anxiety, providing a psychological defense of doctrine and ritual against terrifying feelings of insignificance and chaos. Because fear is a primary motivation in adopting religious beliefs, "the believer may be upset by any suggestion that her adopted belief system is fallible."[39] People close themselves off to new insights and in extreme circumstances respond with persecution. This "dark side" of religion can be a destructive political force. "A believer who sees those who oppose or question her beliefs as aligned with the 'powers of chaos' is likely to treat the public square as a battleground rather than as a forum for debate. Religion, if unleashed as a political force, may also lead to a particularly acrimonious divisiveness among different religions."[40] Fervent beliefs may become fuel for intolerance, repression, hate, and persecution.

Marshall suggests that, by and large, ideas of restraint about religious advocacy, or at least about institutional separation, may have avoided these dangers in the United States. The notion that religion should be "privatized" may dilute intolerant urges and disincline people to try to conquer competing religious beliefs in the political realm. In sum, a disengagement of religion from politics forestalls many of the worst consequences for social life that the "dark side," which is characteristic of much religion, threatens. Although Marshall does not address *anti*religious beliefs, presumably he would want those excluded from politics as well, either because history shows that persecution of religion by antireligion (as in the Soviet Union) has its own "dark side," *or* because if antireligious ideas flourished in politics, religious believers could not reasonably be expected to exercise self-restraint when it comes to religious ideas.

Given the actual history of religious conflict, one cannot doubt that there is some truth in what Marshall says. Whether the "dark side" is as permanent a feature of religion as he believes is more questionable. Without attempting to resolve that question, I will readdress it in subsequent chapters. Here it is sufficient to say that worries of the sort Marshall raises are among the best arguments for principles of restraint for keeping religion out of political life. Whether such principles are finally defensible depends partly on their feasibility, partly on the value of what they would sacrifice, and partly on the persuasiveness of alternative approaches. I have said enough to indicate that a full principle of no reliance on religious grounds would sacrifice religious freedom to a significant degree for many people.

As far as alternative principles of self-restraint are concerned, there are two important variations. Some alternatives compete directly with principles of self-restraint for religion, admitting religious considerations into political life much more than would the principles examined in this chapter. Other alternatives end up excluding all, or most, religious grounds but drawing lines that are not explicitly in terms of religion and excluding some nonreligious grounds. It is to such alternatives that I turn in the next chapter. In chapter 9, I consider arguments that all principles excluding religious grounds are misconceived.

I postpone the issue of feasibility—that is, whether principles are ones people can really be expected to employ—until I have presented other possible principles of restraint, since all the principles raise closely similar questions. Another issue that I largely postpone is the question whether restraint should be mainly aimed at decision (as Audi proposes) or advocacy (as Foley suggests) or should reach both similarly. In chapters 11 through 14, I suggest that this issue is critically related to feasibility and that limits on advocacy are far more feasible than limits on judgment.

7

Excluding Grounds That Are
Nonaccessible, Based on Comprehensive
Views, or Based on Controversial Ideas
of the Good Life

This chapter considers three closely related principles of political self-restraint that are not cast explicitly in terms of religion: those that exclude nonaccessible grounds, grounds deriving from comprehensive views, and grounds based on controversial ideas of the good. The principles of restraint treated here apply to all political subjects. Chapter 10 addresses a principle proposed by John Rawls that applies to constitutional subjects but not to "ordinary" politics.

In discussing nonaccessible grounds, chapters 3 and 4 concentrated on intuitive perceptions about what is true or good that a reasonable person understands would not carry nearly the same weight for an outsider. Here I now present in more detail an argument that such nonaccessible grounds should not play a role in the political process.

Self-Restraint as to Nonaccessible Grounds

The basic argument for excluding nonaccessible grounds has two dimensions. The first is that it is fundamentally unfair to coerce people, or to use the corporate authority and power of the state, when the grounds for doing so are not ones that all those affected could be expected to accept if they made reasonable judgments. The second dimension of the argument is that the political life of a society will be healthiest and most stable if political issues are resolved on premises and grounds that are fully available to everyone in the society.

My initial statement of this argument leaves open whether the appropriate restraint applies to all action by the state or only action that coerces individuals.[1] It also leaves open the way accessibility is to be judged; more specifically, it does not address either whether the grounds must (in some sense) be accessible to every reasonable person, or whether a person judging accessibility is to rely upon his or her own assessment of what reasonable people can understand or upon standards that enjoy common currency in the society. I explore these questions after I consider the basic argument for excluding nonaccessible grounds in more depth.

Higher-Order Impartiality and Personal Convictions

This argument was put in striking form in 1987 by Thomas Nagel.[2] Although Nagel has since written[3] that he has been persuaded by a critique of the article by Joseph Raz,[4] his position bears examining, not least because Raz's critique seems to miss something very important in Nagel's original article.

Nagel suggests that political liberalism rests on what he calls a higher-order impartiality that distinguishes "between what justifies individual belief and what justifies appealing to that belief in support of the exercise of political power."[5] Treating all people impartially within one's own view is not sufficient to satisfy this higher-order impartiality. The inquisitor who orders that a heretic be burned may be treating the heretic impartially, given the inquisitor's belief about what is true. The inquisitor is interested in helping to save everyone's soul. Imposing that penalty may seem the way to save the most souls and perhaps even the heretic's.[6] Higher-order impartiality, however, requires beliefs that "can be shown to be justifiable from a more impersonal standpoint."[7] Nagel explains:

> The idea is that when we look at certain of our convictions from outside, however justified they may be from within, the appeal to their truth must be seen merely as an appeal to our beliefs, and should be treated as such unless those beliefs can be shown to be justifiable from a more impersonal standpoint. . . .
>
> This does not mean we have to stop believing them—that is, believing them to be *true*. Considered as individual beliefs they may be adequately grounded, or at least not unreasonable: the standards of individual rationality are different from the standards of epistemological ethics.
>
> [U]nless there is some way of applying from an impersonal standpoint the distinction between my believing something and its being true, an appeal to its truth is equivalent to an appeal to my belief in its truth. . . . The appeal to truth as opposed to belief . . . must imply the possibility of some standard to which an impersonal appeal can be made, even if it cannot settle our disagreement at the moment.
>
> [One must be prepared] to submit one's reasons to the criticism of others, and to find that the exercise of a common critical rationality and

consideration of evidence that can be shared will reveal that one is mistaken. This means that it must be possible to present to others the basis of your own beliefs, so that once you have done so, *they have what you have,* and can arrive at a judgment on the same basis.[8]

For Nagel, the element of coercion in the political order necessitates reference to this higher-order impartiality. To justify making people do things against their will, an especially stringent requirement of objectivity in justification must be imposed;[9] people need to be "impartial not only in the allocation of benefits or harms but in their identification."[10] This requirement is not met when "part of the source of your conviction is personal faith or revelation—because to report your faith or revelation to someone else is not to give him what you have, as you do when you show him your evidence or give him your arguments."[11] Nagel supposes that the inquisitor would be unable to justify coercion to the heretic without relying on personal faith or revelation. Further, Nagel thinks that in the present state of moral debate, certain moral conclusions, about issues such as abortion, sexual conduct, and the killing of animals for food, rest on "personal moral convictions" that fail the test of higher-order impartiality, even when those conclusions are not tied to religious premises.[12] Nagel concludes that the state should not restrict individuals' liberty with respect to such issues if they are reducible to "a pure confrontation between personal moral convictions."[13] He recognizes that coercion cannot await unanimous agreement to be justified. Disagreements exist, and persist, even when reasons are offered that lie in the public domain. People have been exposed to different testimony and arguments, they have had different experiences, and they assess evidence and arguments differently, so reasonable disagreements result.[14] But "the distinction between a disagreement in the common, public domain and a clash between irreconcilable subjective convictions [is not] too rarefied to be of political significance. Judgment is not the same as faith, or pure moral intuition."[15]

Personal Convictions and Acceptability to Others

Raz's challenge, in part, is founded on an apparent denial that a category of understanding of the kind Nagel describes actually exists. Since Nagel plainly had in mind just the sorts of grounds discussed in chapters 3 and 4, Raz's attack reaches many of the distinctions I draw there. In response to Nagel, Raz writes that although he is sympathetic with Nagel's basic idea that some grounds of coercion might be excluded, Nagel's limits are either too stringent or fail to exclude even the sorts of claims that Nagel had in mind.[16] Raz points out that Nagel's standards do not exclude many claims for religious revelation, those based on ordinary evidence, such as miracles and fulfilled prophecies, which I mentioned in chapter 4. Raz also notes that all commonsense notions of sharing evidence include claims based on personal experience, for example, "I know it snowed in New

York because I was there and saw it." He further recognizes that we hold ourselves open to extrasensory perceptions, such as those of diviners who have found water on previous occasions. He says that even claims of revelation that do not rely on trusted modes of acquiring knowledge can be public, as when thousands testify that they had a similar experience at the same time: "One may think that the fact that many had the same experience at the same time lends credence to the report of each one of them. But it does not differ in principle from the report of a single person of the same experience, even when it was not witnessed by others. Either such reports are acceptable by all, or they are not to be trusted even by the person who had the experience." [17]

Raz is right that such experiences carry some weight for an outsider's evaluation of what is probably true; [18] but he *does not acknowledge* that for perceptions of truth whose accuracy is not testable in the manner of divination of water, the people who have had the perceptions reasonably give them more credit than someone who listens and does not doubt that the claimed subjective experiences have occurred. As I suggested in chapter 4, Saul reasonably gives more weight to his conversion experience than does an outsider who believes Saul's reporting of what he experienced is accurate, that is, accurate so long as Saul's report is purged of conclusionary judgments about the true significance of the experience. The key sentence in the preceding passage of Raz is "Either such reports are acceptable by all, or they are not to be trusted even by the person who had the experience." This sentence glides over the phenomenon of conversion experiences and similar nonreligious intuitions. Raz suggests that a person should trust his own experience only if it is "acceptable by all." If Raz means that the person who has the experience should distrust it if it carries *no weight* for a reasonable outsider, he may be correct. Perhaps if experiences are "not acceptable" at all, they should not be trusted by the persons who had them. Raz could conceivably be taken to go further and endorse the view Ronald Replogle has explicitly defended: namely, that the person who has an experience that yields insight should give the experience *no more weight* than would a reasonable outsider who gives it *some weight*. I argued in chapter 4 that that position is strongly contrary to normal, healthy human behavior; I have claimed that individual experiences pointing toward religious or ethical truths that count only a little for others reasonably count a great deal for the people who have had them. Raz seems to deny that the holder of beliefs will perceive any gap between justifiable bases for his beliefs and reasons that should persuade others; but many (otherwise reasonable) religious people do perceive just such a gap.

The crucial issue about political coercion is whether a person who strongly believes something is true because of this sort of individual experience is justified, when deciding about political coercion, in assigning more weight to the experience than he could reasonably expect an outsider to give it. That is the heart of the question which Nagel raises and which he answers negatively.

Fairness to Fellow Citizens

Nagel's claim is fundamentally one of fairness: coercing people on the basis of grounds they can reasonably reject is not right. Related to this concern may be worries about perceived unfairness and stability. I shall concentrate on the fairness argument, but what I say also has implications for perceived unfairness and stability.

If people at large accepted a restraint against using nonaccessible grounds, they would be giving up a chance to coerce others on the basis of what they understand to be their "personal convictions" in return for relief from coercion on the basis of what others understand to be their personal convictions. The first point to be made is that, in operation, Nagel's principle would apparently call upon each person to consider the accessibility of grounds on which he might rely in politics. If the person is convinced he is offering grounds that all reasonable people should accept, and thinks he is presenting evidence and argument of a generally comprehensible sort for those grounds, he may rely on them, even though most people are not persuaded or do not even think his argument has any force. Thus, the person who thinks reasoned philosophic argument or references to historical events can establish the existence of a certain kind of God would be free to use that premise in political decision and discourse. This, indeed, is a large part of Raz's critique, and it is valid.

Nagel might respond that most philosophers and intellectuals do not suppose that religious truths can be established in this way; but many people who have such religious beliefs believe that these two groups are composed of self-important manipulators of ideas rather than genuinely wise people. Thus, the skepticism of intellectuals about the rational knowability of religious truths leaves many believers unmoved.

If people are to rely only on grounds that are subject to a common critical rationality, the process of decisions about self-restraint would inevitably introduce some unfortunate discriminations. Suppose Claude and Danielle have essentially similar religious beliefs, but Claude thinks each step can be established on the basis of reason and Danielle does not. In a conscientious application of Nagel's principle to political decision and argument, Claude can rely on his religious beliefs, but Danielle cannot rely on hers.

Often a more subtle discrimination would be at work. Few people are rigorously self-reflective about what they believe. This leads some to be "overmodest," assuming that premises in which they believe are based only on intuitions when on further thought they would see that their premises are establishable by reasoned argument to reasonable people. Other people, I suspect a much greater number, believe they have reasonably establishable bases,[19] but would discover under intense examination that personal insight plays a larger role than they have recognized. Practical application of Nagel's principle would tend to work against people who are intellectually honest and self-critical.

More fundamentally, as the Liberal Coalition proposal in chapter 2 reveals, Nagel's claim of unfairness turns out to be circular in its dependence on what people regard as desirable and fair. We saw there that, making an overall evaluation of advantages and disadvantages, people might choose to accept some coercion based on nonaccessible grounds. For people who had reached such agreement, reliance on nonaccessible grounds would not be unfair. To develop this point further, we need (drawing from the discussion in chapter 5) to reflect on situations in which people are coerced. In some, such as Nagel's example of a heretic burned at an inquisitor's order, a basic liberty is impinged upon with no corresponding gain in the basic liberty of someone else. For such prohibitions, people might well insist on a principle of no coercion without grounds that all reasonable people would accept. The practices that I have loosely spoken of as religious impositions consist of those in which religious liberty is directly violated.

In other situations, a question arises whether someone or something deserves protection, and no imposition (in my sense) is threatened. Suppose the issue is to be whether hunting of some species of animals is to be allowed. Each side recognizes that its arguments rest partly on premises that are not publicly accessible. Thinking in advance about such situations, reasonable people might decide that the interests or liberties of hunters are of no greater significance than the interests or liberties of the people who want to save members of the species. Instead of adopting a principle, as Nagel does, that would leave actions unrestricted unless there are grounds for restriction whose force all reasonable people would acknowledge—a principle that would here favor the hunters because their liberty would be directly curtailed by regulation—people might decide it would be better to adopt a principle that the greater number would prevail in their judgments, even when their judgments include nonaccessible grounds.

Another illustration of this point is the distributional issue of how much wealth the well-to-do should share with those who are poor. Again, it is not clear why reasonable people would decide to let all resources stay where they are (or would otherwise be) if there were a division of nonaccessible judgments on what should be done.

To sum up, reasonable people in some liberal democratic societies might, in the absence of religious or similar impositions, reasonably decide to let nonaccessible judgments be used to resolve some sorts of political issues. That is the possibility exemplified in the Liberal Coalition proposal. If people *did so agree*, reliance on such grounds definitely would not be unfair. Of course, if *there were reasonable agreement to the contrary*, as in the Fervent Believers proposal, reliance would be unfair.

In our society, no explicit agreement exists either way. If one asks which perspective is closer to our political history, it is the absence of a principle of restraint; since people have not typically assumed that, they should in political choices censor grounds they think are otherwise appropriate. Anyone who claimed that Nagel's *principle should cover all political issues*[20] would have to say that it represents the best realization of liberty and equality in liberal democracy. Because of the difficulties and discrimination in practical application and the unwarranted comparative advantage for those who would otherwise be immediately restrained by the state (such as the hunters in that example), I believe that the principle in the broad form he suggests is not appropriate. Whether the principle may be wise for some or all *officials* is a much harder question to which I shall return.

An alternative rendering of the Nagel proposal would be that citizens should rely only on grounds that are commonly shared.[21] These grounds would include basic political principles of the society and common modes of reasoning: as John Rawls puts it, shared principles of justice and "practices of common sense and science."[22] Under this approach, a person considering whether to rely on grounds would have to consider whether others actually find the underlying reasons plausible, not only whether *he* thinks all other reasonable people should accept them. A person might thus end up excluding some of his beliefs that he thinks get by the hurdle of his own perception of accessibility. Since more would now depend on what most people actually think, this approach would reduce, but not eliminate, the unfairness and discrimination that would accompany the principle's application; less would rest on what the believer thinks reasonable people *should* accept. This approach, however, might leave many more issues with no resolution on commonly accessible grounds. The presumption in favor of immediate liberty, which I have claimed is not an appealing one for all instances, would have even more practical force.

Self-Restraint about Comprehensive Views or Controversial Ideas of the Good

Liberalism as Neutral between Comprehensive Views or Controversial Conceptions of the Good

Proposals similar to Nagel's have been made with respect to comprehensive views or controversial ideals of the good. As the idea is put by Charles Larmore, "The fundamental liberal principle is that the state should remain neutral toward disputed and controversial ideals of the good life."[23] Although Larmore, himself, does not explicitly discuss the connection between a state that is neutral in this way and the neutrality of input by citizens and legislators in the political process, his full argument suggests that he also supports neutrality of input. Such a view about officials is explicitly urged by, among others, Lawrence B. Solum, who writes that a requirement of public reason applies "to members of legislative bodies in the course of official public deliberation, to executive officers in the course of their official duties, and to judges and other adjudicators."[24] In his central contention that political decisions should not rest on claims that one conception of the good is better than others, Bruce Ackerman's *Social Jus-*

tice in the Liberal State plainly extends the restraint to citizens acting in politics.[25] Before looking at arguments in support of this kind of principle of self-restraint, I consider three preliminary questions about its range: (1) How closely does its exclusion follow that of Nagel's proposal? (2) How are controversial conceptions of the good related to comprehensive views? (3) What is the range of state activities a principle of neutrality plausibly covers?

How, if at all, does the idea that political inputs should be neutral between controversial ideas of the good differ from Nagel's suggestion? Without doubt, the overlap in what they would exclude would be great. The most important difference in application is that under the Larmore-Solum-Ackerman approach, a legislator (and perhaps a citizen) who is making a decision cannot rely on a controversial idea of the good,[26] even if she believes the idea can be fully supported by accessible arguments. If she recognizes that her religious or other conception is one that many people do not share, she is not to rely upon it (despite her opinion that it is accessible).[27]

Does it matter whether a principle of self-restraint is cast in terms of conceptions of the good life or comprehensive views? Some discussions of this are a bit loose. Within the realm of personal morality, we can draw a distinction between obligations people owe to others (for example, one should not lie) and standards for how they should live in other respects (one should pursue excellence in one's activities). One *might* conceive ideas of the good as limited to the latter standards; but those who advocate neutrality between controversial ideas of the good life mean to cover neutrality between controversial moral claims about personal ethics, even when those claims concern matters of personal obligation. Many comprehensive views about the meaning of human existence reach still further, influencing answers to questions such as the proper status of animals and human fetuses. These aspects, with their political as well as personal moral implications, deal with who should count as members of the community of entities to be protected; they really do not fit comfortably into a category of ideas of the good life. Nevertheless, those who talk in terms of self-restraint and public reason mean to exclude the use of comprehensive views as they bear on these subjects. Thus, the claim that legislators should not invoke competing conceptions of the good life probably needs to be understood broadly to cover *some aspects* of competing philosophic conceptions that reach beyond "the good life" understood in any narrow sense.[28] So understood, "conceptions of the good" amount to what I have referred to in earlier chapters as comprehensive views, though in any precise delineation the two concepts differ slightly. For the purposes of this book, I treat principles of restraint that cover comprehensive views as identical to those that cover controversial ideas of the good.

When scholars recommend state neutrality concerning ideas of the good, and self-restraint concerning those ideas when people make political judgments, what range of activities do they have in mind? Given the role of public schools, it seems doubtful if the government in all its functions could possibly remain neutral between competing conceptions of the good life. One could imagine a society in which families and other institutions were so strong that schools could limit themselves to instruction on public responsibilities; but in this society the schools end up being the main teachers of personal morality for many children. How are schools to approach the lives of actively gay (homosexual) men and women? Presumably, the schools in teaching public responsibility should emphasize that all people deserve respect as equal citizens, whatever one thinks about their personal lifestyles.[29] But should the schools present a gay sexual lifestyle as unacceptable, as acceptable but not as good as a heterosexual lifestyle, as "good" as a heterosexual lifestyle, or as a matter of personal choice about whose desirability the school has no view? Or, should the schools avoid the subject altogether? With modern claims for gay rights, it is hard to see how schools can avoid the subject altogether, and, if they do, the implicit message may be that gays are deviants whose lifestyle is unhealthy and wrong. The desirability of a gay lifestyle is certainly an issue of the good life that is presently controversial. It is hard to see how public schools can remain fully neutral about it,[30] and it is hard to see how people can take positions on what the schools should do without relying on their own views about the appropriateness of homosexual relations. In New York City, proposals to implement a "Rainbow Curriculum," which, among other things, teaches young children the acceptability of gay couples, contributed to the dismissal of the chancellor of the schools and led to divisive contests in local school board elections in 1993.

Beyond schools, need the government be completely neutral about the good life in deciding such matters as which arts to subsidize? Can it choose to fund operas and symphonies and what it deems to be good literature, without funding all forms of music and writing? In deciding that certain forms of art are particularly valuable and that some examples of an art are of higher quality than others, it makes judgments about what is good for the producers and consumers of art.[31] In light of these serious questions, the thesis of neutrality about controversial conceptions of the good should be understood as *mainly* directed to actions of the state that coerce individual behavior, as indeed Audi and Nagel have understood the primary force of their proposed principles of restraint.[32] I turn now to arguments for neutrality and self-restraint concerning controversial conceptions of the good (or comprehensive views).

Arguing that "[p]luralism and reasonable disagreement have become for modern thought ineliminable features of the idea of the good life," Larmore suggests that "[t]he state should not seek to promote any particular conception of the good life because of its presumed *intrinsic* superiority —that is, because it is supposedly a *truer* conception."[33] Larmore strongly challenges criticisms that liberalism itself is based on a controversial notion of autonomy in personal life. Rejecting ideas that the proper state somehow *expresses* what is proper in personal life, Larmore says liberalism is a political idea, and the liberal state is a *modus vivendi* for political relations among people with varying ideas of the good life. According to Larmore, "[N]eutrality emphasizes the equal freedom that all persons should have to pursue their conception of the good life."[34] Neutrality is of procedure, not outcome.[35] Given the decisions the state must make, "some conceptions of the good life will fare better than others,"[36] but decisions should not be based on the correctness of any particular conception of the good life.[37]

Since liberalism, in Larmore's account, is political and does not take a stance on controversial questions of the good life, Larmore eschews reliance on reasons for supporting tolerance of diversity that themselves rest on answers to such questions. More specifically, he urges that liberalism should forego appeals to values of skepticism, experimentation (as in the philosophy of J. S. Mill), and individual autonomy (as in Kant's theory).[38] Liberals need to devise a *"neutral justification of political neutrality,"*[39] one that does not itself rest on a controversial conception of the good. Larmore suggests that this justification, which is *not morally neutral*, can be developed from a commitment to converse with others, the kind of commitment emphasized in Habermas's theory about ideally rational conditions of dialogue. Larmore posits a maxim of withdrawing to neutral ground in conversation, "even when the disagreement centers on the more substantial parts of what one understands to be ideal conditions of conversation."[40] Larmore acknowledges that a notion of rational dialogue alone cannot explain why one should bother to continue such a conversation with those with whom one lacks sympathy and who one does not need to persuade politically, but the norm of equal respect for persons may provide a basis for doing so.[41] Larmore indicates that the crucial respect is for persons, not beliefs; and it is based on the capacity of people to work out a coherent view of the world.[42] Our showing this respect equally does not depend on whether people exercise their capacity autonomously and experimentally or instead accept traditions and forms of life uncritically.[43]

Solum argues that the liberal principle that "[p]ublic reasons exclude particular comprehensive conceptions of the good"[44] is contingent on the historical conditions of pluralism.[45] In those conditions, this exclusion is called for by respect for free and equal persons.[46] The use of religious reasons by officials, Solum says, represents an endorsement of their truth and denial of the beliefs of others.[47] Stability constitutes a further reason for neutrality; if restraint is not observed, politics may degenerate into competition for power along religious lines. In answer to the claim that the United States need not worry about instability caused by religious tensions, Solum writes (even before the tragic example of the former Yugoslavia), "A survey of world history and contemporary experience reveals that seemingly unshakable stability can rapidly degenerate into strife and even chaos."[48]

Critique

The arguments for and against self-restraint concerning comprehensive views or controversial ideas of the good for those engaging in political action are substantially similar to the arguments we have already reviewed in connection with a possible exclusion of religious grounds or of grounds that rest on "personal convictions" unsupported by accessible reasons. There are, however, some specific features of Larmore's and Solum's proposals that warrant noting.

Larmore seeks to ground the neutrality principle in a conception that does not itself rest on a comprehensive view. Has he persuasively done so, or at least sketched the outlines of a basis for doing so?[49] He recognizes that the requirements of rational politics alone would not require "carrying on the conversation" with a powerless minority, but he suggests that a recognition of equality based on shared capacity to work out a coherent view of the world may lead us to do so. *Standing alone,* however, this basis for equal respect does not seem promising. Almost all mature human beings have *some capacity* to work out a worldview, but there is a threshold below which some severely retarded people who have reached an adult age lack this capacity. If a minimum threshold of capacity exists, some people will be just over that minimum, while others will have more substantial capacity. Among those with *similar capacities,* some will exercise the capacity more than others. Some people seriously concern themselves with the nature of life, others drift along without reflecting much or even consciously accepting traditional outlooks. Although many defenses of equality rely on moral capacity, it remains unclear why people should be owed equal respect based on a capacity *if* the capacity itself is unequal among people and is exercised to unequal degrees.[50]

This problem *is resolved* by some comprehensive views, most notably by the religious idea that all human beings are equally loved by God and are equal in God's sight, but it seems doubtful if the basic principle of equal respect can itself be grounded without reference to some comprehensive view. Unless Larmore's form of equal respect is simply taken as a starting assumption of liberal democracy, or as a belief held by most people within liberal democracies, it probably cannot be sustained without reliance on some comprehensive view.[51]

Concentrating on judicial decision, Solum has an illuminating discussion of the relation between making decisions and justifying them. He recognizes that at the deep level of fundamental assumptions, people may be influenced by religious or other comprehensive views, but he urges that this is different from explicit reliance on those views. He understands that identifying the use of inappropriate bases is relatively simple for public justifications but not for actual judgments, but his proposed principle of restraint covers both. He reasons that if one grants that justifications should be in terms neutral between competing conceptions of the good, it follows that judgments also should be. Otherwise, the justifications will constitute a kind of lie, misrepresenting the true bases of decision. Someone who argues, as I do later, that sometimes constraints on public justifications should be greater than constraints on bases for judgment must meet this highly plausible challenge to any discrepancy between the two.

Solum puts forward an explicit argument that in situations in which public reasons do not resolve a problem, the liberty of those to be regulated should prevail.[52] Solum claims that the liberty principle is "at the very core of a liberal theory of justice,"[53] but this principle cannot be drawn out of pluralism and equal respect alone. My example of the liberty of hunters, which is opposed to interests in preserving species, shows why the claims of the hunters should have no evident preference. As Amy Gutmann and Dennis Thompson put it succinctly, "Neither action nor inaction by the state should have a privileged status in moral justification."[54] Solum's claim that the liberty principle is central cannot be made without reference to some comprehensive view of human good. Political notions of equal respect do not establish it.

Larmore and Solum treat nonreligious ideas of the good or comprehensive views similarly to religious ones, but they do not quite face up to the difficulty of distinguishing improper reliance on liberal nonreligious comprehensive views from proper reliance on (relatively) *noncontroversial* ideas of the good. In his treatment, Rawls talks about (J. S.) Millian and Kantian liberalism as comprehensive liberal views.[55] Although the Kantian approach would serve as well, I shall use Mill's philosophy to make my point.

Mill's liberalism is substantially consequentialist; it places a very high value on human autonomy, creativity, diversity, and the development of human faculties over time. The values that are central for Mill are not absent from what common reason indicates in our culture. These values are found there, though the comprehensive Millian view may give them a different or more precise magnitude and ordering.[56]

Now, what does the constraint of not relying on a comprehensive view amount to if your comprehensive view is Millian liberalism? You, of course, cannot argue that decisions should be reached in accord with Mill's overall philosophy. And, perhaps you would have to acknowledge the force of factors that are present in public reason that Mill omits or seriously downplays. But for the most part, you could present the factors relevant under both your comprehensive view and common public reason that lead you to one position or another. Presumably, you could even refer to specific arguments in Mill's *On Liberty*, say, about free speech and self-regarding acts, that enjoy a substantial currency independent of whether people regard themselves as Millians in some broader sense. In sum, understanding how a liberal Christian would censor herself is much easier than understanding just how the Millian would censor herself, how she would determine what to omit from the treatment of political matters that would be part of her comprehensive view. Apparently, her censorship would involve restricting a much less significant or sizeable portion of her relevant total understanding. What we can see here is that although Larmore and Solum treat all comprehensive views about human good similarly, and notably treat religious and nonreligious comprehensive views similarly, the nonreligious liberal comprehensive views will suffer much less significant self-restraining censorship than will nonliberal comprehensive views and religious liberal comprehensive views.

8

Acceptable and Unacceptable
Religious Grounds?

Some writers who agree with the idea that all contributions to public political discourse should be accessible explicitly argue that reliance on some
religious premises is appropriate. This chapter discusses two approaches of
this kind, one that treats relevant religious perspectives as subject to fully
rational scrutiny and one that proposes a dialogue among adherents of different religious groups and nonbelievers.

Natural Religion and Politics

Challenging the claim that religious ideas should be omitted from public
debate about political issues, Franklin Gamwell concentrates on the nature
of religious belief.[1] Gamwell rejects the widely held proposition that religious convictions are inherently nonrational or beyond reason, finding "no
persuasive case for this understanding of religion."[2] Like Franklin, Jefferson, and Madison, Gamwell thinks religious convictions are subject to rational examination and are not beyond public scrutiny. Only opinions that
are subject to rational review have a claim on citizens,[3] but religious convictions are not more or less the subject of rational evaluation than other
bases of political judgment. Arguing that public debate should be as full as
possible, Gamwell states that "[t]o seek the political implications of one's
faith, and to advocate both in the public debate, is not only permitted to
but incumbent upon citizens of the Republic."[4]

If Gamwell's assessment of religious convictions were accurate, it
would constitute a substantial argument in favor of religious perspectives
being an explicit aspect of political debate. Drawing from the discussion in
chapters 3 and 4 of the grounds for moral judgment, I first suggest complexities and difficulties with Gamwell's central thesis as it applies to much

85

religious belief. I then consider a problem about religion and politics that exists whatever the ultimate ground of most religious understanding.

Some people self-consciously hold religious views that they do not believe are fully subject to rational evaluation. Gamwell makes clear that he does not draw a distinction between good grounds for truth in the realm of religion and good grounds for truth in the political realm. He thinks religious beliefs without rational grounding are unsound religious beliefs.[5] His view about the political status of these unsound beliefs is not entirely clear. Would it be desirable for them to be withheld from public political debate, or is it fine for them to be put forward, so that other citizens may shoot them down for their lack of rational grounding? If almost everyone accepted Gamwell's rational approach to religion, perhaps an occasional reliance on another sort of belief would do no harm; but if many people are confused about religious beliefs and their grounding, the introduction of explicitly nonrational beliefs directly into the political process may not be constructive.[6]

If Gamwell thinks that only religious claims with rational grounding properly belong in the political process, the question arises what force his argument reasonably has for holders of other sorts of religious beliefs. Gamwell presents no argument specifically related to the political realm.[7] Suppose Faith is unpersuaded by Gamwell's approach to religious understanding and herself holds religious beliefs that are not fully subject to rational evaluation. She will find no reason in Gamwell's discussion to withhold reliance on her religious beliefs in the political process if rationally grounded religious beliefs are assumed to have a place there.

A more subtle question raised by Gamwell's approach concerns what he counts as being subject to rational examination. He speaks of "laws which are informed by the truth that is accessible to common reason and experience."[8] I have suggested that religious experiences are largely explicable to others, but that the person who has had the experiences naturally gives them far more weight than do reasonable outsiders. When a believer offers personal confirmation as evidence of the truth of her religious beliefs, that confirmation serves as some slight evidence for others, but it is much weaker evidence for them than it is for the believer. No fully interpersonal, rational way exists for assessing the weight of such personal experience. If a law were based largely on religious beliefs that were mainly confirmed by personal experiences, those who had not shared in the experiences might *understand* why the law had been adopted, but they would lack a *reasoned basis* for concluding that the law was sound.

How might Gamwell respond to this reality? He might say that as citizens dealing with political subjects, believers should give no more weight to their own personal experiences than would a reasonable outsider. That, however, would require difficult mental gymnastics for the believers. He might say, instead, that such personal confirmation by experience is simply an inappropriate ground of religious belief. That view would stand in opposition to much of the Christian and other religious traditions. Finally, he might claim that explicability assures that a conviction is subject to rational examination. But explicability, without more, yields no test of the weight to be given claims based on a conviction. Thus, if explicability alone were enough to satisfy Gamwell, we could not expect that "full public debate"[9] would provide a very helpful test of what beliefs should be held and relied upon for the adoption of laws.

Reasoned judgment, as I have said, plays an important part in what most people believe about religion; but many people's religious convictions rest partly on elements that are not fully subject to reasoned interpersonal evaluation. Gamwell apparently doubts that confirmation by personal experience is an important source of *true* religious understanding. Many members of our society disagree. A proposal to admit rational arguments for particular religious beliefs into the political process needs to say something more to these people than that they misconceive the nature of religious truth. Gamwell's suggestion that religious claims be included in public political debate seems most appealing when applied to positions that explicitly claim rational, interpersonal foundations. Even here, however, we can see difficulties that relate to the particular character of the political process. Suppose a political advocate says, "this passage of Genesis establishes that the interests of animals do not count, and I know that the Bible is infallible, as I shall establish by a series of rational steps, including miracles and the accuracy of prophecies." The speaker's claims are subject to judgment by interpersonal reason; but a political debate over the treatment of animals is hardly the occasion to run through each of these claims step by step. Casting doubt on the reasoned basis for biblical infallibility will not appear productive to those whose aim is to protect animals. They might worry that even if they succeeded, the speaker would probably cling to biblical infallibility and his interpretation of Genesis, giving up only his belief that these could be fully supported on rational bases. Any genuine dialogue over the import of particular biblical passages for political positions is likely to be between people who accept the authority of the passages but begin by interpreting them differently, not between those who think the passages carry great authority and those who think they carry none.

This problem of useful interaction extends to philosophic arguments about God's existence. A debate that primarily concerns political policy is hardly the best forum to examine those arguments. A more likely result is the trading of insults: "What can you expect from someone who rejects even the obvious existence of God?" and "Anyone foolish enough to think God's existence can be demonstrated lacks judgment."

In summary, if Gamwell wants to admit into public debate all religious convictions that are subject *in any degree* to reasoned analysis, those based substantially on confirmation by personal experience would be appropriately argued. Such an outcome would clutter political debate with many religious claims that are not subject to reasoned interpersonal evaluation. If, instead, Gamwell would encourage reliance only on claims believed to be *establishable* by reasoned interpersonal argument, this would still include many claims about God that rest on philosophic arguments or the infallibility of biblical passages or the authority of religious leaders, when those claims rest upon links in a chain of reasoned argument. Political debate is a very unwieldy vehicle for addressing such claims.

Naturalist Ethics and Politics

I turn now from Gamwell's focus on religious claims themselves to views that emphasize the nature of moral and political claims. A long tradition in the Roman Catholic Church and, to a lesser extent, among some Protestant groups holds that many, perhaps virtually all, ethical and political truths are accessible to common human reason, that understanding of these truths does not require an understanding of religious truth. Although Christian revelation and the church are considered important additional sources of insight about morality and politics, for the most part they provide alternative means to grasp what those outside the faith may also understand. Thus, even if specifically religious claims are not fully evaluable by common reason, ethical and political assertions are subject to such evaluation.

At first glance, this perspective may seem to pose no obstacle to a principle that would exclude religious ideas from political disputes. Believers would simply work through the natural ethical arguments available to everyone and present those arguments, not relying upon or arguing from the alternative religious sources of understanding.[10] Thus, the "genetic" argument for the personhood of the embryo would matter in politics, not church teachings that condemn abortion from the time of conception.

This fairly simple picture raises some difficulties if a principle of self-restraint were to cover how one makes decisions as well as one's public justifications for decisions. In my discussion of what constitutes reliance on religious grounds in chapter 6, I mentioned how religious premises may intertwine with naturalist reasoning, how a belief that God ensouls a fetus at some moment in time might lead one to look for one critical point of changed moral status rather than to suppose that moral status steadily develops. I also mentioned a second problem, that people may believe natural arguments are sound because of religious authority, not because they perceive the intrinsic force of the arguments. A third problem is a variation on the second; someone might find the natural arguments *somewhat persuasive* by themselves, but be *much more certain* of their truth because of religious beliefs. In politics, as elsewhere, one's degree of certainty often matters. A person who is certain that a fetus is already a "human being" may favor restrictions that he would not favor if he thought that that valuation of the fetus was only probably right. These difficulties somewhat compromise the assumption that the religious believer in naturalist ethics can just plunge forward with the naturalist reasons even if religious grounds should not be relied upon. (The difficulties do not, however, threaten self-restraint that is *limited to public justification alone*; a person can offer naturalist reasons in public justification without mentioning religious grounds that support his confidence in them.)

What I consider here is a position that is naturalist to a large degree, but is skeptical of the validity of straightforward universalist ethical argument and seeks to introduce *some* greater explicit reliance on religion in the political process than would any principle of total exclusion. I shall concentrate on a book, *Love and Power*,[11] by Michael Perry, a leading constitutional law theorist who is a liberal Roman Catholic. Perry explicitly concerns himself with public justification rather than grounds of decision, which he calls a "relatively marginal issue";[12] but his central thesis concerns both, since one persuaded by his arguments needs to ask whether the grounds Perry would exclude from public political *debate* should be employed in political *judgments* and should be *discussed within communities of believers*.[13]

The first part of Perry's book is devoted to criticizing the approaches of others. Among other things, he rejects "right prior to good" political theory, arguing that claims about human good must figure in political justification. He argues that ideas of "impartiality" like Nagel's actually unfairly favor those whose beliefs can be supported by reasons that fall within the range of the commonly accepted; they unfairly privilege beliefs that happen to be shared.[14]

Perry's own ethical position combines pluralist and universalist elements. Of special relevance to the political conception that follows, he says, "Any plausible conception of human good—of human well-being, of human nature—must be pluralist."[15] Rejecting the historicist denial of any shared human nature, he suggests that the serious challenge to a notion of common ethical duty is not a nihilist denial of the notion of human good, but is, rather, doubt whether we should care for other people.[16] On this last question, he writes,

> Why should we "love one another just as I have loved you"? The answer, in the vision of the Jerusalem-based religions—a vision rooted in the lived experience of the Jerusalem-based religious communities—is that the Other, too, including the outsider, the stranger, the alien, is a "child" of the one, creator God and therefore "sister" or "brother"; the Other, too, no less than oneself, is therefore of intrinsic and inestimable worth.[17]

He indicates that various religious and other viewpoints are converging toward this understanding of human responsibility. He says that religious visions and theologies "have an essentially political character."[18] His sense of religious faith is a trust in ultimate meaningfulness; religious beliefs are faith mediated by concepts.[19] He quotes Charles Davis approvingly: "Religious beliefs are the changing, limited, culturally particular manifestation of religious faith."[20] Authentic religious faith includes a critical stance toward one's religious beliefs; like other beliefs, they should be the subject of self-critical rationality.

The major theme of Perry's book is an idea of ecumenical politics, in which people speak to one another from their own traditions, but with sufficient basis in community and shared ideas to engage in genuine dialogue. The purposes of dialogue are to declare, persuade, justify, and deliberate. Not every political unit is a genuine political community, capable of ecumenical political dialogue, but in the United States "there are constitutional and religious premises about the human that constitute the intersubjective basis of our political-moral rationality."[21] Dialogue can strengthen the bonds of human community by mediating dissensus,[22] and the very ambiguity of some basic shared values permits a common discourse from diverse perspectives.

For Perry, certain attitudes and virtues go with ecumenical political dialogue. These include cognitive competency (being fully informed); a willingness to probe arguments rather than question motives; honesty; sincerity; and, very importantly, fallibilism (to which "authentic religious faith" is "intimately connected") and pluralism (belief in the positive value of pluralist understandings).[23] In responding to a position that although religious language and symbols should be used for internal discussion, external discussion should be in more universal language, Perry responds,

> [C]learly, external deliberation cannot serve as a significant part of a religious community's self-critical reflective practices unless the community communicates to others, outsiders to the community, its understanding (mediation) of its faith—in particular, its interpretation of its tradition, especially the moral aspects of its tradition—and, moreover, unless it communicates such information in language and symbols that clarify rather than obscure the scriptural and other religious/theological warrants for its understanding/interpretation.[24]

For Perry, two cardinal dialogic virtues are public intelligibility and public accessibility. About public accessibility, Perry writes,

> [T]he virtue of public accessibility is the habit of trying to defend one's position in a manner neither sectarian nor authoritarian. A defense of a disputed position is sectarian if (and to the extent) it relies on experiences or premises that have little if any authority beyond the confines of one's own moral or religious community. A defense is authoritarian if it relies on persons or institutions that have little if any authority beyond the confines of one's own community.[25]

Only positions that are publicly accessible can play a constructive role in political discourse.

Perry addresses more specifically the kind of religious discourse that meets the standard of public accessibility:

> Consider . . . the practice of religious narrative or storytelling as an element in moral, including political-moral, discourse. It is one thing to tell

a religious story—for example, about the Good Samaritan—for the purpose of indicating what a sacred text obligates the listener to do. Even if storytelling for that purpose is sometimes appropriate in a religious community for which the text itself, or a particular interpretation of it, is authoritative, such a practice is sectarian and would certainly be divisive in a religiously/morally pluralistic context. It is another thing altogether to tell a religious story for the purpose of providing some (human) insight into the question of what it means, in some context or other, to be human—truly, fully human. Such a narrative practice, which may even draw on a religious tradition or traditions not one's own, is not sectarian nor any more divisive, in our pluralistic context, than "secular" narrative about how it is good or fitting for human beings to live their lives.[26]

Talking about religious symbols, rituals, and myths is appropriate "so long as . . . [the] stories and symbols are interpreted . . . 'as [h]uman testimonies to [human] possibility itself.' "[27] Perry commends the American Catholic bishops' statement on abortion, *"as the yield of the lived experience of many historically extended communities struggling to discern what it means to be human."*[28]

Apparently in anticipatory response to the worry that ecumenical religious dialogue could lead to the imposition of some religious ideas on those who do not believe, Perry comments that in a pluralist society, no single community's view is likely to be determinative. He further suggests that there should be political tolerance by the state and public, tolerance of beliefs judged false.[29] Coercive political strategies should not be favored, and, because it can cause extreme suffering, "extreme coercion" to make people do what they think is destructive of well-being or forbidden should be rarely employed.[30] The moral aspirations of law should be to minimum morality, and law should protect fundamental interests.[31]

This completes the basic exposition of Perry's *Love and Power.* I shall offer some comments of my own, saving for the following chapter the views of a conservative Christian critic and Perry's response within his conclusion and subsequent writing.

In examining Perry's suggestions, it helps to distinguish the central idea that *some* religious ideas may undergird political decisions and expressed justifications from the more particular account of the appropriate religious ideas and the conditions of ecumenical political dialogue. One might well endorse some parts of Perry's position without accepting others.

I want first to consider what Perry conceives as appropriate religious discourse in politics, to understand what claims connected to religion meet his various conditions. When Perry talks with specificity about appropriate religious contributions to political dialogue, he emphasizes the deep value of religious symbols and myths, endorsing John Coleman's suggestion that these are among the richest sources of our community life; he speaks, too, of religious traditions providing human testimonies to human possibility. He unambiguously rejects the idea that political dialogue should be carried out exclusively, or even mainly, in some universalist natural language. But what he *primarily* has in mind as religious contributions lie at the far edge of what some others, including myself, have considered religious.[32] I have suggested that reliance on religious premises means that one's position is connected to some sort of religious belief or association, in the sense of depending on that belief or association. An atheist who says that the story of Cain and Abel teaches us a lesson about concern for others is not relying on religious premises. Suppose that someone says, "The experience of the Roman Catholic Church over centuries has consistently emphasized concern for fellow human beings; we can take that as important testimony to human nature and morality." A non-Catholic could honestly make such a statement; it relies directly on no religious premise. As Perry notes, modern nonbelievers like Robert Bellah have written about the resources of religious understandings; if nonbelievers appropriately recommend, and use, religious imagery and references to tradition, so can believers. No doubt, believers will generally be more inclined to see the values of these resources and to make arguments in those terms than nonbelievers, but that does not mean the believers are explicitly relying on religious grounds.[33]

Perry is, of course, entitled to have a more expansive view of what it means to rely on religious grounds than do some others. *But,* what is vitally important is to not lose sight of what various people propose *as religious grounds to be excluded.* If, as I suspect, the main things Perry regards as appropriate religious contributions to dialogue would *not* be excluded by many who have proposed principles of restraint for religious grounds, then Perry is much less far away from them than might first appear.

We may ask what Perry's position is on claims that include philosophical arguments for God, historical evidences of supernatural authority, and assertions about the fruits of conviction, when these claims are put forward by believers who regard them as open to common reason. From the point of view of the believers, those claims are accessible. Apparently Perry does not think most such arguments surmount the hurdle of his conditions. In an important passage, quoted above, he says that a publicly accessible position must be neither sectarian nor authoritarian. A defense is sectarian if it relies on experiences and premises that have little if any authority beyond the confines of one's religious community; it is authoritarian if it relies on persons or institutions that have little if any authority beyond the confines of that community. This sounds as if most arguments for specific religious views are excludable.[34] In another passage, Perry suggests that telling a story for "the purpose of indicating what a sacred text obligates the listener to do" would fail the requirement to be non-sectarian.[35] He also says that a defense of convictions would not be publicly accessible if it claimed to be "the yield of some epistemically privileged insight: religious revelation to, or infallible communication with the will of God on the part of, a particular religious community or its leaders."[36] These passages indicate strongly that many religiously based claims fail Perry's test of public accessibility, even though *proponents* believe that each step of the reasoning is publicly accessible.

Most instances of what I consider reliance on religious grounds, and much of what constitutes internal discussions within religious communities,[37] are excluded from public political debates by Perry's accessibility requirements. Is anything left that involves reliance on theological premises? Although I am not certain that they surmount his accessibility standard, I think Perry would approve references to sustained belief in a creator God who calls us to love one another.

This thorny question of what *counts* as reliance on religious grounds raises the further question of why it *matters* that people express their religious grounds in the public forum. Perry, of course, thinks that the religious grounds that meet his conditions will actually contribute to political dialogue. But he also speaks of people declaring, persuading, justifying, and deliberating.[38] Part of the value is that people can express their deepest concerns.

This theme has been developed by Robin Lovin, who asks whether an opponent of nuclear deterrence should say, "My faith tells me that we cannot continue to rely on nuclear weapons for security without betraying a more fundamental reliance on God."[39] He suggests that believers use religious language in political discussions to proclaim an alternative way of ordering human life, to convert secular citizens to their religious premises, and to "articulat[e] an idea of the human good" and how it might be achieved.[40] Lovin provides specific examples that leave doubt both about the size of any gap between him and those who support restraint of religious argument and about the consonance of the uses that he approves with Perry's accessibility condition;[41] but in his understanding of why some religious articulation is appropriate, he and Perry are close together.

Our evaluation of Perry's approval of some religious grounds in political debate and disapproval of others that do not meet his conditions requires an initial judgment whether these two aspects of his proposal are required by premises of liberal democracy, are forbidden by those premises, or fall within a range of social practices that are neither required nor forbidden by them. If they fall within the last category, we must make a further judgment about their appropriateness for the conditions of our society.

It helps to compare Perry's proposal with those of the Liberal Coalition and the Diverse Fervent Believers in chapter 2. The Fervent Believers proposed to exclude religious grounds from political debate, worrying that their use would be too divisive. The attitudes of the members of the Liberal Coalition closely exemplified those underlying the ecumenical dialogue Perry suggests. They, too, thought the benefits of open discourse in religious terms would outweigh its dangers, having confidence in the quality of argumentation and open-mindedness of participants in the political community whose religious views varied from their own. Indeed, the members of the Liberal Coalition had such confidence in the quality of their fellows, they did not feel a need to set the kinds of restraints on political dialogue that Perry suggests.

A major thesis of this book is that both the Fervent Believers' and the Liberal Coalition's proposed understandings of political decision and dialogue are consistent with the fundamental premises of liberal democracy; that is, neither approach is ruled out by these premises. Perry's constrained ecumenical dialogue, falling as it does between these two understandings, is also consistent with fundamental premises, but neither his admission of some religious grounds nor his exclusion of others is demanded by those premises. What remains to be assessed is whether his understanding of political discourse fits well with the conditions of all or any liberal democracies, and most particularly with the conditions of our liberal democracy.

Part of Perry's argument is that his various conditions of dialogue represent the soundest ideas of *religious understanding* and of fruitful communication among religious perspectives. To this extent, his position can be expected to appeal to persons who initially have views about religious understanding closely similar to his or who are persuaded about what he says on that score. Perry's position would not have much force for those who entertain radically different ideas of religious understanding. Building a full-scale theory about rationality, human good, religious truth, and so forth, and showing the theory's implications for political life is, of course, one appropriate philosophic exercise; but the result is not a political theory with independent persuasiveness. A political theory with independent persuasiveness must contain reasons that appeal to persons with different ideas about rationality, human good, religion, and so on.

Some of what Perry says does have independent persuasiveness. A crucial argument for allowing the political expression of religious convictions is that, without it, people would be unable to say what concerns them most about some political issues. Further dialogue both about the immediate political subjects and the underlying divergent religious perspectives will be enriched if these perspectives are expressed. These are reasons that have force for people of divergent persuasions. Perry's exclusions will cut off what matters most to some people, but a reason for doing so is that these expressions will not contribute to constructive dialogue and will be divisive. At the level of independent political theory, one might defend Perry's proposal as involving a sensitive balancing of the values and dangers in pluralist settings of various sorts of religious political discourse. It admits broad reliance on deep background premises (such as religious concern for fellow human beings) and nonsectarian references to the insight of various communities: contributions that leave participants open to learn from others. It does not admit narrower, more dogmatic uses of religious ideas that are likely to cut off discussion rather than enhance it.

Whether one's own appraisal will finally coincide with that of Perry's *Love and Power* will depend on how one assesses the values and risks of various religious contributions and, importantly, the possibilities of intrinsic unfairness and difficulties of application generated by Perry's line between acceptable and unacceptable religious grounds. As we shall see in the next chapter, the unfairness possibility has caused Perry himself to retract his crucial accessibility standard as a criterion for appropriate discourse.

9

No Restraint: Arguments from Religious Freedom, Equality, and Enrichment

It is time to consider again the possibility that no principle of restraint cast in terms of accessibility, religion, comprehensiveness of view, or conception of the good is appropriate. In chapter 5, I presented two simple arguments, based on the liberty of citizens and the desirability of democratic outcomes that reflect the feelings of citizens, in favor of encouraging people and officials to rely on whatever they think is relevant to resolutions of political issues. I also presented responses to those arguments and concluded that at least some principles of self-restraint are warranted in liberal democracies. People should not undertake violent overthrow of government, undermine liberal democracy, or promote unconstitutional consequences. A corollary of the last two principles is that people should not engage in religious impositions. In the chapters following we looked at various proposed principles for more substantial restraints and at supporting arguments for them. Among the grounds for judgment and justification that *each* proposed principle is intended to exclude are faith-centered reliances on revelatory religion. These grounds are obviously religious, they are significantly not accessible, they involve a comprehensive view and a controversial conception of the good. If it turns out that these reliances should not be excluded, then *no* proposed principles of the kind mainly discussed in this book will be sound. This chapter investigates contentions that such faith-centered reliances and justifications should not be regarded as improper within American democracy.

Defenses of this position are made from explicit religious premises and from a broader point of view, and I look at both kinds of defense. I begin with a critique by David Smolin, an evangelical Protestant, of Perry's approach in *Love and Power;* this critique indicates reasonably fully Smolin's own sense of how political life should be regarded.[1] I then turn to other authors, including some who do not rest their arguments on religious conceptions. Finally, I comment on Perry's response to Smolin, which represents a sharp change of his view on the main subject of this book.

A Conservative Traditionalist Challenge to Ecumenical Dialogue

Smolin undertakes his examination of political dialogue from premises radically different from those of Perry. Most importantly, Smolin rejects completely Perry's view of authentic religion. Smolin asks, "Why should those who consider Perry's distinction between religious faith and religious belief to be heretical be persuaded by a vision of dialogue premised on acceptance of this distinction as the mark of 'authentic religion'?"[2] He disagrees with Perry's commitment to individual autonomy and to self-revising of autonomous individuals.[3] In contrast to Perry's conviction that religious beliefs should be continually subject to rational reexamination, Smolin says, "[M]y own religious perspective would view the attempt to establish reason as a criterion apart from God as a flawed and even irrational attempt to elevate the human mind above the divine mind."[4] Smolin regards liberal Christianity as unstable, because the attempted mix of modernist premises with loyalty to God is bound to result in an increasingly secular identity.[5] Smolin urges that "[t]he very nature of scriptural religions like Christianity, Judaism, and Islam is that they posit an extremely public and accessible revelation of God";[6] from this Christian perspective, the main barrier to acceptance of Christianity is not insufficient understanding but a failure of will stemming from sinful human nature.

Smolin's conception of appropriate relations of government and religion is less than fully separationist.[7] (Although Perry does not address himself explicitly to the subject, he apparently approves the basic constitutional stance taken by the Supreme Court since World War II: that as a matter of interpretation of the religion clauses and sound political philosophy, the government itself, in its official pronouncements and acts, should not favor one religion over another and should not favor religious belief over nonbelief.) Smolin importantly accepts institutional separation of the government and religious institutions; he also accepts freedom of speech and practice for members of diverse religions and for nonbelievers. He does not provide detailed views on the range of constitutional issues of church and state, but he does suggest that the prevailing establishment clause test—under which a practice is declared unconstitutional if its purpose or primary effect is to advance religion or if it entangles religion and government unduly—should be abandoned in favor of a test that would make "coercion" the critical feature of establishments of religion.[8] He also comments that "[s]elf-government means that a Christian people will have, in some sense, a Christian government."[9]

In light of these basic premises, Smolin's criticism of Perry's conditions for ecumenical dialogue is hardly surprising. He argues that "Perry has used his own vision of good religion as the standard for admission to

political and legal debate."[10] Perry has excluded the theologically conservative theists—including Protestant evangelicals, fundamentalists, and penta-
costals, and traditionalists (some Roman Catholics, Anglicans, and Luther-
ans)—who are "most active in trying to displace the cultural hegemony of
America's highly secularized elites."[11] Those excluded, including himself,
will naturally protest that the exclusion is unfair.[12]

Smolin recognizes that Perry, responding to an earlier letter of his,
moderated somewhat in his conclusion to *Love and Power* in respect to
the "conditions" of fallibilism and pluralism. Perry there says, "Perhaps
fallibilism and pluralism are better understood, not as prerequisites *to* ecumenical political dialogue, but as attitudes or positions for which it is
sometimes fitting to contend, depending on the particular question at issue,
in ecumenical political dialogue."[13] This may initially appear to be a considerable concession to theological conservatives, most of whom have
greater confidence in the truth of their beliefs than Perry's ideal and do not
regard pluralism as positively desirable, since everyone's holding the correct religious views would be preferable. Smolin points out that typical
conservative views will still fail Perry's condition of accessibility. Even
though their religious claims are intelligible and widely understood, conservatives advocate grounds that Perry disqualifies as sectarian and authoritarian.

Smolin believes that the political arena cannot be lifted out of the crucial cultural struggle between modernist approaches of various stripes and
theological conservatism. Any exclusion of Perry's kind unfairly privileges
one side in political life. Smolin does believe that translating religious concepts into broader mediating language can often be useful in facilitating
common life with those of different beliefs.[14] One properly approaches
this and other questions about self-restraint from the perspective of one's
own religious position, not conceiving some set of limits that applies to all
citizens.[15] Although Smolin strongly prefers a victory for conservative theism over modernism, he thinks that "there are fair rules of dialogue and
conflict to which Americans could overwhelmingly agree, under which either traditional theism, or liberalism-as-autonomy, could win cultural hegemony."[16] In answer to worries of the sort William Marshall raises about
a politics of religion (discussed in chapter 6), Smolin writes, "Allowing
religious conflicts to affect government's promotion of the temporal peace
will not, as some fear, lead to the intensification of conflict to unmanage-
able levels."[17] Such worries, he argues, are ill-founded, given the American
history of de jure and de facto establishments of religion from the colonial
era until World War II. Among other protections of minorities is federalism, which would allow different states to adopt different stances in respect
to religion and political and moral issues for which religious outlooks are
important, such as abortion, fornication, and homosexuality.[18]

Smolin's religious understanding and his assessment of relevant social
facts lead him to conclude that political life is full of issues for which religious truth is highly important and that civil discourse can occur even if

people employ full comprehensive views that are radically opposed on some vital issues. His sense of the irreconcilability of fundamental outlooks suggests that he sees politics as less of a mutual learning process than does Perry, though he does believe basic terms of "civil peace" can be accepted by believers and nonbelievers.

Not all theological conservatives will find themselves accepting Smolin's stance on political choices and dialogue. Some may envision a more active role for the state in promoting the "true religion" than he does and favor a politics that is both based on religious perspectives and aimed at the public success of those perspectives.[19] Others may believe that liberty of religion involves greater self-restraint in the use of religious premises for political judgment than does Smolin.[20] Still others may worry more about the dangers of serious divisiveness or violent religious conflict or be concerned that their own beliefs and values will suffer impositions if political dialogue involves a give-and-take on religious truth. These conservatives may wish, as did the Fervent Believers in chapter 2, to protect their own religious beliefs and communities by keeping most or all explicitly religious grounds out of political debate. They may do so even if they agree with Smolin that, as far as *judgment* is concerned, citizens and "government officials cannot act without reliance on implicit moral and factual assumptions that derive from various competing religious views."[21]

In one crucial aspect, Smolin's position replicates Perry's. Both rely heavily on a particular religious understanding and then proceed to draw out implications for political dialogue. But each also makes arguments that appeal to those of different religious views. Smolin's basic argument *of this sort* is one of fairness. If the conditions of public political dialogue are not to be unjustly stacked in favor of modernism, conservative theist grounds of political positions—sectarian or authoritarian as they may be by Perry's categories—must be admitted. Since open inquiry and fair access of all points of view are critical features of liberal democracy, this fairness argument is one that should have substantial force for those whose perspectives on religion differ greatly from those of Smolin.

Fairness and Enrichment

Others from a variety of perspectives have concurred with Smolin's opposition to a principle of self-restraint, believing that no defensible model of good citizenship calls upon people to forego reliance on grounds that seem convincing to them. Some writers have focused on the conditions of public political discussion. Maimon Schwarzschild urges that the dangers of religion in political life vary with history.[22] Although Enlightenment thinkers may sensibly have feared the Christian religion of their time, religious thinking and argument do not pose a comparable threat to modern liberal institutions. Schwarzschild says, "Religion seems an odd choice as prime threat to liberalism at the end of a century that has been so greatly dominated by struggles over Communism, fascism, and extreme nationalism."[23] In our pluralist societies, the dominance of one religion is not an immediate danger; what seems precarious are things that "modernity sometimes seems to sweep away: meaning, connection to the past, identity, community, purpose, the spiritual side of life."[24]

Jeremy Waldron contrasts Aristotelian and Millian models of public deliberation.[25] The Aristotelian model, which resembles that of John Rawls, involves, as Waldron puts it, "the idea of *shared modes of reasoning*, a common matrix of public understanding on which various views of various people can be laid out, compared, contrasted, and synthesized."[26] Waldron says that John Stuart Mill's "suggestion is that people simply fling their views and opinions into the public forum of ideas and, whether others understand them precisely or not, they will have their effect, and the truth will emerge by a sort of invisible-hand process."[27] Although perhaps citizens should address each other as thinkers and reasoners, not just subliminal recipients, Waldron thinks that people should not have to make their contributions in terms of any prior consensus. Appeals to religious considerations are ones we cannot expect others to accept, but many of our theories of basic rights, property, and justice stem from religious roots. Contributions that draw explicit religious connections can enrich a debate that may now be ultimately secular.[28]

Sanford Levinson notes the similarity between claims of those with strong religious commitments to be included in public dialogue and claims of feminists and critical race theorists.[29] In an illuminating review of Perry's book, he concludes, "[It] [i]s . . . possible . . . that this whole quest to discover legitimating criteria that will determine what types of discourse should be admitted into the public square is fundamentally misguided."[30]

Writing from a more explicit religious perspective, Daniel Conkle emphasizes that free exercise and free speech rights include the right of religious believers to influence law and public policy.[31] Without proposing a principle of self-restraint, Conkle does suggest that "some religious arguments have more to offer than others, and that they accordingly are entitled to more attention and public consideration."[32] He offers procedural, structural, and substantive criteria of evaluation. The procedural criterion considers a religion's method of thought. Since fundamentalists of various hues lack the openness of mind that is necessary in a dialogic decision-making process, "[w]e should be wary of fundamentalist involvement in the political process."[33] Modernist religious thinking is not problematic, but since it adds little to secular philosophy and politics, it is not a type of religious involvement "that we should especially praise."[34] Religious reconcilers, as Conkle calls them, take religious sources much more seriously than modernists but are open to competing sources of truth; they "have the potential for enhancing, elevating, and perhaps even ennobling American public life."[35] The "structural" dimension concerns a religion's orientation to society, politics, and law; examination of questions about that dimension yields similar conclusions about the political contributions of fundamentalists, modernists, and reconcilers. Substantive criteria involve evaluation of substantive positions on public issues; Conkle acknowledges that such evaluation will inevitably be partly theological.

Some writers perceive grave defects with the arguments made by those who propose restraint. They challenge notions of accessibility and commonly shared premises as they relate to fundamental evaluations. Steven Smith comments on criteria of accessibility offered by proponents of restraint:

> "Accessibility," it turns out, has little to do with the beliefs, values, and reasons that the actual citizens in a democracy *do* in fact understand and use. Complex scientific calculations and abstruse philosophical notions may be "accessible" even though ordinary citizens may find them foreign or implausible, but religious values that are widely accepted (and understood even by many citizens who do not accept them) are not. "Accessibility" becomes little more than an appealing catchword denoting the theorists' preferred mode of political discourse.[36]

Closely related to this point about accessibility is a claim that citizens do not have a common stock of values and techniques for determining facts from which to draw. Many secular philosophies rest every bit as much on unestablishable premises as do religious points of view.[37] If Kantian claims are to be allowed in the political process, explicit religious claims cannot fairly be excluded. Larry Alexander has written of a "unity of epistemology," suggesting that there is no difference in reason as applied to liberalism and religious views.[38] He urges that liberalism and religion are on the same epistemological level, that liberalism is one sectarian view among many.[39]

What of the argument that we share *some* common values and ideas of discerning truth, and that relying on these in politics is appropriate when they yield answers to problems? Steven Smith answers that this way of putting things itself misleads. Religious believers do not, he says, accept the idea that common considerations, uncolored by religious values, should control decisions; rather, "[t]he religious citizen supports not two severable propositions but rather the single, complex proposition that secular and religious influences must both play a part in public decisions."[40] On this view, no genuine common denominator exists on which it is fair to rely.

The claim that we lack common premises might be limited to fundamental convictions about value, but some writers extend the claim to scientific methods as well. Commenting on the Supreme Court's decision that teaching creationism in public schools represents an establishment of religion, Stephen Carter acknowledges that belief in biblical infallibility, not independent scientific examination, leads creationists to reach the conclusions they do, conclusions that reject widely accepted scientific ideas about evolution and about the length of time the universe has existed.[41] Carter sees the creationists as relying upon a different hermeneutical method for understanding the world.[42] According to Carter, liberalism's neutrality "is really derogating religious belief in favor of other, more 'rational' methods of understanding the world."[43] Similarly, treating evolution and creationism as two competing paradigms, Frederick Mark Gedicks says, "The allocation of creationism to the marginalized world of subjectivity, and evolution to the privileged world of objectivity, is merely the exercise of social power rather than a natural, value-neutral distinction."[44]

These challenges to any liberal principle of restraint raise profound questions. Since evaluation of some aspects is simpler after an examination of the views of John Rawls, I return to these questions in the next two chapters; but I offer some brief comments now.

No liberal principle of "neutrality" is itself neutral; it requires some value judgment of its own that cannot be neutral. Whether that value judgment must invoke a comprehensive view (or a controversial conception of the good) or can somehow be based on other sources is a subject I have discussed in connection with the views of Charles Larmore. That issue comes up more pointedly in Rawls.

Without doubt, *some* secular philosophies have no stronger basis in interpersonal reason than do some religions. *Unless* a special reason were adduced to exclude religious views, a plausible principle of restraint would have to reach many nonreligious views. Understood in a certain way, I agree with Larry Alexander's claim about the unity of epistemology. Some claims about religion are based on standards of truth that are similar to standards of truth for some nonreligious moral and political claims. However, I believe chapters 3 and 4 demonstrate that some claims of truth are self-consciously less subject to interpersonal evaluation than are others. Many people make claims about morality, for example, that love is preferable to hate, that they think can be defended on the basis of an interpersonal reason. Interpersonal reason does not establish that others should give the same weight to personal conversion experiences as those who have the experiences. If the "unity of epistemology" constitutes a denial of such differences, it is mistaken.

Belief in the literal truth of the account of creation in Genesis, assured by biblical infallibility, and belief in evolution, assured by science, are, without doubt, competing paradigms, but it does not follow that they are equally subject to validation by interpersonal reason. This particular disagreement is colored by gaps in the scientific record of evolution *and* by the belief of many people that biblical infallibility itself *can be established* by a chain of interpersonal reason. I want first to make my analytical point with a much simpler example. Some years ago, many people believed that the Shroud of Turin, with its remarkable imprint of a human body and face, was the cloth used for the burial of Jesus. The Roman Catholic Church allowed a very small part of the cloth to be subjected to the process of carbon dating. This revealed that the cloth came not from ancient times but the medieval period. For most people who thought about the subject, however little they understood the scientific dating process, this was very weighty evidence that the cloth did not have an imprint of Jesus and had not been used for his burial. Suppose someone said, "In general I trust carbon dating, which I know has very substantial evidence in favor of its accuracy; but God can certainly perform miracles, and my faith tells me that on this occasion God preserved the original burial cloth and miraculously affected its physical composition so that it would appear to be 'dated' to a later time." If all the person presents is his experience of faith, his "competing paradigm" is not absurd or illogical. It is, however, less subject to interpersonal *reason,* indeed to interpersonal evaluation at all, than the conclusion based on carbon dating, which people accept either because they grasp the scientific basis of carbon dating or because they trust the nearly uniform view of scientists that carbon dating is roughly accurate. On some views, at least, evolution (even the controversial claim of evolution from one species to another) is supported by interpersonal reason in a way, and to a degree, that creationism is not.

If people *generally* accept some scientific methods or value judgments, is it fair to rely on these to the exclusion of other methods or values that some people, but many fewer people, strongly believe are as valid? Steven Smith is right that this common-denominator approach can involve elements of unfairness. To consider whether the common-denominator approach *is defensible,* one has to know much more about the actual views people hold and about the likely effects of judgments and arguments based on positions that reach outside what is shared in common. That, indeed, is one of the lessons of chapter 2 and of chapters subsequent to this one.

Perry's Response

In response to the challenge made by Smolin and others, Michael Perry has shifted his position. Without retracting his opinions about what constitutes bad theology and bad epistemology, Perry, in a recent essay, abandons his "middle ground exclusivist ideal."[45] Perry explicitly applies this thought to say that one should not posit an ideal that would render beliefs like David Smolin's an inappropriate basis for political choice.[46] Instead, those beliefs need to be met on their merits.

Although Perry does not himself put it exactly this way, his position of no restraint is softened or qualified in various ways. He notes, as he did in *Love and Power,* that liberalism-as-tolerance disfavors coercive political strategies (Smolin also had expressed support for modest use of coercion); he says that those of a mind to do so may seek to have laws grounded in consensus, and he approves David Hollenbach's argument that the role of religious discourse "in public" in pluralist democratic societies is "much more in public culture than in public argument specifically about political issues: to help build a public consensus about what kind of people 'We the people' should aspire to be,—with what values, commitments, sensibilities."[47] None of these points is a genuine qualification to his admission of various religious positions into political debate, however, because each is a recommendation from his own overall perspective.

When he turns to judicial opinions, Perry comes closer to an explicit qualification of sorts. It is not that he here favors some religious beliefs over others, as had his conditions of ecumenical dialogue. Rather he indicates that a judge should infrequently rely on any controversial moral beliefs, religiously grounded or not; even when reliance seems unavoidable, "my suggestion is not that she also give the controversial belief (perhaps religious) that in her view supports the controversial moral belief, much less that she undertake a theological or philosophical defense of the supporting belief."[48] Perry clearly does not envision extended theological arguments in opinions, and he apparently does not propose even a statement that a judge is relying on religious grounds. If judges may rely on such grounds as "Citizens owe a duty to their less fortunate neighbors" but should not reveal that their underlying basis is religious, judicial opinions might not look different from how they do now. Were judges to note their reliance on such underlying bases, this would represent a move away from an ideal of publicly persuasive reasons for opinions (*especially* majority opinions) that still has a powerful hold in the legal community. Someone might respond that the accessible religious arguments Perry favors do not rely on reasons other than those that all can reasonably evaluate, but Perry has *now* said he would not exclude faith-centered claims of revelation as bases for political decision. If these began to appear in opinions, even in the shorthand form of "My basis for this belief is the authoritative Word of Genesis," that would mark a genuine change in conventions about opinion writing.

Perry does not tackle the related topics of preambles, committee reports, presidential signings of bills, administrative determinations, and so on, in which actors in other branches of government make formal statements of justification. He implicitly approves, I believe, statements of religious justification made by individual legislators.

There is a very important possible qualification in Perry's present "inclusivist" position. Perry acknowledges that some religious styles may not show due respect for fellow citizens.[49] Does he think that argument in these styles is inappropriate in our liberal democracy? He does not develop the point, but since equal respect is a fundamental norm of liberal democracy, a basis for decision that denies such respect would seem to be an inappropriate ground for decision and argument. That, indeed, is the thrust of my claim in chapter 5 that a ground that seeks to reintroduce slavery is inappropriate. In a democracy people are at liberty to rely on and even argue such grounds, but other citizens correctly deem such grounds as not consonant with the premises of our society. If we can identify religious arguments as failing to show due respect, we can say they are at odds with liberal democratic premises, even though the proponents believe that following God's will overrides such considerations *or* themselves believe that their grounds *do show equal respect.*

Preliminarily, we can say that Perry is correct in claiming that liberal democracy does not by its very nature require the neutralist position or some exclusivist middle ground like ecumenical politics. The inclusivist model supported by authors mentioned in this chapter and by Perry's most recent writing is not at odds with basic premises of liberal democracy. Whether it is actually a position to be preferred for liberal democracies in general or our own liberal democracy depends on some nuanced factual judgments. Later chapters make some of the relevant judgments.

10

Self-Restraint on Fundamentals

The Approach of John Rawls

One approach to principles of self-restraint in political life is to distinguish among political issues: citizens and legislators should limit themselves to common grounds in respect to some range of fundamental issues, but may employ religious and other comprehensive views in making ordinary political decisions. This approach, suggested by John Rawls as an ideal of democratic citizenship, deserves careful attention, and not only because it now forms an important part of the philosophy of the leading political theorist of the recent era.[1]

Although its elaboration is complex, the basic idea of Rawls's approach is simple. It is that the fundamentals of political life should be more or less agreed upon and set outside ordinary political wrangling. A corollary of this "setting outside" of basic fundamentals is that when people must determine the implications of the fundamentals, they should do so according to a common reason that does not involve disputed comprehensive views.

In considering Rawls's position, one needs to distinguish between two closely related issues: the reasons why people might *accept* basic principles of justice and the reasons that they properly use to develop (or possibly change) these principles. The second issue is our primary concern, but I initially say a few words about the first.

Many people read Rawls's *A Theory of Justice* as claiming a methodology for arriving at *the most rational* principles of justice;[2] but in subsequent writings, Rawls has made clear that his more modest aspiration is to set out principles for liberal democracies, ones that best capture the fundamental idea of "a system of fair social cooperation between free and equal persons."[3] If this is the grounding of Rawls's more concrete principles, the question arises why a citizen should accept the principles if his comprehensive view suggests an altogether different basis of social life *or* an unusual understanding of how the fundamental idea of fair social cooperation applies. Imagine that a fervent religious believer thinks that theocracy may be preferable to liberal democracy or accepts Rawls's fundamental idea of fair social cooperation, but thinks that treating people as free and equal means giving all people the strongest encouragements to adopt the true faith. Why should such a person accept principles of justice that an incomplete common reason suggests?

Rawls's response is that appropriate principles of justice are ones that are sustained, or at least could be sustained, by an overlapping consensus of comprehensive views.[4] These principles, initially developed as a "free-standing political conception" for the basic structure of society,[5] fit with a wide range of comprehensive views likely to arise in a liberal democracy.[6] Pluralism of comprehensive views will inevitably exist in liberal democracies, and social life is not likely to go well if the proponents of any one view seek predominance. A comprehensive view is "reasonable" if it acknowledges the freedom and equality of citizens on which political liberalism rests. A democratic regime can be enduring or stable only if a substantial majority of its citizens freely support it.[7] If people understand this, they may accept principles of justice other than those their comprehensive views might initially have inclined them to favor. They may realize that efforts to create a theocracy[8] or to provide strong inducements toward one set of religious beliefs would be unfair and highly disruptive.

Rawls asserts that many people in a society will accept principles of justice because these fit with their *reflective* full or partial comprehensive views;[9] others will believe the principles are appropriate without direct reference to nonpolitical aspects of their particular comprehensive views.[10] Principles of justice can be argued for as valid, or desirable, or appropriate without reliance on any particular comprehensive view,[11] though the validity of these principles will depend largely on their capacity to fit with an overlapping consensus of comprehensive views. It is in this sense that Rawls argues that political philosophy need not be metaphysical. In a well-ordered society, a plurality of comprehensive views will support the basic political structures and ideas of justice (though some unreasonable comprehensive views will not be supportive).

One aspect of the principles of justice in a liberal democracy will be a principle of common reason. Rawls says, "There is no reason . . . why any citizen, or association of citizens, should have the right to use the state's police power to decide constitutional essentials or basic questions of justice as that person's, or that association's, comprehensive doctrine directs."[12] When citizens talk with all their fellows about such matters, they are to look to what is commonly shared, not to what divides them.

What precisely does Rawls imagine as the reach of the overlapping consensus of reasonable comprehensive views? In some of his earlier writing, it appeared that the consensus might embrace highly specific principles of justice, including such features as fair equality of opportunity and the "difference" principle, as developed by Rawls. In *Political Liberalism*, Rawls explicitly recognizes the possibility of a much weaker shared understanding, such as acceptance of basic constitutional procedures.[13] He envisions the full overlapping consensus as reaching more deeply and broadly than that. Apparently, however, it will leave room for some disagreements about important issues of justice. In the chapter on public reason, Rawls assumes that other liberal views about social justice will compete with his ideas of fair opportunity and the difference principle; and I assume that the overlapping consensus is to be capacious enough to embrace a variety of perspectives on these subjects.

My main interest in Rawls's thesis about an overlapping consensus lies in how it relates to his theory of public reason. About that relation we can conclude preliminarily that citizens properly consult their comprehensive views to determine whether they accept political structures and principles of justice; however, in public discussions of applications of shared principles to particular circumstances, comprehensive views are to recede in favor of public reasons.

Rawls's basic position about the overlapping consensus has been challenged by critics, including Michael Perry[14] and Joseph Raz,[15] who urge that viable political philosophy must depend on at least a partial comprehensive view of human good, that it cannot be free-floating. They and others have expressed doubt whether an overlapping consensus on fundamentals is close to existing now in the United States, is generally feasible, or is necessary or particularly valuable for stable liberal democracy. I shall save direct comment on these problems for the next chapter, but a similar problem concerning the lack of connection between politics and comprehensive views arises in the context of appropriate political discourse within a society.

I turn now to that subject, to Rawls's account of public reason and fundamentals. Rawls talks of public reason as the reason of citizens sharing equal citizenship.[16] Justifications in terms of public reasons "appeal only to presently accepted general beliefs and forms of reasoning found in common sense, and the methods and conclusions of science when these are not controversial."[17] One employing public reasons does not appeal to comprehensive religious and philosophical doctrines, but rather "a reasonable balance of public political values."[18]

According to Rawls, the work of the Supreme Court exemplifies the use of public reason, and that is the "sole reason" the Court exercises;[19] for others, the requirement to use public reason is less constraining. It holds for those engaging in political advocacy in the public forum, and for candidates and elections; it does not apply to personal deliberations and reflections, or to reasoning within associations such as universities or churches, where religious, philosophical, and moral considerations of many kinds properly play a role.[20]

For citizens and legislators, "the limits imposed by public reason do not apply to all political questions but only to those involving what we may call 'constitutional essentials' and questions of basic justice."[21] Regulation of property, preserving animals, and controlling pollution are not included in this category. A liberal principle of legitimacy and a duty of civility require that on fundamental questions, principles and policies can be supported by public reason. Expecting that values specified by a fundamental political conception will give a reasonable public answer to all, or nearly all, questions about constitutional essentials, Rawls says, "There is no reason why any citizen, or association of citizens, should have the right to use state power to decide constitutional essentials as that person's, or that association's, comprehensive doctrine directs."[22]

Rawls indicates what he means by constitutional essentials in the following passage:

> There is the greatest urgency for citizens to reach practical agreement in judgment about the constitutional essentials. These are of two kinds:
>
> a. fundamental principles that specify the general structure of government and the political process: the powers of the legislature, executive and the judiciary; the scope of majority rule; and
> b. equal basic rights and liberties of citizenship that legislative majorities are to respect: such as the right to vote and to participate in politics, liberty of conscience, freedom of thought and of association, as well as the protections of the rule of law.[23]

As far as questions of basic justice are concerned, Rawls asserts that some principle of opportunity and a social minimum providing for the basic needs of all citizens are essentials, but more stringent aspects of his own theory of justice (namely, fair equality of opportunity and the difference principle)[24] go beyond the essentials.[25] Rawls explains that settling the constitutional essentials dealing with basic freedoms is urgent, that telling whether these essentials are realized is far easier than telling if principles governing social and economic inequalities are realized, and that gaining agreement about what the basic rights and liberties should be is also comparatively easy: "These considerations explain why freedom of movement and free choice of occupation and a social minimum covering citizens' basic needs count as constitutional essentials while the principle of fair opportunity and the difference principle do not."[26]

Clarifications

The principle of self-restraint implicit in Rawls's ideal of democratic citizenship would, like Thomas Nagel's proposal, restrict use of reasons that are not publicly accessible, religious grounds being treated like other grounds in this category. Rawls makes clear, in contrast to Nagel, that direct reference to comprehensive views is out, even when those who hold them believe they can be arrived at by common reasoning. Rawls thus avoids the particular criticism that it is unfair for the holder's own belief about whether common reason can establish his comprehensive view to become the standard for whether he may rely on the view. Rawls's approach is *more modest* than Nagel's in that the strict version of the principle of self-restraint mainly reaches only constitutional essentials and basic issues of justice, and mainly reaches only public justifications and voting.

In respect to the *precise coverage* of the requirement to limit oneself to public reasons, four points need clarification. The first concerns the range of persons and contexts for which the requirement reaches all topics. The second is the status of basic questions of justice that are not covered within constitutional essentials. The third is the importance of public reasons for situations other than those when the requirement to employ such reasons strictly applies. The fourth is the degree of constraint that compliance with a standard of public reasons involves, when the standard strictly applies.

Rawls assumes that courts should limit themselves to public reasons in all circumstances.[27] Such reasons should be the exclusive mode of justification, and of internal deliberation as well. Rawls contrasts courts with legislators and citizens, who may bring other reasons to bear on nonfundamental issues, like the treatment of animals. In this connection, Rawls does not discuss actual statutory language, or the content of reports of committees of Congress and of administrative agencies, or the language in which the executive branch formally proposes the enactment of legislation. Would he think that the justifications in such official pronouncements should be restricted to public reasons for all subject matters? The range of what such documents appropriately say is somewhat broader than the typical judicial opinion, because preambles to statutes, committee reports, and the like, need not draw justifications from preexisting law, as do most judicial opinions.[28] In a society with many reasonable comprehensive views, it is highly doubtful whether any particular comprehensive view should be presented as a major justification for new legislation; but perhaps a committee report might point out that a provision to protect animals fits with many comprehensive views that are widely held in society. Such a justification might be found in judicial opinion, but it would be unusual.[29] If what Rawls says about courts and public reason is sound, certain other kinds of official documents are appropriately cast in some (perhaps broader) form of public reason, even when they do not deal with constitutional essentials or issues of basic justice.[30]

The second question about covered topics concerns the relationship between "constitutional essentials" and "questions of basic justice." Rawls says that the requirement of public reason applies to both of these.[31] Midway in his discussion he concludes that some principle of opportunity and a social minimum providing for basic needs—certainly matters of basic justice—are among the constitutional essentials.[32] Fair equality of opportunity and the difference principle, crucial aspects of his own political conception of justice, fall outside the constitutional essentials. Do the constraints of public reason apply only to the constitutional essentials, which include *minimum* requirements of basic justice, or do the constraints *also apply* to advocacy about matters of basic justice, such as fair equality of opportunity and the difference principle, that go beyond the constitutional essentials? This is an important practical question because many political issues will turn on controversial conceptions of justice that reach beyond the minimum. Particularly since these issues will be sharply contested, it matters whether people must concentrate on public reasons in public justifications for their positions. Rawls plainly intends the constraint of public reasons to apply to advocacy about these issues of basic justice that reach beyond the constitutional essentials.[33]

The third question concerns the status of public reasons for topics when other reasons may be used. At an early point, Rawls talks as if he is beginning with the clearest illustrations of a concept of public reason and is uncertain to what extent the relevant restrictions apply to a broader range of political issues.[34] He also says that it is usually highly desirable to settle political questions by invoking the values of public reason. Later, however, he indicates that "[c]itizens and legislators may properly vote their more comprehensive views when constitutional essentials and basic justice are not at stake."[35] I take his comments in the following way: that the general preclusion of justifications in terms of comprehensive and other nonaccessible reasons applies for legislators and citizens only to constitutional essentials and basic questions of justice, but that, more generally, commonly accessible reasons should have a kind of priority in liberal democratic politics.

I turn now to the fourth question: what does the constraint of public reasons amount to for the topics to which it strictly applies? Here we need to consider the behavior that the constraint covers, and more particularly, the relation between grounds offered in justification and the actual grounds of decision. Some passages suggest that Rawls is concerned with public justification rather than decision. He says the limits of public reason do not apply to personal deliberations and reflections about political questions, or to reasoning within associations; the limits apply only to public political advocacy.[36] That sounds a little like people can make up their minds on various grounds, so long as they publicly discuss the issues in terms of public reasons. However, other passages make clear that this is not Rawls's full view. At a number of places he talks about voting as covered; the ideal of public reason calls on one not to vote one's simple preferences and interests or even what one thinks is right and true by comprehensive convictions.[37] Many legislators never have to explain particular votes, and many citizens do not even reveal their votes. The constraint on voting clearly indicates that the principle extends beyond publicly stated advocacy and justification.[38] Rawls's reference to courts as exemplars of his concept of public reason strongly suggests the same conclusion. Courts, in general at least, are supposed to be guided by the reasons they state. Rawls does not imagine that judges on an appellate court have fulfilled their duty if they have self-consciously determined their decision by a comprehensive view they happen to hold in common and then have offered entirely different public reasons in a majority opinion. For judges, public reasons should guide decision as well as debate and opinion writing; and Rawls holds up judicial practice as a sort of model.

Rawls's discussion leaves a bit of uncertainty on one subject that is critical to the relation between actual grounds of decision and public justification—whether the proponent of a position must himself believe in the public justification he offers. Rawls writes that the ideal of citizenship imposes a "duty of civility—to be able to explain to one another on those fundamental questions how the principles and policies they advocate and vote for can be supported by the political values of public reason."[39] He says that "[w]hat public reason asks is that citizens be able to explain their vote to one another in terms of a reasonable balance of public political values."[40] Imagine the following situation: Joan believes that for possible criminalization of some late abortions, various positions can be supported as consonant with a reasonable balance of public reasons. Her comprehensive view leads her to believe that maximum criminalization is desirable. She thinks a reasonable defense of that position can be made in terms of public reasons, but her own sense of the *balance of public reasons,* taken alone, is that they support a different position. Is it appropriate for her to vote for the position that fits her comprehensive view and support the vote with an argument of public reasons in which she does not fully believe? In Rawls's language, Joan could "explain" her vote for maximum criminalization "in terms of a reasonable balance of public political values," but her explanation would not be persuasive to her. I believe that Rawls has in mind a sincere justification, one which the speaker actually credits.[41] If this is accurate, Joan is not fulfilling her responsibility to rely on public reasons if her basis for believing in maximum criminalization is the statement of a religious authority, and she offers arguments of public reason that she thinks are reasonable but finally unpersuasive. Suppose, however, religious authority leads Joan to conclude that certain arguments of public reason really are persuasive, although she does not grasp from their own terms why that is so (as a Roman Catholic might believe natural law arguments against abortion are valid, although she realizes she would not reach this conclusion in the absence of the church's position to this effect). Joan now does believe in the force of the public reasons she states. This is enough to satisfy Rawls (although Joan would not pass Audi's requirement of secular motivation, discussed in chapter 6).

In light of the apparent need for a *sincere* justification in terms of a balance of public reasons, Rawls's comments that the limits of public reason do not apply to private reflection and associational discussion are somewhat less permissive and important than they appear at first glance. The primary way that citizens *act* to resolve political issues is by public advocacy and voting and by urging legislators to vote. If decisions by citizens and legislators on how to vote are to be determined by public reasons, just what is the significance of discerning in reflection, or in discussion with cobelievers, the implications of one's comprehensive views for particular political issues? Rawls, focusing on the abolitionists and Martin Luther King, does discuss the question of whether people properly offer reasons related to their comprehensive views *as well as* public reasons. He comes down in favor of the inclusive view that such reasons may be offered, concluding that it "best encourages citizens to honor the ideal of public reason and secures its social conditions in the longer run in a well-ordered society."[42] Nevertheless, the way one reflects by oneself and discusses with cobelievers will be deeply affected by a standard of public reasons for appropriate decision making. For example, if we assumed that Supreme Court justices are supposed to decide by public reasons, we might be disconcerted to learn that three Roman Catholic Supreme Court justices were discussing with each other exactly what the implications are of Roman Catholicism for a particular constitutional issue. Thus, Rawls's limiting of the requirement of public reasons to voting and public advocacy is less significant than one might initially suppose; that requirement would infect thought and discussion of relevant issues in all settings.

Criticisms

With these clarifications, and perhaps slight extrapolations, we are ready to consider more fundamental questions about Rawls's approach. I discuss three related problems: (1) the need for, and possibility of, agreement on constitutional essentials; (2) the nature and problem of interpretation of essential principles; and (3) difficulties with crucial lines of distinction.

Agreement on Essentials

Is it necessary for people in a liberal democratic society to agree on constitutional essentials? Is it desirable for them to do so? In approaching these questions, we may usefully keep in mind the present-day United States. No doubt, some liberal democratic societies are so homogeneous that very wide agreement on constitutional essentials can coexist with some differences in comprehensive views—perhaps Sweden is a modern example—but Rawls mainly imagines societies much more diverse than Sweden. With its continuing substantial immigration from all parts of the world, the United States includes people of tremendously varied backgrounds and outlooks on life; it is more typical of the problem Rawls puts to himself.

In theory at least, a diverse society might manage if people agreed generally that political change should be peaceful and accomplished according to existing constitutional devices, even if they considered all substantive matters, including basic constitutional requisites, as up for argument. Raz suggests that agreement on constitutional essentials is not so important to stability: "Rather, affective and symbolic elements may well be the cement of society, and to these one has only to add the little power individuals have to affect social affairs."[43] But, even though a society might be moderately stable with widespread disagreement about the wisdom of basic constitutional arrangements, Rawls is correct that *if* agreement can be achieved on basic essentials, *if* some fundamental matters are taken off the agenda, that will *contribute to stability and coherence.* Whether such agreement is *feasible* depends partly on the expansiveness of the subjects to be covered and the place of an idea of common reason.

I shall concentrate on freedom of religion and separation of church and state, but the issues I discuss are representative of those involved with most "constitutional essentials." I want initially to consider a minimal version of agreement on these two related essentials about religion and then to address a much fuller version of possible agreement. The minimal version includes agreement about what would generally be regarded as the most direct violations of religious liberty and separation of church and state: agreement, for example, that the state should not forbid people from adhering to particular religious beliefs or to practices of worship,[44] that no particular religion, such as Presbyterianism, will be denominated the state religion, that church officials will not by dint of their positions automatically hold important government offices, and that government officials will not automatically hold church positions. If that is what we mean by agreement on religious liberty and church-state separation, agreement in the United States is very great. Since existing agreement on these subjects is so widespread, it really does not matter too much whether public discussion and potential voting directly *about them* includes or excludes substantial reliance on comprehensive views.

A fuller version of religious liberty and church-state separation might include matters such as "no government promotion of religious truth," "no substantial direct aid of religious schools," and "no prayer in public schools," *and* the idea that elaboration and development of ideas of religious liberty and church-state separation will be carried forward in terms of common reason. Agreement about these matters is obviously a lot harder to attain, and certainly is not close to existing now in the United States. Many people think the government should promote Christianity in certain ways, that the state should give substantial aid to parochial schools, that prayer should be allowed in public schools, and that decision of these issues themselves should be based substantially on reference to comprehensive views.[45]

We might conceive of agreement as being much more abstract. People would agree that citizens should enjoy religious liberty and that church and state should be separate, but without reference to details. Agreement on such abstract ideas may exist now in the United States, but this agreement has limited significance when many people have very definite ideas on how to fill in details, and these ideas powerfully conflict with each other.

We can, thus, imagine agreement on constitutional essentials in liberal democracies, but such agreement is likely to be limited to general abstractions and to what constitute blatant violations. There is bound to be important *dis*agreement about a range of debated applications. Public judgments and discussion about that range of possible applications will greatly affect the political life of the society; and constraints set by public reason will matter.

Interpreting Essentials

The problem of *interpreting* essentials can be illuminated by considering the position of someone who favors public school classroom prayer and extensive financial aid to parochial schools. Such a view might be seen as (1) *rejecting* all plausible understandings of religious liberty and church-state separation, (2) offering a genuine interpretation of these essentials but one that is out of accord with what a balance of public reasons would indicate, or (3) offering an interpretation from the perspective of a comprehensive view on questions for which public reason is indecisive.[46]

I shall explore briefly the possibility of rejection. Advocates of prayer and aid do not regard themselves as rejecting all plausible understandings of religious liberty and church-state separation. They point out that their views have enjoyed wide currency and even been dominant for long periods of the country's history. Suppose, however, that we persuade those who urge prayer and aid that their position is a move *away from* any plausible account of religious liberty or church-state separation,[47] or both.[48] So long as they continue to believe that their approach is desirable and enjoys powerful historical support, why should they not feel they remain free to advocate it? Here, once again, we face the question of why a citizen need feel loyalty to institutions and practices that are at odds with those his comprehensive view seems to recommend. The citizen facing this dilemma will need to examine how much room his comprehensive view leaves for loyalty to existing institutions when other possible social arrangements seem to fit better with the comprehensive view. To put the point a bit differently, the person will have to ask if his *reflective* comprehensive view calls for disloyalty to existing institutions in these circumstances. He may finally decide that these institutions actually do fit his comprehensive views best; or that the institutions should be accepted as a compromise necessary in the circumstances, although they are less than ideal; or that he should conform with the rules of the institutions while working to change them; or that he should feel free to decline compliance altogether, insofar as that is possible.

Let us suppose, instead, that the position offered is one reasonable interpretation of constitutional essentials. Not only does the advocate of prayer and aid provide an account of what he thinks religious liberty and church-state separation should amount to in our society; we agree the account he provides is a plausible one. To give this alternative maximum persuasiveness, we might imagine that the person supports aid to parochial education primarily because of its substantial secular value, and that he supports school prayer as an accommodation to the exercise of religion of those who want to pray that interferes only minimally with those who prefer not to pray in school. We *might* conclude that public reason does not tell us how the concepts of religious liberty and separation should be interpreted in these doubtful areas, and that people must inevitably rely on comprehensive views to resolve those questions. That understanding, which I think may well prove accurate for some controversial problems about the state and religion, would increase the difficulty of defending any position that people should self-consciously try to have their political judgment determined by public reasons.

I want to consider the alternative that more strongly favors Rawls's recommendation that citizens rely on public reasons in decision and discourse. That possibility, which I believe holds for some problems, is that public reasons, taken alone, do suggest one outcome, but that people who rely on comprehensive views to color their understanding of constitutional essentials and publicly shared principles may reasonably arrive at a different outcome. Since Rawls himself talks about failures to realize constitutional essentials as relatively easy to identify, perhaps he doubts that such situations will arise;[49] but I believe they may, so long as constitutional essentials are understood to cover more than the most gross violations of concepts like religious liberty and church-state separation.

I shall illustrate this point by reference to abortion, an issue Rawls explicitly considers. He says:

> Suppose . . . that we consider the question in terms of these three important political values: the due respect for human life, the ordered reproduction of political society over time, including the family in some form, and finally the equality of women as equal citizens. (There are, of course, other important political values besides these.) Now I believe any reasonable balance of these three values will give a woman a duly qualified right to decide whether or not to end her pregnancy during the first trimester. The reason for this is that at this early stage of pregnancy the political value of the equality of women is overriding, and this right is required to give it substance and force.[50]

Rawls suggests that public reason would, on balance, support a broadly permissive approach to abortion for at least the first trimester. I am not certain what Rawls is assuming about the status of the embryo/fetus; but suppose Joan takes the following position:

> Political values cannot tell us how much a fetus should be valued; they are either radically incomplete *on this question* or suggest that a fetus is probably of much less value than a newborn baby. On either understanding, women should have substantial freedom to have early abortions. But I *know* from my comprehensive view that a fetus deserves as much moral consideration as a newborn baby. On that understanding, either a woman should not have a legal right to abortion, or the appropriateness of such a right is highly debatable, and a broad right to abortion should not be considered required by constitutional essentials.

This illustration shows how comprehensive views can influence someone's sense of the application of fundamental values. In Joan's view, the fundamental value of protecting "innocent human beings" against "willful killing" colors how equality for women should be regarded (or constitutes a value that here competes with full equality). Thus, someone's comprehensive view can lead her to a different understanding of the full content of a constitutional essential than she would reach if she stuck to public political values alone.

A person might see some church-state issue similarly. He might, for example, suppose that if one stayed with public reasons of equality of citizenship and church-state separation, one would think they were best promoted by not having substantial aid given to religious schools, despite the valuable general education these schools provide. However, thinking that religious salvation is of overarching importance for human life and that religious schools help promote that, he might decide that substantial public aid is, on balance, desirable, and represents a better understanding of religious liberty and church-state separation.

In more typical cases people will not try to figure out what political values alone would indicate; their judgments will be infused by their transcendent perspectives. Since Rawls's restrictions reach *how one votes* and *whether* one publicly advocates a particular outcome, rather than just *how* one advocates an outcome one decides to support on other grounds, his constraint on public reasons is significant, requiring people who wish to comply with an ideal of citizenship to support positions they think are indicated by a balance of public reasons. But, for reasons I explore in this and subsequent chapters, it is highly doubtful that people should feel so constrained, attempting to reach interpretations of essentials that correspond with a balance of public reasons alone, even when their comprehensive views lead them to other plausible interpretations.[51]

Rawls does not deny that people may sometimes face conflicts between their own comprehensive views and public reasons, and that they must resolve these conflicts in light of their own comprehensive views. Thus, he might treat my examples simply as (somewhat complicated) conflicts of this sort. But I think their force goes beyond this; it calls into question the desirability of a standard of public reason that asks citizens to aim for justifications on particular issues that do not rely on comprehensive views.

Difficult Lines of Distinction

Serious technical problems arise out of difficult lines of distinction drawn by Rawls. Examination of these lines raises further doubt about the theoretical defensibility of his position and about the feasibility of its practical application.

One distinction in Rawls's schema is between what are constitutional essentials, on the one hand, and what are interpretations and applications, on the other. Church-state examples can be troubling in this respect. A principle of "no government promotion of religious organizations" might be considered an essential or an interpretation of the essentials of religious liberty and church-state separation. For ordinary purposes, this particular distinction is elusive, depending on the level of generality at which some basic right or fundamental principle is cast. But this distinction is important for Rawls in two ways. First, the essentials are deemed to be off the political agenda; people can argue about interpretations but for the most part they accept the essentials. Second, if the subject of why existing essentials should remain as such does arise, one is free to explain that one's own comprehensive view (part of the overlapping consensus) supports a political conception that includes such essentials. Yet, if the issue is interpretation, one must rely on public reasons (using one's comprehensive view only to provide supplementary reasons for a position). Thus, imagine someone whose religious view strongly indicates that government should give some support to religion. He may say, "I cannot accept this essential, so I am not part of the overlapping consensus. There is an alternative I could accept. Were it adopted I could embrace all the essentials." Or, he may say, "Support is consistent with a proper view of the essential of church-state separation, but I must make this claim based only on public reasons." There is a kind of incongruity in saying that people may appropriately look to their comprehensive views to decide whether they support an existing political conception, including its constitutional essentials, but that comprehensive views must take a decidedly back seat when the details of the essentials are in controversy. If the proponent of aid may reject an essential based on a comprehensive view, why should he not be able to reject an unfavorable interpretation of an essential based on a comprehensive view?

An even more central distinction for Rawls is between constitutional essentials and basic issues of justice, on the one hand, and ordinary political issues, on the other. The first problem with this distinction for legislators and citizens involves discerning which issues are covered by constitutional essentials and which are not. Rawls manages fairly successfully to establish plausible criteria, but troublesome borderline cases will be inevitable. If abortion falls within the range of constitutional essentials, what of research on and implantation of fetal tissue and the enforcement of surrogate motherhood contracts? People may not always be sure whether an issue they discuss is an aspect of constitutional essentials or basic issues of justice, requiring reliance on public reasons.

A second, more serious, difficulty with this distinction concerns a frequent relation *between* constitutional essentials (and questions of basic justice) and other issues. Argument about constitutional essentials bears on the disposition of other issues. An issue, such as, say, fetal research and implantation, may not be about constitutional essentials, but its discussion may involve some *arguments from* constitutional essentials, such as the appropriateness of abortion. Should *those arguments* rely primarily on public reasons, although other arguments may employ comprehensive views? The permissibility of abortion and whether the fetus counts as a full human being are part of the constitutional essentials; these questions may be relevant to evaluation of fetal research and implantation, because these practices may be more offensive, and their possible encouragement of future abortions much more disturbing, if the fetus counts as a full human being and abortion is not a protected right.[52] Should all arguments about encouraging abortions rely mainly on public reasons?

Rawls, I believe, has not yet faced the extent to which interpretation of constitutional essentials infects ordinary political argument. It would be odd to say that you can freely use religious (and other comprehensive) perspectives to argue about constitutional essentials when the essentials are not directly involved (the fetal research issue) but you should not freely use such perspectives when the essentials are directly at stake (the permissibility of abortion issue); but it would also be odd to say that you can use any religious arguments for "nonessentials" *except for* any argument that draws from constitutional essentials. This intermixture of issues presents a troublesome feature of Rawls's distinction that resists easy resolution.

Even when the distinction among issues is clear and issues fit in one category or another, without the perplexing intermixture problem, the idea that different sorts of considerations may be brought to bear on different issues is troublesome. Legislators and citizens are told that all sorts of reasons they may properly treat as highly relevant over a wide range of political issues should be largely excised from their decision making and public discussion concerning constitutional essentials and basic issues of justice. Even if Rawls's underlying theory is otherwise sound, it is not one whose force is intuitively obvious or compelling. Most citizens and ordinary legislators in all branches of government would probably find it strange that references to sources of truth for most political issues were in some degree barred to them for a particular category of issues, whose members are not always *so easy* to identify. This difficulty seriously compromises the practical usefulness of Rawls's distinction among issues.

Finally, Rawls's approach requires that one decide what counts as public reasons as compared with comprehensive reasons. The problem about religious comprehensive views is relatively minor. Rawls assumes that in genuine liberal democracies, citizens are not going to accept *with near universality* any particular Christian view, or Christianity in general, or Islam, Judaism, Hinduism, and so on. Nor will they accept theism as opposed to nontheism. Thus, the exclusion of comprehensive views bars direct reference to Christian, Jewish, Islamic, theist, or atheist premises. Subtle questions arise about the status of religious stories and references to religious traditions as sources of general human or particular cultural understanding, but the discussion in chapter 8 indicates why, when they are carefully presented in the right way, such stories and references can fall within the domain of public reasons.

A more serious concern arises over nonreligious comprehensive views, particularly liberal nonreligious comprehensive views. As I explained in chapter 7, when someone urges that the value of autonomy be respected, it may be virtually impossible for him and others to tell whether he is relying on a particular comprehensive perspective or the widely shared value of autonomy in our culture. Liberal nonreligious comprehensive perspectives are bound to "suffer less" from a principle of self-restraint than both religious views and nonreligious, nonliberal views. This difference may reasonably be thought to involve a kind of inequity.

Stability and Fairness

I have suggested some substantial problems with the principles of self-restraint that Rawls has proposed, and most especially with the line between ordinary political issues and issues that involve constitutional essentials and basic questions of justice. The basic arguments for his approach are ones of political stability and fairness. I shall take my discussion of Nagel as responsive to claims that self-restraint is required by fairness, and here treat only the argument from stability.

Rawls has suggested, convincingly in my view, that diversity of comprehensive religious, philosophical, and moral doctrines is a "permanent feature of the public culture of democracy."[53] If the followers of these various doctrines feel distrust and fear toward those of different views, that is a strong reason to settle on a political culture of common reason, at least for essentials. (This is the conclusion the Diverse Fervent Believers reached in chapter 2.) But suppose people hold widely differing comprehensive views in circumstances of mutual interest and approval; they trust and want to learn from each other (more or less like the liberal groups supporting the Liberal Coalition proposal or like Perry's reasonable fallibilists). In such a culture, references back to comprehensive doctrines would not be particularly threatening. Whether such a culture could exist in a society *as* diverse and *as* prone to hostility and violence as ours may be doubtful; but it is too early in the history of liberal democracy to write off that possibility for all liberal democracies. We should not suppose that the only means by which liberal democratic societies can unite in stability and mutual respect among citizens is by coalescing around a relatively full version of constitutional essentials and an ideal of common reason; some broader acceptance of the relevance of comprehensive views in all political dialogue is a reasonable alternative.[54]

11

Autonomy, Generality, and Foundations of Principles of Restraint

In the following four chapters, I will state and defend principles for restraint concerning grounds for political judgment and advocacy. Here, I draw some general lessons for theorizing about such principles. These lessons, largely revealed by the analysis in the last few chapters, concern the autonomy of claims of political theory, the appropriate level of generality for principles of restraint in a single society and over time and place, and the underlying values from which principles of restraint should be developed. Although I concentrate on the subject matter of this book, much of the discussion bears more generally on how one does normative political philosophy.

Autonomy of Political Principles of Restraint

A vexing problem about the relation between comprehensive views and politics, one highlighted by Rawls's theory and the challenges to it, is whether any political principle of self-restraint can stand independently of comprehensive views. My comments, directly addressed to the relation between religious views and political principles, but also applicable to the relation between other comprehensive views and political principles, show why one needs to resist the temptation to fall into one oversimplification or another.

We can distinguish between the methods by which one determines the validity of a principle and the status of the principle in relation to other standards. Is truth (or validity) in political philosophy known in ways different from religious truth? Is political truth intricately related to religious truth or does it have some independent place? The unexciting answer to each question is that, despite *some* commonalities among people, their understanding of these relations varies greatly, mainly depending on their particular understandings of religious or other comprehensive truth. I shall deal with the two questions in turn.

Ways of Discovering Truth

For *some people,* the manner of knowing much political truth is virtually *identical* to the manner of knowing much religious truth. Malcolm might say, for example, "The way we know most of what we know about God and about how we should live is by interpreting an authoritative text, the Koran. We use exactly the same means to know how to organize society and resolve competing claims of justice." To present a rough analogue, everyone might have great confidence in the founder of a summer camp who left detailed instructions about how people should occupy their time and about camp organization and discipline. The subjects would be different but the manner of deciding what should be done would be the same; one would read and interpret the founder's directions. So long as the subjects were dealt with in similar detail,[1] the interpretive exercises would be closely similar.

For *almost everyone,* the ways to determine religious truth and political truth are significantly linked. One linkage involves "negative checks." What we confidently believe about ordinary facts and ethics serves as a check on what we will accept as religious truth and as sound political philosophy. Our ethical and factual beliefs may, of course, shift as we become persuaded of religious or political claims; but ordinarily we are hesitant to accept claims that fly in the face of our beliefs about the world and how we should live. Similarly, our religious beliefs are a check on our political beliefs and vice versa. We do not accept claims that we recognize as seriously incompatible.[2] Of course, people rarely scrutinize their sets of beliefs with great rigor, and they often hold views that do not fit together comfortably. Nevertheless, few people accept grossly contradictory beliefs; members of Christian groups that emphasize the severe and inherent sinfulness of human beings do not subscribe to political philosophies that rest on the capacity of people to become completely unselfish during the march of human history.

Another linkage in methods of discovery is more positive.[3] Most people use methods for evaluating political principles that are similar to methods they use to determine some religious truths. The search for religious understanding typically involves various levels and techniques. Reasoned deliberation from fundamental premises, for example, so important in secular political philosophy, is one common method for ascertaining some religious truths.

Despite connections between ways of understanding religious and political truth, many people believe significant differences exist between criteria for religious knowledge and criteria for sound political principles. Some who believe that conversion experiences and other individual, "nonaccessible" insights are crucial sources of religious truth do not believe that these sources are important for discovering the truth about desirable principles of governance.[4] In contrast to others who treat political issues similarly to religious questions (believing, for example, that felt response to prayer is the best way to approach thorny political issues), these people rely much more heavily on "ordinary" modes of reasoning for their fundamental views about politics than for their religious understanding. That understanding, which depends in part on "privileged insights," leaves open many possibilities in politics, and they think that central claims in political philosophy, like claims in math and science, are subject to arguments that are publicly accessible.[5]

Someone who reaches a conclusion about the extent to which claims of religious truth are subject to the same techniques of understanding as are claims of validity in political philosophy may accurately express his own view; and one of these views may indicate the correct perspective on how *valid judgments* are made in the two realms. But *any single vision* of the relation between assessments of religious and political claims will misdescribe the richly variant ways in which people regard the quest for understanding about these subjects.

Relative Status

The question of how truth in each realm is discovered is no more central for this book than the related question of the relative status of religious (and other comprehensive) views and political principles. Those who deny that any principle of political restraint can stand alone are mainly denying that a political principle can stand independently of one's comprehensive perspective.

A typical modern religious view is comprehensive, addressing itself not only to theological possibilities such as the existence of God, but encompassing some perspective on how to lead a good life and how to treat one's fellow human beings.[6] Whether any particular religious view directly addresses political organization and justice, some political principles will invariably fit better with that view than will others. At a minimum, then, a religious view will have *some bearing* on acceptable political principles.[7]

As a comprehensive view, a religious perspective is not only broad in what it covers, its significance is overarching. If one's religious convictions call for certain practices, and one has well-ordered beliefs,[8] one thinks the practices should be instituted;[9] it is not as if other considerations can outweigh the religious ones. Given that religious views are both comprehensive and paramount, no room exists in someone's reflective understanding for a political principle that is actually at odds with one's confidently held full religious convictions. To this degree, the argument against the autonomy of a political principle is sound. For the person who accepts a comprehensive religious position, no domain of sound political philosophy is totally removed from sound religious understanding.

There is, however, much more to say. As I have already noted, one's religious views may not speak directly about political organization and justice. One may think that the main techniques for deciding these issues need not rely on religious premises themselves and are compatible with a wide variety of religious premises, though not all.[10] One can thus believe that political philosophy is autonomous in the sense that sound principles for what people should do in politics do not depend on propositions about God or other controversial religious subjects. Of course, one who is rigorously self-reflective "will believe" in this form of autonomy only if his religious views fit with that understanding. Many religious believers do think they can reach important conclusions about political organization and justice that do not depend on disputed religious premises.[11]

A related point concerns social conditions. A political theory must be appropriate for the society to which it applies. Suppose that Faith believes that ideally everyone would accept the true religion (her religion), and that if people did overwhelmingly accept that religion, the government would appropriately support it. In her actual society, however, a plurality of beliefs exists and only one-sixth of the people accept the true religion. Under actual conditions, Faith might think it appropriate for the government to withdraw from claims of religious truth.

We can imagine Faith accepting this principle of withdrawal in one of two ways. She might regard it as a second-best compromise, even as applied to actual circumstances. In this understanding, Faith would think it preferable for the government to support the true religion, which is accepted by only one-sixth of the people; however, realizing that she and her cobelievers do not have the political clout to achieve this result, Faith is willing to settle for the government keeping its hands off religion. This sort of attitude predominated when the principle of toleration first developed in Western Europe. The second way Faith might accept the principle of withdrawal is as an actual requirement of justice, given pluralist conditions. She might suppose that it is inappropriate for the state to support a religion accepted by only one-sixth of the population, even when that sixth happens to be right in its religious view. Such support would inadequately respect freedom and consent as grounds of human community. Thus, Faith's understanding, her *overall understanding including her religious convictions*, would include principles of respect for nonbelievers that might call for principles of justice in religiously diverse societies different from those appropriate in societies in which the correct religious view overwhelmingly predominates.[12] In this understanding, Faith's sense of justice for pluralist societies does correspond with her full religious views; but it does not follow that Faith thinks the principles of justice can be easily derived from religious truth.

If principles of justice are to regulate society, they may need to have fairly wide acceptance. As we saw in the last chapter, that is a central proposition in Rawls's political philosophy; he has sought to develop principles of justice from premises that are widely shared in liberal democracies, and do not depend on any particular religious or other comprehensive perspective. Faith, or any other particular individual, might accept political principles that fit with widely shared premises because that seems an appropriate way to show respect for fellow citizens.

We may conclude that if Faith is rigorously reflective, acceptable political principles will have to be consonant with her overall religious view; they will not be autonomous in the sense of floating freely and unaffected by her religious views. No doubt, as people reflect on both religious and political principles, interactive influences are common;[13] but the status of someone's political principles and the techniques she uses to determine them may be largely independent of the religious truth in which she believes. Principles of justice for diverse societies may have a fairly remote relation to many particular religious views (except insofar as those views include notions of equality and of respect for the autonomy of nonbelievers). Some of Rawls's critics have claimed[14] that people's defensible views on justice will bring comprehensive understandings, including religious views, more directly to bear than Rawls calls for with regard to constitutional essentials. My comments on this complex topic in chapter 10 and here suggest that the feasible divorce between comprehensive understandings and political issues is less complete than Rawls suggests, but is greater than some critics acknowledge.

I have focused thus far on the relation between an ordinary individual's comprehensive view and her political principles and suggested that, if she is reflective, she will measure the latter against the former to some degree. The stance of the political theorist may be somewhat different. The theorist will, of course, not suggest as true or valid any political principles he thinks fail to correspond with a true or valid comprehensive view; but he *may* self-consciously present political principles that do not rest on any particular comprehensive view. He may offer these in the hope that they will appeal to people with diverse comprehensive views. This kind of normative political theory stands more detached from particular comprehensive views than does the evaluation of proposed principles that individual citizens undertake. That, indeed, is one lesson of the recent work of John Rawls, and it also captures the aspirations of this book. I shall comment shortly on *why* such an aspiration makes strong sense for principles of self-restraint and public reason within liberal democracies.

Generality of Political Principles about Decision and Argument

In this section, I consider two related questions about the appropriate generality of political principles of restraint. One question concerns the kind of principles appropriate for a particular time and place; the other concerns the range of application *over* time and place.

Generality in the Present: Practicality and Breadth of Appeal

Various principles of restraint have been suggested for modern liberal democracies. Since most of those writing on this subject have been Americans, their implicit reference, if any, has been to the contemporary United States.

In discussing possible principles, I shall assume that a crucial standard is whether they could be recommended as appropriate for real people in an actual society. We can imagine principles of self-restraint that might work for highly conscientious, self-reflective citizens who have a nearly full understanding of the reasons behind the principles, and are able and willing to apply them with precision. Perhaps theorizing about political orders containing ideal people has some value; but political principles can be finally recommended only if they are suitable for real people, as they are or as they might become.

We have seen from the prior discussion in the book that possible principles of restraint in politics can be cast in various ways, differing as to kinds of grounds, degree of exclusion (or disfavoring), persons affected, behavior covered, and range of subjects. Here, roughly, are the possibilities for recommended restraints:

1. *Kinds of grounds.* People should not rely on nonaccessible grounds, religious grounds, grounds deriving from comprehensive views, or controversial ideas of the good, or some combination of these. (The idea of public reason, as explicated by Rawls and summarized in chapter 10, would exclude all grounds based on particular comprehensive views, including religious views, *and* any additional grounds that are nonaccessible.)

2. *Degree of exclusion (or disfavoring).* People should try to decide without any kind of reliance on the excluded grounds; or should try to use public grounds and rely on excluded grounds only when public grounds are indecisive; or in all instances should give greater weight to public grounds but can give some weight to disfavored grounds; or should not rely directly on excluded grounds, but may appropriately be influenced by them in their approach to public reasons.

3. *Persons affected.* The persons who should not rely on excluded grounds include judges, legislators, executive officials, politically active citizens, all citizens, or some of these but not others.

4. *Behavior covered.* People affected should not rely on excluded grounds in argument or decision or both; they should not rely in all or some of the political roles they perform; they should not rely directly on excluded grounds believed by themselves, or they should not rely on excluded grounds believed by others (as a legislator might rely on the religious beliefs of constituents), or both.

5. *Range of subjects.* People should not rely on excluded grounds for all political subjects, or only for constitutional essentials and questions of basic justice, or for some other subset of all political issues.

This brief review suggests the great number of conceivable principles of restraint that might be recommended. And there is, of course, the very important alternative of no restraint, that people may rely on any grounds of judgment they believe are appropriate.

In the remainder of this chapter, I shall focus on choices about legislation and assume that legislators and citizens should be governed by similar principles of restraint. I qualify this simplifying assumption to a substantial degree in the following chapters, when I present my own position, but those qualifications are unnecessary for the points I make here. These points illustrate why one needs to think in terms of political principles that can be recommended to actual citizens and officials and that are appropriate for the society in which one lives.

One kind of problem of appropriateness for actual people concerns feasibility of application. I suggested in the last chapter that having different permissible grounds for "constitutional essentials" and ordinary political issues largely founders on the problem of practicality. The issues are intermixed, and people cannot comfortably extirpate sources of understanding for constitutional essentials that they properly bring to bear for other issues, even when they can determine which of the two kinds of issues is presented and blending is not a difficulty.

A different problem about appropriateness for actual people concerns the reasons presented to justify a principle of self-restraint. This problem infects the suggestion that people should limit themselves to naturalist (or rationalist) arguments in political discussion because ethical (and perhaps religious) judgments should themselves be based on naturalist (or rationalist) grounds (as discussed in chapter 8). Someone who thinks all ethical judgments should be based on natural arguments regards all nonaccessible means of reaching such judgments as mistaken. From this perspective, no special principle of exclusion for nonaccessible reasons is needed for politics because nonaccessible grounds for moral judgments are inappropriate at the outset. One way to take *some* arguments made by Michael Perry, Franklin Gamwell, and Robin Lovin is the following.[15] A sound comprehensive philosophy is naturalist about ethical and social judgments. Other approaches to morality and justice are misguided. Therefore, all good arguments in the political process should be of a naturalist sort, permissibly colored by some religious claims. Under such an approach to the subject, all misguided and mistaken arguments should be excluded.

So understood, this approach definitely does not yield an *independent political principle*. If someone thinks a naturalist approach to ethics is mistaken or very incomplete, that person will not yet have been given reasons to eschew other than naturalist arguments in politics. If one thinks of political principles in liberal democratic societies as needing to appeal to people of different ethical understandings, it would not be a plausible *political* principle simply to say, "Rely on naturalist arguments, and their religious accompaniments but do not rely on other grounds for political positions."

Such a principle, without further justification, could be persuasive only to those who already believe or are persuaded that naturalist grounds are correct and other claimed grounds are incorrect.

It *may be reasonable,* independent of one's own particular views about religion and ethics, to emphasize the importance in a pluralist society of public discussion in terms of grounds that are accessible to others. Thus, "Do not publicly rely on grounds that are not accessible to others" is a plausible political principle with a wider range.[16]

If one is to suggest a principle about reasons for political decisions that is more than a corollary of religious and ethical views concerning the validity of methods of reason, then one must present grounds for the political principle that have appeal to persons of religious and ethical views different from one's own. The principle must also be one that people of various views are actually capable of applying.

The need for breadth of appeal is especially great if the principle one invokes depends on reciprocity of performance. Some principles should guide one's actions no matter what other people are doing. For example, it is not desirable to rely on grounds for political decisions that are intrinsically inadequate, such as astrology, even if many other people are relying on such grounds. Most of the principles of restraint we have considered are not like this. They call on people to decline reliance on grounds that they believe are sound bases for reaching decisions, and to do so in the interest of fairness to others, as well as consequential considerations such as stability. Imagine that a society was divided evenly between people with strongly divergent comprehensive views *C* and *S.* Suppose it were clear that everybody believing *C* was determined to employ that comprehensive view directly for all political subjects. Fairness to believers in *C* would hardly require adherents of *S* to refrain from using their comprehensive view. Barring some powerful relevant difference in the nature of the comprehensive views, fairness would call for parallel behavior by adherents of the different views. The final appropriateness of self-restraint would depend on the prospect of reciprocity, restraint on one side being matched by restraint on the other. This feature of reciprocity helps us to understand why a theorist proposing restraint may wish to step back from his own comprehensive view, presenting reasons that will seem persuasive to holders of a range of comprehensive views. (An alternative is to develop reasons from the particular perspective of one's own comprehensive view, with the expectation or hope that these will have force for people with other comprehensive views.) Insofar as theory influences behavior, we are unlikely to achieve reciprocal restraint unless people of different views recognize similar substantial grounds for restraint.[17]

Application Over Time and Place

I now turn to the domain of coverage of possible political principles of restraint. We may distinguish here (1) fundamental principles good for all social orders, (2) fundamental principles for liberal democracies, (3) practical principles good for all liberal democracies, (4) practical principles good for a time and place, and (5) prudential strategies for effective persuasion. We can quickly exclude the first possibility as not directly relevant for our topic. A social order founded on a narrow claim of religious truth would certainly not exclude religious grounds from political decision. A social order founded on belief that inexplicable insights are the best sources of truth in all domains would not exclude all nonaccessible insights as grounds of political judgment. Of course, such social orders *may* themselves be indefensible. But if that conclusion is to be the basis for a principle of restraint, it must rest on some much broader argument about what are acceptable social orders.

Roughly what I mean by a fundamental principle of liberal democracy is a principle that is basic enough so that a failure to recognize it would either disqualify a government from being a liberal democracy or would constitute a very serious defect. Notions that citizens are essentially equal, that they should have opportunities for political participation, and that they should enjoy liberty of speech and religious exercise are such fundamental principles. By a practical principle good for all liberal democracies, I mean some principle that does not appear to be fundamental, but which always will prove to be desirable to follow. A practical principle good for a time and place is one that should be accepted by citizens in some social orders at certain stages of their history. A prudential strategy for effective persuasion is not by itself a *principle* of restraint at all (although it might conform with a principle of restraint); it is the most effective means to achieve one's political objectives. Thus, it might be said that in a pluralist society, the most effective means to persuade others is usually public argument in nonreligious accessible terms. One could believe this without thinking that any principle of restraint is called for; indeed, as we shall see, if it is very clear to everyone that effective strategy dictates accessible argument, that may actually be a reason not to have any political principle against nonaccessible argument.

What I have said so far in this book indicates my belief that self-restraint about the use of religious or nonaccessible reasons is not part of a set of fundamental principles for liberal democracy. Were a liberal democratic society made up of people with essentially similar views about religion who thought religious perspectives were important for social policy, they would not bar all reliance on those perspectives. A similar position might be taken by people who had highly diverse religious views (so diverse that no one feared imposition on the basis of any set of religious premises), a history of harmonious religious interaction, and a strong common interest in dialogue about religious views. These, indeed, were roughly the conditions that led to the Liberal Coalition proposal for Sretna Bosna. Although denying religious freedom is by definition illiberal, it is not necessarily illiberal to rely upon nonaccessible religious understanding to decide that factory farming as presently constituted is immoral and should be stopped, or that certain forms of genetic research should not be allowed.

Someone might concede this much and claim that nonetheless some principle of restraint is appropriate for all liberal democracies, given the nature of people and social orders. If freedom of religion exists, diverse religious views are bound to emerge and continue; religion engenders such strong passions that it will inevitably be a source of tension; and that tension will be aggravated by reliance on religious grounds in political decisions and arguments. Relatedly, social unity in liberal democracies will always be fragile enough so that argument in terms of nonaccessible grounds will be harmful. In such ways, someone can argue that favored principles of exclusion will be apt for all liberal democracies.

Full examination of such a thesis would require a lengthy excursion into the conditions of liberal democracies that I shall not attempt. I am inclined to believe, however, that within liberal democracies, the vitality of religion and confidence in nonaccessible sources of insight can vary so greatly that no simple political principles about these are good for all such societies. Further, if the human race and liberal democracy manage to survive a few more centuries, liberal democracy in the 1990s will have been in its comparative infancy, with origins strongly related to religious controversy. It is still too early to predict the range of conditions in which it may flourish.

I spent two weeks teaching in Holland in the summer of 1991. Students in that fairly homogeneous society told me that very few people took religion seriously any longer, that tolerance was high and religious tension virtually nonexistent, that religious arguments for political positions would be wholly ineffective. In these respects, I suspect that a number of Scandinavian countries are now similar. In such conditions, there would seem no good reason to suggest an exclusionary principle of restraint concerning religious grounds. The same conclusion might hold if most people *were* religious, but accepted highly rationalist forms of religion based on naturalist arguments. Of course, the absence of a need for self-restraint about religious grounds, in particular, does not necessarily rule out the need for principles of self-restraint governing all comprehensive views. Nevertheless, we need to acknowledge that what principles of restraint, if any, are appropriate may depend on time and place, on a sense of the present makeup of a society, of its history, and of its likely evolution.

If this is correct, judgments about appropriate principles for the United States at this time cannot be based solely on abstract conclusions about liberal democracy and the nature of religious, comprehensive, and nonaccessible bases for judgment. Religion is of urgent importance to many people in this country. The population is highly diverse and becoming more so. In some sections of the country, one or two religious perspectives are dominant enough so that imposition is a serious danger. Although religious violence is now rare, we are not yet close to a state of bland tolerance. These realities provide the setting in which we should examine possible principles that would reach religious grounds.

Such an examination raises once again the question of autonomy. Can judgments about appropriate political principles stand independently of comprehensive religious and philosophical schemes? Yes and no. There are general arguments for and against some principles of restraint that appeal to people of widely differing religious and other comprehensive views. Few thoughtful people in liberal democracies will welcome religious conflict or the suppression of religious liberty. On the other hand, the slightest risk of these dangers would not appropriately bring on restraint in decision and public justification. One's own religious view will have much to do with whether or not one thinks that open religious controversy is healthy, that religious criticism of secular culture is of great importance, and that helpful dialogue about deeper subjects will be significantly promoted by religious argument over particular political issues. How one *weighs* the various arguments for and against restraint may depend to a considerable extent on one's own comprehensive view.

Thus, we can conceive of powerful arguments for and against self-restraint that float nearly free of grander philosophical assumptions because their force is so widely accepted or is linked so closely to basic premises of liberal democracy. We can also imagine fairly wide acceptance of some rough principles of restraint among partisans of differing comprehensive views. However, a refined assessment of arguments for and against particular principles of restraint will be affected by comprehensive views, and the principles that are accepted will somehow have to fit with most of those views.

I have suggested that history and present social relations will matter for appropriate principles within any liberal democracy. Of particular importance, as chapter 2 showed, will be the various kinds of religious convictions and the degree of mutual interest and acceptance among their adherents. Accounts of whether people conceive themselves to be under principles of constraint will be some evidence of what will work in a society, but they also have a more immediate relevance.

Descriptive accounts of past and present attitudes can matter for the normative theorist in two different ways. Suppose a theorist is trying to decide what would be *the most appropriate relations* between religion and politics in the United States. He would need to pay attention to our constitutional structure, social institutions, and religious diversity; but he might reach conclusions that deviate a great deal from present practices. Thus, the theorist might say, "There has been a considerable intertwining of religion and politics in American history. This continues to the present, and in some respects is even increasing. Nonetheless, the healthiest relations would be ones in which religion is a matter of private conviction and cultural debate, but politics is a separate domain."

The theorist might instead ask a different question, one about what individuals now have a duty to do. He might ask, for example, whether a legislator, here and now, has some kind of moral duty not to rely on her religious premises in reaching decisions. Here, actual practices have a more direct bearing. I have suggested that reciprocity is important for principles of self-restraint. If most legislators feel free to rely on religious premises *and* that has long been an assumption of American governance, saying that an individual legislator now has a moral duty not to do so would be hard (unless one could point to unjust domination by those sharing the legislator's views). After all, if this legislator stops relying on her religious convictions, she may have legislation determined by the religious convictions of others. Even if her refusing to rely on her convictions would be desirable in helping to bring about a politics more free of religion, she may have no present duty to act that way. In brief, past and, especially, existing practices matter a lot for what we can reasonably demand or ask of those presently involved in political life; they will also matter, but they may matter less, for suggestions about ideal relations in the United States or some other liberal democracy.

Criteria of Judgment

The next four chapters suggest principles of self-restraint nuanced to different roles and the conditions of American society. The question was put to me by a reader of a previous draft: What is the measure against which someone could assess the soundness of your specific conclusions? The question is a troubling one and the answer is not simple. Various considerations, already mentioned in the book, guide my judgment. One is belief in a robust freedom of religion, and the further belief that an aspect of the full exercise of religion includes political action that is guided by one's religious convictions. Other considerations grow out of conditions of pluralism: the inequality and disrespect that members of minorities may feel if they believe that major political decisions are made on grounds that they cannot accept, the sense they may have that they are being imposed upon as second-class citizens. Further considerations involve productivity of political discussion and relative stability. There is little point in having irreconcilable and bitter disputes about unresolvable subjects as the centerpiece of the practical art of politics. Considerations of feasibility are of major importance: plausible principles must be ones that most relevant people can live up to in substantial degree much of the time. As I have explained, a critical feature of proposed principles of self-restraint and public reason is reciprocity. A principle of this sort cannot be feasible unless it is attractive to people of widely diverse comprehensive views and political ideologies and unless people who restrain themselves can have some confidence that others are acting likewise. That problem is the main focus of the next chapter, where I argue that limits on discourse are much more enforceable than limits on judgment. I assume that present understandings matter. I think they are some guide to what is appropriate in a society otherwise constituted as ours is. They are certainly of vital importance for what we can reasonably expect of people here and now.

These various considerations genuinely point in different directions, a lesson that I hope the first parts of this book teach forcefully. There is no easy resolution that captures everything of value in each relevant consideration. A choice for or against restraint sacrifices something of value. But the problem is much more complicated than a single overall choice. The priority and weight of considerations turn out to look quite different in regard to people who occupy different positions and exercise different responsibilities. And present understandings certainly vary according to position and role. Thus, the relevant choices turn out to be highly specific. The judgments I offer in the following chapters reflect my own assessment of how the considerations bear in various concrete contexts. Because of the very nature of the enterprise, if I have accurately captured what is the nature of the enterprise, anything in the way of conclusive demonstration is foreclosed. Even if I persuade a reader about what matters, he or she may assign a different priority or weight to considerations, because of disagreements about values or over complex social facts. Such disagreements can lead to rejection of concrete conclusions that I offer.

This reality raises again the value of a theorist's developing an argument of political philosophy that is detached from a specific comprehensive view. Of course, disagreements over conclusions might exist among people with similar comprehensive views; but how may variances in comprehensive views figure in the assessment of considerations I have noted? I believe that they undoubtedly will figure. That is, I do not think the priority and weight of the considerations I have suggested can be assessed on some political basis that is completely free of controversial comprehensive views. If this much is true, proponents of different comprehensive views, all of whom embrace liberal democracy, will reasonably disagree about the precise amount of self-restraint that is most desirable. It follows that the theorist's own estimation of priority and weight (in this case mine) will be affected to a degree by his comprehensive views. Thus, his presentation must inevitably be somewhat incomplete unless he ties everything else to his comprehensive view. I find no difficulty in acknowledging this. It may still be better to offer this slightly incomplete picture than to attempt to develop the comprehensive view itself and explain how it ties to subtle matters of debatable judgment, an enormously complex task that might bear little fruit. In any event, I have thought it best to offer the considerations without invoking my own full religious understanding. That understanding does fit with the conclusions I draw, but it certainly does not yield them in any straightforward way; and it seems to me that the assessments I make could be widely shared by people whose comprehensive views are strikingly different.

12

Self-Restraint in Decision and Advocacy and Public Roles

Previous chapters have indicated many possible principles of self-restraint with respect to reliance on nonaccessible, specifically religious, and comprehensive (including religious) grounds. These principles may bear on the political decisions someone makes, on his public advocacy, or both. Earlier chapters also have set the broad parameters within which resolutions should be offered, ones focused on the contexts of particular liberal democracies at particular stages of history and addressed to people of differing religious and philosophic persuasions. In the rest of the book, I suggest principles that are fairly flexible in context and that can give way in light of other powerful considerations. These principles are not too far from present practice, as I understand it, and that indeed has much to do with why I am comfortable offering them as recommendations for action here and now.

In this chapter, I comment on what may seem tangential personal illustrations. I believe these examples show how self-restraint works, why self-restraint in advocacy is much more attainable than self-restraint in decision or judgment, and why exercising greater self-restraint in advocacy need not amount to insincerity. I also set the stage for the following chapters by outlining briefly various roles and functions in liberal democratic governance.

Two Incidents

My most direct experience in governing has been in academic associations.[1] One must be wary of drawing analogies too easily, but reflection on what is appropriate for these smaller governments may illuminate possibilities for the general government. My account of two incidents suffers some in-

134

accuracy because of faulty recollection, but the details about which I am unsure are not crucial.

At Swarthmore College, when I was a member of the student government, a wide variety of student organizations received money out of general student fees to invite outside speakers and put on programs. The Student Council allocated money among the organizations.

One of the organizations receiving money was the Christian Fellowship; its speakers participated in programs in which worship was an important component. Perhaps because Swarthmore was a college with strong religious (Society of Friends) roots and because virtually every organization that students wanted to create received some funding, the idea that all students lent slight support to forms of worship in which only some engaged did not strike many as a problem. However, during this particular period the Christian Fellowship decided to require members to subscribe to some statement of faith. Within the fellowship there was some disagreement about how stringent the statement should be. As a member of the fellowship, I felt that any criteria that would exclude students who considered themselves to be Christians would be inappropriate for the one formal Christian organization on campus, an organization receiving general student funding. After some heated discussion, the organization did adopt fairly "generous," that is, inclusive, standards of what one needed to believe for membership; it was difficult to imagine someone considering himself or herself to be Christian who could not subscribe to the simple statement of belief. Nonmembers were free to attend all events, but only members could vote to elect officers and on other matters that came for decision before the full organization.

When the time came for the yearly allocations of student funds, some members of Student Council believed money should not be given to any organization with an exclusive membership. During the council's discussion of the issue, no one talked about whether the Christian faith was true or whether religion in general was beneficial for humankind. Members of the council who held no positive religious beliefs tended to be the strongest opponents of funding. Members who belonged to the Christian Fellowship tended to be the strongest proponents. Nevertheless (or therefore), the discussion did not evolve into an argument about the merits of Christian discussion and worship as compared with other activities, such as those sponsored by the Film Club. No doubt, *part* of the reason why this did not happen was strategic; arguments for or against the activities of the Christian Fellowship could only harden opposition and might put off those who were uncertain. But part of the reason certainly was a sense that the Student Council's job, beyond some minimal standard of review, was not to pass on the merits of funded activities.[2] The basic argument against funding was that general student funds should not go for activities with an exclusive membership. The contrary argument was that it was proper for the Christian Fellowship to include only those who seriously regarded themselves as Christians. Otherwise, it was conceivable that the organization could be "captured" by those who were anti-Christian and who wished to under-mine the organization—in a manner that did not seem possible for the Film Club or the radio station. Though I supported funding, I saw even then that the opponents had a substantial argument, and I am not sure how I would resolve the issue now.

My recollection about my self-conscious motivation is less clear than my memory of the discussion, and I do not know how others saw their own positions. I do not recall specific conversations with friends who were members of both the council and the fellowship in which we explicitly discussed the issue in terms of the importance of having funding for fellow-ship activities; but I believe that mattered to me, and that I did not scrupu-lously try to disregard its importance. I also would have felt I had let down colleagues in the fellowship if I opposed funding or remained neutral. What I thought was good from my own complete perspective and the point of view of the fellowship coincided with what I thought was right from the Council's point of view, and I did not agonize too hard over whether that answer would have seemed right if I were an atheist and thought all religion was foolish superstition.

My second incident comes from about fifteen years ago at Columbia Law School, when individual constitutional rights were being taught in a second semester of Constitutional Law. A number of us, six or seven (four or five in a given year), were teaching the course; our schedules were highly coordinated because we periodically had lectures before the entire group of nearly three hundred students. For a few years we had planned the last two (!) sessions on cases under the free exercise and establishment clauses of the First Amendment. (This was an era when religion clause interpretation was less active than it has since become.) A number of pro-fessors, squeezed for time, ended up doing nothing on those cases, except what was covered in a large lecture I gave. One year a tentative proposal came around to omit the religion cases altogether. With some zeal I op-posed this idea in a memorandum, saying that it was one thing to omit the material because of unplanned time pressure, quite another to decide in advance to do so. I argued that given the important place of religion and state-religion relations in the country's history, the continuing significance of religion in the lives of many citizens, and the absence of any separate course on the subject in the curriculum, one could not defensibly leave the topic out of a syllabus covering individual rights in general. Whether I actually persuaded anyone or the others decided it was easier to continue their unplanned omissions than to fight with me over the two planned days, the religion clause cases stayed in the syllabus. In none of the circula-tions or conversations did anyone talk about whether religion was actually important to human life, and I *definitely* did not think a positive answer to that question was required to sustain my position. Again, *my reasons* for not getting into that question were partly strategic; but I would strongly have doubted whether contention about it was appropriate dis-course within a faculty of diverse backgrounds and beliefs. Although I was fairly certain that differences in respect to that underlying question had something to do with the original proposal and my reaction to it, discussing whether to keep the religion clause cases in the course hardly seemed an apt occasion to debate the merits of religious beliefs.

Decision and Public Justification

These two incidents show how one's complete grounds for action may differ from one's public justification or advocacy. On both occasions, I explained my position and advocated it in a manner that made no use of my religious beliefs, any comprehensive view, or any nonaccessible ground. I appealed to considerations that I thought would be taken as relevant by all those with whom I had joint responsibility for a decision.

One crucial difference between one's public advocacy and one's actual grounds for judgment is that advocated grounds are evident to everyone who listens (although subtle undercurrents of manipulation may not be apparent). If one conceives of possible principles of restraint as exercising some kind of reciprocal force, one quickly sees that restraint on one's public advocacy has a kind of "enforceability" that restraint on one's decision lacks. If I employ my comprehensive view in dialogue—"The Christian Fellowship should receive money partly because it helps foster valuable religious practices on campus"—others can respond that such an appeal is totally inappropriate or can bring their own comprehensive views to bear— "We certainly shouldn't support an organization that chooses to be exclusive and is perpetuating harmful superstitions."[3] No such "enforcement" is possible as to privately held reasons: those asked to exercise restraint can never be sure whether others, particularly their opponents, are doing so.

The second, more fundamental, difference concerns efforts to apply principles of restraint. In both the college and law school circumstances, I understood the difference between making a directly religious argument and making arguments that had wider applicability, and I was comfortably capable of abiding by a principle restricting the former. Perhaps if someone had pushed me hard enough, I would have been forced to acknowledge that I might have taken a different view if I strongly believed that all religion was mere superstition; but discourse over particular political issues is rarely an occasion for acute and probing dialogue over the full structure of people's thoughts. (Of course, this *might* change if conventions about what is said changed.) In both situations, I did regard myself as subject to some kind of principle limiting the kinds of arguments that were appropriate to make to a diverse group. I was far less clear at the time whether I should try in developing my own position to discount my own religious beliefs in judgment. I *could* have tried hard to imagine how I might have regarded the issue if I had a decidedly negative view about religion, if I were uncertain or indifferent, or if I were in some original position not knowing whether I would hold religious beliefs when I became a real human being.

If, as I supposed, the Swarthmore Student Council did not have the responsibility of serious review of the merits of various student activities, perhaps I should have tried to look at the issue free of any opinion about the worth of what the Christian Fellowship was doing. But the issue was whether an organization should be able to be exclusive in its membership. Evaluating *this* without some understanding of, and sympathy or lack of it for, the organization would be hard. Suppose the Film Club had said it would admit as members only those who subscribed to a statement that they were genuinely devoted to the art of film. I suspect my view would have been different. I can now think of grounds that are independent of my own religious beliefs that would have allowed me to treat the two groups differently; but I did not then have a strong sense that those beliefs were entirely irrelevant. Putting aside self-interest is not easy, but I have voted in faculty meetings for things, most notably appointments, that have been contrary to what I have regarded as my self-interest. Overcoming bonds of association and one's overall view of what is right is much harder.

To generalize my experience, people have great difficulty trying to face particular political issues free of the push of their religious or other comprehensive views. It requires an exceptional discipline to do so with any success. It is doubtful whether one should recommend to ordinary people a self-restraint that is so hard to perform.

The very difficulty of this self-restraint reinforces the concern about effective reciprocity. People have trouble understanding why others disagree with them so often. I have heard it said that everybody thinks they have a good sense of humor. Maybe so, but I think more people are confident about their "good judgment" than their sense of humor. People need continuing education to be persuaded that others with the best of motives can disagree with them radically. It is so easy to leap to the conclusion that one's opponents are willful, or at the very least pursuing some illicit self-interested agenda. If someone is conscientiously trying to purge his own position of religious or comprehensive views, but finds (surprisingly) that his position ends up being the one that fits best with those overall views, how far is he going to believe that his opponents have managed to discount their comprehensive views? I *do remember* thinking that those who opposed funding of the Christian Fellowship and those who were inclined to extirpate religion clause cases from our semester of constitutional law probably were affected by a low view of the value of religious practices. *If* it is very hard to discount one's own comprehensive views *and* one is disinclined to attribute such success to opponents, people are likely to feel that if they try too hard, they will be unfairly disadvantaging the comprehensive views from which they begin.

If this natural distrust can operate in the relatively congenial setting of the Swarthmore Student Council, as I knew it, and the Columbia Law Faculty, as I continue to know it, how much more are they likely to operate in the rough and tumble of real politics when issues of vital importance are at stake? It is demanding a great deal to ask people strenuously to aim to distance themselves from their comprehensive views when they will inevitably suspect that their political opponents are failing to do so.

Any differential that calls for greater self-restraint in discussion and advocacy than in decision raises a "sincerity" problem, one to which I shall return in subsequent chapters. We can see from the two illustrations that whether there is *genuine deceit* depends on expectations. If people think the influence of certain reasons is appropriate and likely, but they do not expect the explication of those reasons in public justifications, someone's failure to mention the reasons does not involve deception. It does, however, mean that the disclosure of bases for decision is less complete than it could be. In both my examples, I believed in the public reasons I offered; what I did not reveal is the extent to which my evaluation of those reasons might have been affected by my religious beliefs. (Given my understanding of the two theories, I probably passed Rawls's test of public reasons sincerely offered, discussed in the previous chapter, but I may have failed Audi's test of secular motivation, explained in chapter 6.) The gap between actual disclosure and full disclosure would have been greater if I had offered public reasons that I did not find persuasive to support a decision reached on entirely different religious grounds. Nevertheless, my disclosure of my own underlying grounds of judgment was not complete. Full disclosure should ordinarily be regarded as a virtue. If less than full disclosure is to be recommended, one must present reasons why a discourse in terms of commonly shared or accessible reasons is desirable. Whether sufficient reasons exist is a crucial question for the remainder of the book.

Self-Restraint and Positions People Occupy in Liberal Democracies

Any discussion of the appropriate place of various kinds of grounds for political decision and advocacy must pay due respect to different positions people occupy. In succeeding chapters I concentrate on judges, then legislators and ordinary citizens, and finally religious groups. I treat members of the executive branch as their responsibilities connect to those of judges or legislators.

The most important subject for our inquiry is legislation. Except for public referenda and the like, legislation is voted upon by official legislators. In the United States, chief executives exercise some sort of veto power, and in all modern democracies much proposed legislation comes from the executive branch.[4] Officials within the executive branch and administrative agencies, some of which enjoy independence from the executive chain of command, further exercise a kind of legislative power when they fill in gaps left by the legislature. The executive also, of course, has the responsibility to administer the law and to enforce both legislative and judicial judgments. We can roughly distinguish between the executive's administrative and enforcement functions and its functions of proposing legislation and legislating in the gaps. In their two legislative functions, executive officials differ in important respects from individual legislators. When the executive legislates within the gaps, it must follow the directions of the legislature; that makes it subject to guidelines that are much more constraining than the constitutional limits that affect legislators deciding upon proposed statutes. Another critical distinction is that the executive is singular.[5] The executive represents "the government," or at least a branch of government, in a way that is not true for individual legislators. Lying behind the executive and legislators are the citizens, to whom public officials are supposed, in some sense, to be responsible. Filling out the picture are courts, and administrative bodies that resolve disputes like courts. Courts "apply" the law and, in English-speaking countries, develop their own common law to cover matters unregulated by the legislature. Original decisions in courts about the law are usually made by a single judge. Intermediate appellate courts have three, or maybe five, judges; supreme courts for the state and country tend to have nine, or seven, judges sitting on a case. Litigation is very expensive.

In reflecting on appropriate self-restraint, it is simplest to begin with courts, because, as Rawls suggests, they are exemplars of public reason.

13

Judicial Decisions and Opinions

A Model of Constrained Sources

If anyone is constrained in the reasons they should employ for decision and argument, it is judges. Considering judicial practices illustrates some issues clearly in a way that helps understanding of more complex problems regarding legislation. As chapter 3 pointed out, the restraint on judges is obvious in easy cases, where the existing law calls for straightforward answers; but it has been typically assumed that judges are substantially constrained even when the right result for a case is highly arguable.

In modern American judicial practice, the sources of judgment provided in the *official justifications* of opinions are certainly highly constrained; there are many conceivable reasons for deciding one way or another that you will not find in judicial opinions. Further, it is widely assumed that judges should be constrained in their own use of sources for *reaching* decisions, whether these sources are publicly revealed or not.

Both the reality and desirability of these constraints have been challenged for a long time. They are now sharply attacked by some feminists and critical legal scholars, among others. The "reality" challenge is that the myth of limited sources creates a delusion of law's objectivity, whereas in fact legal decisions result from class advantage, social prejudice, and personal quirk. This delusion tends to reify and legitimate standards that should be exposed for what they are, the frail consequences of an all-too-human enterprise. A more openly personalized practice of decision and justification would better convey what already happens and would burst unhealthy myths.

The "desirability" challenge is that insofar as judges are genuinely constrained in the way the myth supposes, they disregard some important features of particular cases. Decisions should be better tailored to a full appraisal of individual circumstances. Thus, more personalized decision would actually encourage more humane treatment of those caught within the coils of the law.

By contrast to these challenges, the traditional model posits as a desirable aspiration an ideal that legal decision not depend on the personality of the judge. The aspiration is not fully achievable even if all judges are intelligent, well-trained, and conscientious, but it is worth striving for by emphasizing that bases of legal judgment should be open and available to all. I take the traditional model as my starting point for the narrower subject of religious and comprehensive convictions, both because I believe it is more sound normatively than its competitor[1] and because it continues to enjoy very wide acceptance among judges and lawyers.

The Exclusion of Religious Convictions from Opinions

Identifying what judges do is very simple in one respect. Writing opinions is an important aspect of the judicial function, especially the appellate judicial function. The opinions of higher courts are published for everyone to see. In the nineteenth century, one could find references to Christianity as a part of the common law, and judges occasionally mentioned Christian teachings to help support legal conclusions. One does not often find such mentions today.[2] A judge may refer to Christian tenets to help put a legal problem or doctrine, or social attitudes, in a historical perspective, but she is not likely to say that an otherwise debatable legal conclusion is correct because it conforms to Christianity or some other supposedly true religious understanding. Few opinions rely directly on religion in this way. Judges assume that people in this country have variant religious views, and I think most judges also assume that basic differences among religious views are not resolvable on the basis of shared forms of reasoning. Thus, no particular religious view is seen to be embedded in the legal materials themselves or to be part of some common understanding or technique of reason that stretches beyond the legal materials but can be a source of guidance.

Within opinions, nonreligious personal moral convictions have the same status. At least so labeled, they are not used in opinions. A judge does not say, "I am holding that this infringement on speech violates the First Amendment because I know personally it is morally wrong." It is true that in a well-known case, the Supreme Court said that it was holding evidence inadmissible that was obtained by "pumping" a suspect's stomach because the police conduct "shock[ed] the conscience";[3] but even in that case the opinion suggested that almost anyone's conscience would be shocked, not that the justices had some special insight into what was morally shocking. In any event, such language is highly unusual. We can say, then, that within the vast majority of judicial opinions, religiously grounded convictions of the judges themselves are treated like other kinds of personal moral convictions of the judges: they are excluded. The reasons that are given are ones that are claimed to be available to all judges, reasons deriving directly from the legal materials themselves, or from shared cultural values, or from modes of making judgments that do not depend on special or personal insight.

If judges *should* self-consciously rely *only* on reasons that appear in opinions, one of two conclusions would follow from my report of present practice in opinion writing. If that practice is sound, judges should not rely directly on religious bases and personal convictions in making up their minds. If judges may sometimes rely on religious bases, then the practice of opinion writing should change to reflect that. But there is another, third, option. Simply put, it is this. Sometimes the materials and arguments available to all judges will be indecisive *and* judges may recognize this. They may then be compelled to decide on the basis of something more personal. Nevertheless, opinions involve a kind of ceremony of justification in terms that are available to all. According to this third option, sometimes judges may appropriately rely on personal moral convictions even though their opinions make it seem as if they are relying only on sources available in the same way to all judges. This option happens to be the one that I accept. Even though, very occasionally, personal factors may self-consciously enter decision, judges appropriately acknowledge the aspiration to rely on public reasons by putting forth a public justification that is limited to those kinds of reasons.

In my statement of the third option, I have so far left open the question whether religiously grounded judgments (and other comprehensive views) are among the personal moral convictions a judge might employ in this way. I have previously taken the position that judges may sometimes rely on religious convictions, but should be very hesitant to do so.[4] The basic position that judges may rely on their own religious convictions has been forcefully developed by Stephen Carter.[5] I state and examine his argument, and also consider a somewhat different use of religious values defended by Scott Idleman.[6]

Reliance on Religious Convictions and Other Moral Convictions

Professor Carter first calls attention to the present political understanding, or myth, which is quite different from his position. He imagines a federal judicial nominee who is known to be deeply religious and whose religion leads her to reject abortion, the death penalty, and most military conflict. She is asked, "If we confirm you and you become a judge, will you be able to separate your religious beliefs from the task of judging?"[7] As Carter says, if she wanted to be confirmed she would have to answer, "Yes." Senatorial questions of modern Roman Catholic justices and their responses fit Carter's assumption.[8] I am not quite sure whether the participants in such exchanges really believe it, but certainly the present public story is that religion should not count at all in judging.[9]

Carter argues that unless judges are to strive to reason without regard to *any* of their own moral convictions, "the separation question, along with its required answer, carries an implicit trivialization of religious faith, and a denigration of religion as against other ways of knowing."[10] If the ideal judge were what Carter calls an "objective judge," one who tries to interpret legal materials in light of interpretive rules of the community, then the judge's religious views *would not be disfavored*. They would not be disfavored because the judge's effort would be to decide free of all personal moral convictions. Carter says, however, that most informed people do not think judges can put aside their own preconceptions, and perhaps most do not think it is a desirable ideal. He posits as an alternative the "morally reflective judge" who "engages quite self-consciously in a form of reasoning best described as moral philosophy."[11] The central "question, then, is whether one can make sense of a rule prohibiting judges from relying on their moral knowledge if it happens to have an explicitly religious basis."[12]

I want to pause here before proceeding to the heart of Carter's argument. The comparison of the "objective judge" with the "morally reflective judge" actually raises two kinds of differences. One concerns what judges are capable of doing, the other concerns what they should strive to do. *Can* judges decide free of personal moral convictions? The answer is that they *cannot entirely*; fundamental beliefs will influence decision even when judges conscientiously try to exclude them. In this respect, religiously grounded beliefs are not qualitatively different from other beliefs; deeply held religious convictions will sometimes have an influence on judgment. This undeniable conclusion is supported to a degree by empirical studies linking religious affiliation to judicial decision in some categories of cases.[13] One of the most interesting findings has been that, among federal district court judges in the South between 1954 and 1962, Roman Catholics, members of a church that condemned segregation, were more likely to issue integrationist rulings than Protestants. The influence of religious convictions on judgment means that the "separation" questions and their typical answers are naive (or cynical) in suggesting that total exclusion is a realistic possibility.

The unavoidability of some influence does not settle, however, the degree of influence, and thus does not settle what judges should *aim* to do. Class prejudices and deep-seated personal resentments will also affect judgment, but the judge should strive to discount or overcome them. Any ideal for judging calls for exclusion of factors that cannot be totally excluded despite a judge's best efforts. The important questions about personal moral convictions are not whether judges are capable of excluding them altogether but whether they should try, and not whether judges can fully distinguish religious convictions from other personal moral convictions but whether they should try.

I shall pass quickly over the important question whether an ideal of judging would allow some use of the judge's moral convictions. This question is complicated, but I believe a model of decision must include some reference to what is right (or what a judge believes is right) as a matter of moral and political philosophy, independent of the legal materials.[14] Carter believes that the present jurisprudence of fundamental rights commits us to this position, and he assumes it in most of his discussion.

Within such a model, can religious convictions defensibly be treated differently from other convictions? Carter says no. He argues that a liberal theory that would exclude religion imposes a rationality requirement in public dialogue, which "effectively privileges a materialistic, analytical form of reasoning over other ways of knowing."[15] This skews public dialogue "so that everyone has a voice except those people whose epistemology rests on faith."[16] Carter rejects notions that people who are religious have less open minds than others and that discussions of religious differences are peculiarly unresolvable and conflict-producing; he finds no good reason to treat religiously grounded beliefs differently from other moral convictions. He urges that the liberal's notion of dialogue is implicitly antireligious, and that, given the quality of serious religious faith as "ultimate concern," it is perverse to insist that the devout citizen abandon religion upon entering the public realm.

In evaluating Carter's argument, we need to draw some distinctions among moral convictions and among practical conclusions and ways of arriving at them. As we have seen, the main difficulty with religious arguments is not that they are difficult for nonbelievers *to understand*. Nonbelievers *usually* have a pretty good idea what believers mean. Rather, the difficulty is that just insofar as the force of arguments depends on a particular religious understanding, Christian, Jewish, Moslem, and so on, their force will not be acknowledged by those who do not accept that understanding. Further, many people think that some central differences are ones of faith and upbringing, that no *adequate reasoned basis* exists for choosing among a number of religious views, and between any of those and atheism or agnosticism.[17] What is worrisome is that if a judge relies on religious beliefs, she will be resolving a legal case partly on the basis of a belief about truth that she cannot expect others to share and, perhaps more crucially, that she does not think is supported by arguments that reasonably should persuade others.

We can imagine a judge doing "moral philosophy," as Carter puts it, in three different ways. One would be to start with her own most fundamental beliefs and to reason in light of those. If the fundamental beliefs themselves rest on some kind of faith, and she so understands them, then they have a status that is similar to religious beliefs. Someone might say it is all right to rely on such personal moral beliefs but not religious beliefs because people are closed-minded about religion and religious disagreements cause conflict; but I shall pass over these concerns here. I agree with Carter that *such* personal convictions should not be privileged over religious convictions in judging.

The second way a judge might do moral philosophy is by drawing from basic premises of our social and political order. Facing some instance of "hate speech" that lies at the border of the First Amendment, she might say to herself that equal respect for persons and liberty of expression are fundamental values of our society, and she might ask how those values could best be fulfilled in the case. This *might* entail some reasoning in moral and political philosophy that goes beyond what is embedded in the legal materials and beyond what are aspects of the present "interpretive rules" of the community. She might believe that in performing this exercise she is relying on deep values that are shared, and she might even believe she could put such reasoning in an opinion (though she might think, instead, that legal opinions should generally refrain from such abstract philosophical theorizing).

The third way a judge might try to do moral philosophy and its applications is to limit herself to *ways of reasoning* that are generally accepted. Thus, in deciding how much protection various animals should have, she might regard as relevant how much they can feel and think. In deciding about ecology, she might entertain ordinary scientific evidence about the future of the earth. These ways of reasoning draw on common assumptions; they are different from relying on a religious judgment about what animals count the most or on a scriptural prediction about the end of time.

Considering these different ways to approach practical moral problems that judges may face suggests that the basic reason for preferring some premises and ways of reasoning over others is that they are shared in our political culture, not that they are *necessarily* a better way of knowing altogether. I accept that basic reason, so I believe reliance on *some kinds* of moral and political philosophy is easier to justify for judges than reliance on their own religious beliefs.[18] I shall indicate in a moment just where this leads me.

Professor Carter would reject much of what I have just said. He does not mention reliance on independent political philosophy that begins from basic premises of liberal democracy as somehow deservedly less controversial than reliance on religious beliefs. And what he says about "creation science," summarized in chapter 9, leads me strongly to doubt he would agree that there are common ways of reasoning whose use is easier to justify. In discussing the case in which the Supreme Court held invalid a state statute requiring that creation science be taught equally with evolution, Carter says that creation science may be bad science, but he urges that neither that nor the religious motivation behind legislative endorsement of creation science should have led the Supreme Court to conclude that the statute violated the establishment clause.[19] On my analysis, if extremely little ordinary scientific evidence supports creation science (with its claim that the earth has existed a much briefer time than virtually all scientists assume), creation science rests on premises and ways of reasoning that many people reject. Evolutionary science, on the other hand, rests on methods of doing science that are widely accepted. Even the believers in creation science do not reject these mainstream scientific methods for most

purposes; they believe, however, that they have a higher source of understanding for the particular set of questions that creation science answers.[20]
Carter sees the creation science issue as one instance of whether rationality
will be unfairly privileged. I would emphasize our culture's shared ideas of
rationality in science. The constitutional fate of the creation science statute
is not the same question as what factors judges can reasonably rely on
when cases are difficult to decide; but I think Carter would not accept my
assertion that there are shared ways of reasoning (outside the law) that
judges should rely on more freely than they rely on their own religious
convictions.[21]

A proponent of judicial reliance on religious values could rightly say
that my comparison of the use of religion and of moral philosophy has, up
to now, been misleading and unfair. I have suggested that judges have reason to rely on moral philosophy that draws from basic premises of our
social and political order or rests on generally accepted ways of reasoning
rather than on their own religious convictions. But I have so far failed to
discuss reliances on religious values that are analogous to the preferred
moral reasoning or are even an aspect of it.

There are four uses of religious values that do not directly employ
the judge's own religious convictions. First, community attitudes about a
particular practice are important; judges look to dominant (that is, mainly
Christian) religions, which condemn the practice and have done so for
some time. Second, judges must themselves evaluate a practice; fundamental moral ideas drawn from dominant religions are one standard for discerning the basic premises of our social order. These are taken as a starting
point for further reasoning. Third, judges must themselves evaluate a practice; they take a wide agreement among religions that the practice is bad as
evidence of that conclusion. Fourth, judges must themselves evaluate a
practice; they draw from a wide range of religions to establish theological
conclusions, and they reason from these conclusions to condemn the
practice.

The first use I have suggested here is clearly appropriate. *One* form of
evidence of what people now believe about a moral problem and of what
they have believed over time is the teaching of the religions to which they
subscribe. Of course, one cannot simply equate the two. The Roman
Catholic Church now condemns artificial contraception, but many (probably most) American Catholics think it is morally acceptable. Still, church
teachings are one source of insight about community morality. (I assume
here what I shall argue in the next chapter: that moral opinions formed by
citizens on the basis of their religious views may appropriately count for
what the law should be.)

The second use also is appropriate. In our culture, as in most others,
religion is intertwined with our deep moral premises. Ordinarily, one can
identify these premises, such as the idea of universal human respect, without looking at religious sources; but the sources are undoubtedly of causal
significance and reference to them in the effort to discern fundamental cul-

tural values is proper. Indeed, an adamant refusal to look at religious sources will give a distorted picture of how our culture has developed and may offend those for whom the religious sources are the central basis for moral values.

The third use of religion is more debatable. Here judges use religious values not to decide what is *regarded as wrong or right in our culture*, but *to determine what is really wrong or right* in some transcultural sense. We can imagine a judge evaluating a practice by asking how it is regarded by diverse moral approaches, such as Aristotelianism, Kantianism, and utilitarianism. If all approaches condemn a practice, that would be *some* evidence that it is really immoral, and a judge could ascertain that without choosing among the approaches. Since many of humanity's major approaches to morality are aspects of religious understandings, a judge might similarly ask how a practice is regarded among important religions. If the practice is one about which religions say little directly, say genetic engineering, a judge might ask how the practice corresponds to fundamental moral premises that the religions endorse. At least if one is willing to entertain an assumption that moral judgments most human beings make over time are probably right, then *this use* of religious values seems appropriate. (I add this caveat because if one believes, for example, that most social morality throughout history and up through the present is mainly the product of unjust oppressions, then judgments and values drawn from historically important religions might be thought to be corrupted rather than substantial evidence of moral truth. One might, of course, attempt some division of elements that result mostly from oppression, say central themes about male-female relations, and elements that are mostly free of this stain.)

If judges were attempting to use religious moralities to discern what really is right, they would have no reason (without some further justification) to give predominate weight to the religions that happen to be primary in this country. This is the conclusion of Scott Idleman, who says that "a judge's evaluation of a religious value or assertion should conform to a thorough and balanced analysis, not unlike a judge's evaluation of any other source of insight."[22] Idleman urges that "because American society and its judicial system are heavily Judeo-Christian in background, especially Protestant Christian, impartiality may only be possible when a judge *does* survey the landscape of religious thought and, when making her decision, takes account of this survey."[23] Taking this proposed universalist approach is just the opposite of what judges should do if seeking to discern the values of their own culture. For that task within the United States, Christian values should dominate. I believe there remain considerable difficulties in deciding what religions are to count and for how much, but in principle, consulting present major religious systems of the world for help about moral judgments is acceptable.

The fourth use of religion is similar to the third, except that the starting points for reasoning about the morality of practices would be theological propositions about God or the nature of the universe drawn from various religions. Although the precise line between moral and theological premises is less than sharp, this use would generally not be appropriate. It seems unlikely that discovery of some congruence in theological presuppositions will help to resolve the disputed morality of some practice. People of different religions probably have a greater commonality of moral beliefs than theological beliefs. Moreover, judges are ill-suited to derive moral propositions from theological premises. This last use of religious values is at least as doubtful an exercise as the judge's use of her own religious convictions.

My own conclusions are that shared premises and ways of reasoning have priority and that these will get judges all of the way in the vast majority of cases. These include some ways of moral reasoning, including reasoning that employs the moral values found in major religions. My category of *personal* moral convictions ends up being substantially narrower than Carter's. Nevertheless, I do agree with him that sometimes judges may have to rely on personal moral convictions. I also agree with him that for reasons of fairness, and because a religious person can hardly ask what her personal moral convictions are, apart from her religion, we should not regard religious convictions as having a status different from other "personal" convictions that reach beyond shared, or public, reasons.

To say that judges may sometimes have to use religious and other personal convictions does not settle whether they should self-consciously do so. One reasonable position is that the situations when legal and other public reasons are genuinely indecisive are so rare and so hard to identify that judges will perform best if they assume that the resolution of any given case can be achieved by those reasons alone, and proceed on that assumption. I am inclined to a different view, believing that on exceptional occasions the indecisiveness of legal and public reasons will be sufficiently apparent to allow a judge to make a self-conscious use of personal convictions.

Of all officials, judges are the most carefully disciplined in restraining their frame of reference. Asking them to try to decide exclusively, or nearly exclusively, on the basis of authoritative materials and publicly accessible reasons is not too great an imposition. Indeed, that is how, in the main, judges now see their responsibilities. If any room exists for self-conscious reliance on personally held comprehensive views, religious or other, it is (1) when, *if ever,* this approach seems directly indicated by the materials themselves or somehow reflects their best interpretation;[24] (2) when, if ever, the judge finds himself or herself in the unusual situation of perceiving the authoritative materials and public reasons as being evenly balanced or radically indecisive, and the judge must decide one way or the other; and, finally, (3) when, if ever, the judge finds "the law" to be so abominable that he or she feels a duty to subvert it in some way, as a judge during the era of slavery might have thought slavery was so evil according to his comprehensive view that he evaded legal requirements to return slaves.[25] With these possible exceptions, the judge has a duty to disregard comprehensive views and nonaccessible reasons in favor of public reasons in intracourt deliberations and in deciding how to vote.

In the rare circumstances when a judge might properly rely in a self-conscious way on controversial religious or comprehensive views, or on nongeneralizable, nonreplicable intuitive insights, should that appear in a judicial opinion? Since different judges will have different views, such reasons would have no comfortable place in a majority opinion. I believe that even when the opinion represents the voice of a single judge, the opinion should symbolize the aspiration of interpersonal reason and be limited to public reasons.[26] (I will defend this discrepancy between internal bases of judgment and publicly stated justifications in the next chapter.)

The executive performs administrative and enforcement functions and engages in quasi-judicial determinations. The guidelines for executive performance of these functions should be similar to the guidelines for judges, and for similar reasons.

14

Decision and Advocacy by Legislators and Citizens

In this chapter, I turn to the more central problems of possible principles of self-restraint for legislators and citizens. I also treat briefly presidents (and other chief executives) and administrative officials. In the next chapter, I address the place of religious organizations.

Two important reasons lead me to consider most citizens in this chapter. One is that comparisons between citizens and government officials help illuminate appropriate standards for each. The second reason involves a more direct relationship between legislators (and elected executives) and citizens. Legislators should exercise some combination of their own judgments and deference to the judgments and expressed interests of citizens, especially their own constituents. Thus, the concern about possible self-restraint by legislators is twofold: (1) Should they rely for judgment and use in public advocacy upon their *own* comprehensive views and nonaccessible reasons? (2) Should they rely upon and use in public advocacy the convictions of citizens that are grounded in this way? A sharp discrepancy between what legislators and citizens appropriately rely upon would create an unfortunate tension. The main practical way in which citizens act upon their views is by voting. If it were completely proper for citizens to form views in any way they pleased and to vote accordingly, but legislators were not supposed to rely on citizen views based on nonaccessible and comprehensive grounds, citizens would appropriately vote out of office (and for that reason) legislators who rightly declined to pay attention to citizens' views developed from nonaccessible and comprehensive grounds. This would be an anomalous and regrettable combination of ideals for political behavior; further, given the politician's dominant aim to be reelected, this combination of ideals would not be likely to prove practically feasible.

I shall shortly examine possible principles of restraint for legislators and citizens, but I first want to emphasize an important difference in how comprehensive views may be employed.

Society and Politics

Religious and other comprehensive views are not just for purely personal life. All religious and other comprehensive views have significant implications for how we should live toward others; most have implications for how we should encourage others to live; most have implications for political organization and justice. These views differ greatly on the efforts one should make to bring others around to one's own way of thinking. Historically, the Christian faith has been strongly evangelical. Significant parts of the New Testament call upon believers to witness to their faith. This aspect of Christianity has been important through the ages since then, although many liberal Christians feel rather uncomfortable with making any personal efforts to "convert" nonbelievers. In contrast to Christianity, Judaism, so far as I understand it, makes little effort to convert nonbelievers, and almost discourages rather than welcomes converts.

In any vital society, competing comprehensive views will be discussed. The alternative to their serious consideration will be cultural dominance of a shallow, thoughtless pattern of life, akin to that portrayed on a great many American television programs. Thus, we need to think about any principle of self-restraint with the clear understanding that any norm that people keep their comprehensive views to themselves is wholly unacceptable. Not only within associations of like believers but also more broadly, people should speak to the implications of their comprehensive views, including their political implications. For example, many comprehensive views have powerful implications for distributive justice and environmental policy. It would be unacceptable to ask people to be silent about these.

A defensible principle of restraint must make some rough distinction between this general cultural interplay of comprehensive views and narrower debates over particular political issues that are up for decision in one way or another.[1] Specific debates within the legislature obviously fall within the latter category; so do virtually all speeches by legislators to their constituents. Matters become a bit more elusive when one talks about discourse by private citizens.

Formal Legislative and Executive Acts

I will suggest standards of restraint for formal legislative acts, legislative discourse, citizen judgment, citizen discourse, and determinations by individual legislators. In connection with government officials, I present some relevant evidence about behavior by legislators and presidents of the United States.

In some circumstances other than court judgments and opinions, a branch of government acts corporately for the government. The most important example is when the legislature adopts a statute. Bases for the statute may be stated within the statute itself, most often in a preamble. During the legislative process, committees issue reports, each of which represents the corporate judgment of at least a majority of the committee. Those who think the government should promote particular religious views may disagree, but I believe that in these expressions, only public reasons are appropriate. And, on present constitutional understandings, if religious grounds figure prominently in a statute or committee report, the statute may well violate the establishment clause. A similar conclusion applies if the executive branch issues regulations with legislative effect, or an agency proposes legislation, or the president issues an official message explaining his signing or veto of a bill. Whether officials should be similarly constrained in their individually stated bases for judgment is a more complicated question, to which I next turn.

Present Practices and Attitudes of Federal Office Holders

I begin my consideration of legislators and executives with a sparse account of present practices and attitudes among federal officials. Getting a grasp of these is not easy. Kenneth Wald says, "[I]t is remarkable to discover how little attention has been devoted to the study of the religious factor in congressional behavior."[2] Booth Fowler begins a discussion of religion and political leadership by noting that "there has been little study of how much religion counts among contemporary officeholders, not to mention the higher reaches of the bureaucracy, when it comes to policy making."[3] He also cautions about the difficulty of discerning religious influence, since no study "can catch all the unconscious influences past religious upbringing or experience may contribute."[4] Most national political leaders have claimed affiliation with mainline churches. Just how far religion matters to their political life is very hard to determine, however. A disquieting illustration of this truth is found in Richard Nixon's fairly close relations with Billy Graham; in retrospect it may appear that Nixon was mainly using Graham rather than being seriously influenced by him. According to Fowler, Jimmy Carter's commitment to "born-again" Christianity was evident in his campaigns, but he did not try "to apply his religion in policy terms in the White House."[5] Carter's background beliefs in human sin and fallibility, humility and love, and a calling to servanthood affected him; but for Carter there were "no obvious policies that follow from a recognition of sin or a belief in love."[6] Ronald Reagan said at a prayer breakfast at the 1984 Republican convention, "[T]he truth is that politics and morality are inseparable. And as morality's foundation is religion, religion and politics are necessarily related."[7] He did not, however, often make explicit religious arguments for particular political positions. He embraced conservative Christian positions on some important subjects, such as school prayer and abortion, but did not devote much political capital into enacting those into law.

A chart from a 1981 *Psychology Today* that correlates the religious views and voting positions of members of Congress shows, Fowler says, that "religious sentiments are at work in their politics."[8] The chart indicates, for example, that 80 percent of "people-concerned religionists" are civil libertarians, compared with only 32 percent of "legalistic religionists" and 30 percent of "personal religionists"; 23 percent of the legalistic religionists and 28 percent of the personal religionists are pro-choice on abortion, 87 percent of people-concerned religionists take that position; only 19 percent of the last group, 84 percent of the legalistic religionists and 78 percent of the personal religionists support a strong military. Similar correlations were found in a study that distinguished "individualism-preserving" religious views from "community-building" views.[9] Other studies indicate relatively little correlation between denominational membership and votes on many issues, but on some issues, most notably abortion, there is a striking relationship between religious affiliation and legislative votes.[10]

House Speaker Thomas P. O'Neill "long contended that his commitment to the disadvantaged is related to his religious training and belief,"[11] and North Carolina Senator Jesse Helms "insists that much of his work . . . derives from his religious convictions."[12] Mark Hatfield, a Baptist with a spirit close to radical evangelicals, "has outdistanced all others in arguing in and out of Congress for a religious approach to politics and matched it in a long career in which he has attempted to fulfill his mission."[13] Hatfield, for example, early opposed the war in Vietnam and has said that "God demands 'a love for the poor and dispossessed.' "[14] Although religion is far more central to Hatfield than to typical members of Congress, Fowler says he "*is* characteristic in that he illustrates that religion does matter from within Congress and the presidency a good deal more than we once thought or, perhaps, than was once true."[15]

We may add to these accounts some other relevant facts. During the 1992 campaign, and especially at the time of their convention, Republicans urged that their stands on "family value" issues and some others were more consonant with a view of the United States as "God's country" than were the opposing positions of the Democrats. The party's use of religious leaders, most notably Pat Robertson, and of religious discourse drew a plain connection between party positions and what was religiously correct. More pervasively, many political leaders in the country have called on God for support, reminded citizens (less frequently) of God's judgment, conceived the "mission" of the country in religious and quasi-religious terms, and used biblical imagery and stories to make points. Without doubt, our religious heritage affects how legislators, as well as citizens, understand politics and the place of this country, even when a particular political position is not directly related to a religious belief.

In judging the attitudes of national political leaders, it is hard to know just what to make of these accounts and other easily recognizable facts. Fowler asserts that religion undoubtedly influences decisions of officials, even when they do not say so. I do not doubt the truth of this influence, but I think the correlations between religious convictions and political positions provide less convincing evidence than he supposes. The reason is that as people become adults, particularly people with strong political interests, they may incline toward churches and ideas of religion that fit comfortably with their political views. Many Protestants attach no heavy significance to the denominational affiliation of their parents and their childhood. Roman Catholics feel more tied to their church, but Mary Hanna found a split between Catholic legislators who emphasized "strict codes of conduct, rules and guidelines" and those who "stressed Christian love, compassion, and concern for one's fellowmen."[16] We would need much more information about individual legislators to know how far religion is influencing political judgment and how far the reverse is happening. Of course, even assuming religious views influence political judgment to a considerable degree, that does not establish that the legislators themselves see the connections or that they self-consciously take religion into account.

Another important point concerns what Fowler leaves unsaid. He speaks of the difficulty of discerning religious influence on policy judgments. This is not because he is skeptical of statements about underlying grounds; it is not that he sees a plethora of religious arguments and doubts whether people are serious about them. No, legislators tend not to offer religious arguments for specific laws and policies. When well over half the members of the Senate debated resolutions to authorize the use of military force against Iraq in January 1991, none made explicit religious arguments.[17] In 1992 approximately thirty members of the House of Representatives spoke on the highly charged question whether a veto by President Bush of a bill authorizing abortion counseling and referral should be overridden.[18] Only Robert Dornan urged explicit religious grounds for his anti-abortion position.[19]

Why are religious arguments so infrequently made? One logical possibility is that religious convictions just have little relevance to public policy decisions. We know this is not the case. We understand the implications of various religious perspectives for many political issues, and we observe the wide range of issues on which churches take positions. Fowler comments interestingly that President Carter disappointed many evangelicals who expected a closer connection between his religious convictions and public policies. Fowler notes that Carter saw the social message of Christianity in broad terms that did not yield easy policy conclusions and that this largely explains the divergence between his practice and the expectations of some religious people. I think this misses something. Carter made clear his own religious convictions, but my recollection is that he did not analyze policy problems in religious terms when he was speaking as president. Granted that his religious convictions did not yield straightforward policy conclusions, nevertheless I would expect that when he discusses matters like nuclear policy, human rights, and affirmative action at meetings of the Plains Baptist Church, where he has long been a member, he brings religious considerations to bear. During the 1976 campaign Carter emphasized "his intention to respect separation between personal religious values and public policy,"[20] and as president he made arguments that did not depend on specifically Christian assumptions.

I believe it is a fact, and a significant fact, that most political leaders, most of whom have religious convictions, do not often employ religious discourse within legislative chambers or in public analysis of particular issues of policy, even when the religious convictions they hold seem to bear on the issues of policy. The 1992 Republican presidential campaign was something of an exception, but one that called forth objections among many Republicans as well as Democrats that no party should claim to be especially in tune with God's views.

Of course, the judgment not to use religious discourse may possibly be purely strategic, an estimate of what will be most effective to persuade people. But if so many Americans are religious, would not religious discourse by legislators be more common if some people did not have deeper reservations about it? Officials may have reservations themselves. They may feel that as representatives of a diverse population, they should use a common public language and not rely on particular religious views. They may also worry that too much religious talk could jeopardize the constitutional status of legislation. Officials may instead, or in addition, feel that many constituents and legislative colleagues think such discourse is not proper and that these constituents and colleagues may be offended by religious arguments.

My present sense is that there is some understanding shared by most high officials and many citizens that *serious, practical political discourse* by officials should be nonreligious. It is harder to tell if there is any similar sense that a legislator's even relying on his or her own religious convictions is inappropriate, or should be disfavored in comparison with other grounds. But whatever may be true of undisclosed reliance, we now have at least weak conventions that disputes by officials over national laws and policies should be carried on in nonreligious terms.

Discourse by Legislators

I turn now from this descriptive analysis to the normative question whether officials should exercise self-restraint in their discourse. I concentrate on legislators, assuming that chief executives should be guided by similar standards. If there is any difference, executives should regard themselves as *more* constrained, because they speak for all the people in a fuller sense than does any individual legislator. *Nonelected* executive officials who are performing rule-making responsibilities probably should have still less, if any, scope to rely publicly on their own comprehensive or nonaccessible grounds.

When legislators speak on political issues, they represent all their constituents. Their explicit reliance on any controversial religious or comprehensive view would be inappropriate. If they argue in terms of reliance on comprehensive or nonaccessible grounds, the losers are likely to feel imposed upon in the sense of being excluded, even if the specific issue does not involve imposition, in the sense of burdening religious practice. Intense religious politics in the United States probably would not produce extensive outright violence, but we are still far from harmonious mutual respect and tolerance. Religious divisions are still very significant in many regions, and people are acutely conscious of whether they are in a majority or minority. Given all the reasons why people find themselves living in particular places, the existence of a federal system with opportunities to move to different states is not a sufficient protection for those in a minority.

Speech that relies explicitly on religious or most other comprehensive views is not likely to contribute directly to the resolution of immediate political issues. Some such speech may actually be unintelligible to legislators and to citizens who do not share the underlying position that is presented. These listeners may be incapable of understanding the premises that guide the legislator. Even when such speech is intelligible, in the sense of reasonably well understood, it functions as a kind of conversation stopper in political dialogue. If a Roman Catholic legislator places heavy reliance on a papal encyclical in a debate over regulation of genetic research, what is a non-Catholic legislator to do? Discussion about such regulation is hardly the time for subtle analysis of the implications of the encyclical or whether Roman Catholicism is misguided as a religion. The same can be said of a legislator's explicit reliance upon "maximum happiness utilitarianism," a nonreligious comprehensive view. Finally, at least for many religious arguments, the speaker seems to put himself or herself in a kind of privileged position, as the holder of a *basic* truth that many others lack.[21] This assertion of privileged knowledge may appear to imply inequality of status that is in serious tension with the fundamental idea of equality of citizens within liberal democracies.

If explicit arguments by legislators based on religious and other comprehensive views are not particularly helpful for the resolution of pressing political issues, neither are they likely to contribute much to deeper knowledge. Legislative chambers are certainly no place to work out disagreements over religious (and other comprehensive) premises, so we cannot expect that explicit speech in terms of religious premises will contribute much to the religious understanding of legislators. But might legislative speech in terms of religious premises in and out of legislative chambers contribute to the religious understanding of citizens? I am very doubtful. The discourse of legislators on particular political issues is likely to be fairly simplistic, even manipulative, about underlying grounds. Not often will it contribute to wide religious understanding; more frequently it will contribute to divisiveness and feelings of exclusion. Legislators discussing particular issues should mainly employ public reasons. Let me be clear, again, that by "religious discourse" I am limiting myself to a fairly narrow use of religiously grounded arguments to sustain legislative judgments. I mean explanations that connect particular religious premises to conclusions of policy; I do not mean all use of religious imagery or mention of religious tradition. Also, my remarks do not cover officials calling on God's help in deliberations or participating in wider cultural discussions of the significance of religion for human life and moral values.

My recommendation of self-restraint may be challenged as restricting important knowledge for citizens and as interfering with the religious liberty of legislators. Perhaps citizens need to know the bases on which elected officials decide issues. As long as legislators and elected executive officials state their grounds honestly, citizens can decide whether or not to keep them in office. Therefore, it is desirable for officials to state religious (and other comprehensive) grounds that influence them. This model contains something appealing, but it underestimates the harm of a religious politics in the present United States. I am not suggesting that elected officials actually conceal the most fundamental grounds of their convictions, either when in office or running for office. In this respect, I think Jimmy Carter was an apt example. In contrast to John Kennedy, he did not assert that his religious beliefs were irrelevant to his political functioning, and he made clear his deep Protestant evangelical beliefs. Nevertheless, when he proposed particular laws or policies, he spoke in terms of public reasons accessible to everyone. On specific issues, it may be appropriate for legislators to declare that they are affected by underlying religious grounds, but they should make their arguments in other terms.

Any impingement on the religious liberty of officials from this kind of self-restraint is modest; and the number of people suffering any impingement is very few in comparison with the broad population that may enjoy the benefits of self-restraint. Officials occupy roles that involve representing the entire body of diverse citizens. In many respects, their bases for public action are more limited than everything that counts in their personal lives. As I hope to have argued persuasively in the previous chapter, self-restraint in public speech is much less demanding than self-restraint as to actual grounds of judgment. Further, if my brief descriptive account is roughly accurate, a principle of restraint like the one I have proposed exists presently for much of the politics among officials in the United States. A principle that is already widely accepted and observed is feasible and is not regarded as an intolerable interference with the religious liberty of most of those occupying political office.

Although I do not wish to place too much emphasis on this, the present bureaucratization of Congress, as well as the executive branch, supports such self-restraint among legislators. Members of Congress spend a very brief time each week on legislative matters; almost all of the relevant work is done by committee and personal staff. Whether or not civil rights laws require it, I think we expect such staff to be hired without regard to the religious convictions of applicants. Thus, members are dealing with diverse staff who do not share any uniform comprehensive view. Of course, each staff person might conceivably try to work from the perspective of the comprehensive view of his or her member of Congress, though this would certainly be extremely complicated for committee staff and would not work very well even for personal staff. The norm of nondiscriminatory hiring linked to a substantial bureaucracy fits best with an ideal of public reason as the working discourse for consideration of laws and policies.

I have not yet addressed official judgment, as contrasted with official discourse. Although that subject may seem to follow closely, I postpone it until I have considered private citizens. The reason is that the appropriate stance of citizens bears considerably on how legislators should decide.

Judgments by Citizens

The main way in which most citizens who participate at all in political life act upon their determinations is by voting for candidates. They do not typically address issues one by one. I have suggested how difficult it is on any particular issue to try to sift out one's religious, comprehensive, and nonaccessible bases. That is a lot to ask of ordinary citizens. To ask them to do this for numerous issues that might affect their votes for one candidate or another in primaries and general elections would be asking much more. Then, there is the unfairness I wrote of in chapter 12. If most citizens suspect that their fellows are not successfully purging these grounds of judgment in favor of the grounds of public reason, why should they undertake this serious form of self-denial?

It is reasonable to expect that citizens will give a kind of priority in weight to public reasons. However, they should not be expected to rely on public reasons exclusively when issues are difficult, even if the issues involve disputes about applications of constitutional essentials. Citizens properly give effect to what they believe are valid sources of understanding, even though they recognize that these are not shared.

As I have said, important reasons of liberal democracy oppose any impositions that discourage religious exercise or promote particular religions, but most decisions about status (say, of animals or the environment) or distribution of resources or military policy do not involve that sort of imposition. Protecting animals or increasing welfare because people's comprehensive views suggest that that should be done is not an imposition on those of contrary view.

Although a rough understanding prevails that legislators should not *debate* in terms of comprehensive grounds, no such understanding exists about citizens deciding on such grounds. Some people do object to the place religious premises play in opposition to abortion, but many others think that is fully appropriate; and many (perhaps most) of those who object to religious premises in positions on abortion lack any consistent view about the place of religious and other comprehensive views, favoring their use to support policies they approve.

Some readers of my earlier work have assumed that I wanted to allow religious premises to figure only in rare instances.[22] I had meant to indicate that appropriate reliance was substantially wider than that, but I did speak about a kind of radical inconclusiveness of public reasons for some issues as triggering proper dependence on religious convictions. I now believe that comprehensive views and nonaccessible grounds can appropriately figure in resolution of the broad range of political issues that ordinary citizens face. Self-restraint in judgment is much more restrictive of religious liberty than self-restraint in public discourse; and a restraint on citizens reaches a vastly greater number of people, each of whom has an immeasurably slight effect on political life, than a restraint on officials. These would be sufficient reasons to reject such a restraint, even were the restraint more feasible than it is.

Citizen Discourse

Most citizens never get involved in advocacy of political positions, beyond talking to family, close friends, and associates. In those personal settings, people should feel free to express their reliance on any grounds they find compelling; they should not regard themselves as limited to public reasons. If ordinary citizens write to legislators, they must reasonably expect that what will matter is how they come out on issues, not their lines of analysis. Except within small communities, they cannot expect that legislators will personally read their letters, or that anyone will engage thoughtfully with the ideas expressed. For this reason, citizens need not worry much about how they express themselves, so long as the grounds leading to their decisions are consistent with basic premises of liberal democracy that they accept.

Some citizens, whom we may call quasi-public citizens, consistently engage in analysis and advocacy of positions on political issues. Media commentators and editors are the most obvious of these; presidents of large corporations and organizations also take positions on many political issues; some law professors do so. These citizens enter a public debate that is much broader than what the ordinary citizen usually experiences. These citizens also are reasonably sophisticated in their understanding of public discourse and political life, and they have experience in many settings of expressing less than their full feelings about subjects. The discipline of self-restraint in expression is not especially demanding for them. Although self-restraint on their part is less important than self-restraint by public officials, they appropriately state grounds for positions that lie in public reason when they address the entire public on particular political issues.[23]

Perhaps distinguishing between two kinds of quasi-public citizens is valuable. Some are quasi-public representatives. The presidents of Columbia University, the American Medical Association, and General Motors not only have a public role that role involves representing large and diverse constituencies. Even *within* their organizations, they are likely to restrict themselves to forms of public reason; that they should do so before the wider public audience is a fairly easy conclusion. Other quasi-public citizens do not represent anyone, or at least do not do so in this direct way. George Will is a national columnist with substantial influence, but he presents his views as only for himself. I am inclined to think that having such a broad audience and impact brings a responsibility to speak the language of public reason when one directly addresses political subjects, but that conclusion is debatable. (Apart from the general criticism that such restraint is too restrictive of liberty, it may be suggested that for the work of many columnists, the line between participation in general culture and political argument is too thin for a recommendation that religious grounds figure in the first discourse but not the second.)

One class of quasi-public citizens falls outside my conclusions here: those whose profession (chosen by others or self-chosen) is to speak from religious and other comprehensive perspectives. They are the subject of the next chapter.

When ordinary citizens occasionally engage in broader political advocacy, say by writing letters to newspapers or participating in open school board meetings, they also should emphasize public reasons. Self-restraint on their part, however, is less important than among quasi-public citizens.[24]

Determinations of Legislators

Determinations by legislators raise hard issues. I shall first address decisions by legislators that rely on reasons of citizens. If citizens properly rely on comprehensive reasons to develop positions on political issues, legislators will often become aware of these positions. They may not know exactly the grounds on which citizens rely; but if they do discover that the grounds rest on comprehensive views, religious or other, the legislators should not then disregard them. However, because there is some value in resolving political issues on the basis of public reasons, a legislator probably should afford more weight to a citizen position that is grounded in public reason (when that position is otherwise similar), than to a position grounded in a controversial comprehensive view.

What of direct legislator reliance on religious and other comprehensive grounds? The basic counters on each side are the same as for citizens' reliance: the desirability of decision based on public reasons against the difficulty of relying just on those reasons, and the desirability of freedom for people to rely on all grounds that seem relevant. The basic considerations are the same, but the comparative balance is quite different. An individual legislator is vastly more important to legislation than an individual citizen. If decision on grounds of public reasons is a good thing, restraint by one legislator contributes much more than restraint by one citizen. Further, even if the issue is not one in which imposition is directly raised, one may think a form of unfairness occurs if legislators, as public officials representing everyone, rely on their own comprehensive views. Since legislators are in the business of being officials, they can be called upon more sensibly to exercise the discipline of self-restraint in decision than can ordinary citizens. They will also have a better sense of whether *their own fellows* are trying to comply with a principle of restraint than will citizens. For all these reasons, the argument is substantially stronger than it is for citizens that legislators should regard themselves like judges, not only justifying but making judgments on the basis of public reasons.[25] If legislators perceive a clear distinction between what they think public reasons would indicate and what their comprehensive views indicate, they should generally follow the dictates of public reason. *Nevertheless,* ordinary legislators each play a relatively small part in what legislation is adopted. A plurality of inputs is acceptable. More than judges and executive officials (who represent the whole people even in their legislative functions), legislators should feel that giving some weight to their comprehensive views is often appropriate.

I want to pause over what may seem to be a kind of anomaly in what I have said about the degree to which legislators should rely on comprehensive views. I have suggested that positions based on comprehensive views somehow have a higher status when they come from citizens rather than from the legislators themselves. How can this difference in treatment be justified? One basic premise is that citizens properly do rely on such grounds with some frequency. A second basic premise is that legislators should accord some weight to the judgments of citizens because they are the judgments of citizens. The following challenge might be made to the second premise:

> When legislation involves a trade-off of interests, it is fine for legislators to accord weight to the expressed interests of citizens (especially constituents). *But* when the issue is what is right (as in whether the country should send troops to Bosnia), legislators should decide what is right for themselves. If they should not rely directly (except to a limited degree) on comprehensive grounds, they should not rely on citizen judgments so formed as an indication of what is right.

I agree that legislators should not take citizen judgments based on religious and other comprehensive grounds primarily as some kind of evidence of what is really right in an independent sense. Rather, I am suggesting that when the issue is (to put it very crudely) one of right or wrong rather than balancing interests, a legislator should care to a degree what citizens believe is right (on whatever grounds are appropriate for them). The weight the legislator accords is to the fact of this belief. In this view, no incongruity exists in a legislator's giving weight to citizen opinion formed in a manner different from how the legislator should form his or her individual political opinion.

The Problems of "Insincerity" and Incomplete Reasons

My suggestions in this chapter raise the sincerity problem I mentioned briefly in chapter 12. Although I have proposed significant correlations between what people actually rely upon in making up their minds and what they explicitly rely upon in public discourse, I have also acknowledged that some discrepancies are proper. Does this not approve an insincerity that will itself be damaging to political discourse and decision? Insofar as the issue is genuine deceit, the problem is largely circular, because so much depends on existing expectations (a point made in chapter 12). If citizens expect fully candid disclosure of actual grounds of decision, then restraint in discourse not matched by restraint in decision will mislead. However, if people regard forms of discourse as having particular functions in the political process, they will not necessarily expect that public advocacy will reflect all bases of decision. Let me give two kinds of examples. In most personal conversation and in the meetings of some small groups, people (or some people) feel they should include their degree of doubt or confidence about courses of action that they favor, actually stating arguments for the position contrary to that which they take and conceding the weight of those arguments.[26] That plainly is not the approach of most judicial opinion writing and of most public political discourse. Having decided, people state the arguments in favor of their position with great force and downplay the weight of opposing grounds.[27] This practice is so common, and so commonly understood, that engaging in it is not insincere; no one takes the stated positions as reflecting the true weight of grounds in the speaker's or writer's mind.

Another feature of legal opinions is that innovative steps are substantially concealed in language that suggests that a principle is already to be found in prior cases. This practice, again, is so common that it is not properly conceived of as insincere (any more than saying "I had a very good time" even when one felt awkward and out of place is insincere).

If people understand that public political discourse is largely to be cast in public reasons, an official's or citizen's public reliance on those reasons is not deceitful, even when unstated grounds derived from comprehensive views matter to his determination. If, however, people positively deny the influence of grounds that they know have moved them, they are dishonest.

The omission of some reasons in discourse does undoubtedly give them less exposure, makes them less a subject of dialogue. Here lies the crucial distinction between culture and the narrow political process. What is the comparative likelihood in the two domains of deep and fruitful dialogue over the meaning of life? I might say much more about this, but I believe that *constructive* dialogue on deeper concerns is much more likely in other settings than the resolutions of political issues,[28] that putting forth opposing religious positions and other comprehensive views in narrow political debate will often lead to acrimony, a hardening of lines, and less fruitful interchange about the comprehensive views themselves than the omission of those views in political debate.

It is true that if the deeper bases for judgment are not a serious part of political dialogue, people will often be stating reasons that they regard as somewhat incomplete. A critic of my position may argue with some force that if the stated grounds are incomplete, others will lack a full basis to reach a resolution on an issue. But there is little point in developing "more complete" grounds, if the extra grounds developed are unlikely to enlighten others, may hinder constructive dialogue, and will probably cause feelings of exclusion and alienation. We must accept that resolution of political issues will often depend on compromises and votes, that the aim for complete and uniform understanding that reaches through to comprehensive grounds is unrealistic and even naive. The benefits of self-restraint in discourse that extends beyond self-restraint in judgment are sufficient to warrant the drawbacks of that discrepancy.[29]

Significance

I need to say a few words about the *significance* of the principles of restraint I have proposed. First, as I have formulated them, they contain a good deal of flexibility. For example, legislators are permitted to rely on comprehensive views but should give greater weight to grounds rooted in public reasons. I mean the principles to be flexible in another way. They are one of a number of guides to action. When guides to action come in conflict, their weight or priority in context must be assessed. Sometimes, as when a policy that is deeply outrageous from a moral point of view has been followed or is being considered, the reasons for explicitly bringing a comprehensive view to bear may be greater than reasons for restraint. Even those who are persuaded that principles of self-restraint are sound may find reasons strong enough to break them on occasion.

15

Religious Organizations and Political Life

This chapter deals with the involvement of religious groups in politics. The topic bears a close relation to the previous chapter; what religious groups should do politically depends partly on what should count as good reasons for officials and citizens to make up their minds. Of special relevance are my conclusions that citizens are properly influenced by religious and other comprehensive views and that legislators properly take such judgments of citizens into account.

In most of the book I have indicated that when I talk of religious views I mean to include as well other comprehensive views. Religious organizations are highly important in American society; organizations that could be said to represent and promote other comprehensive positions are not. In this chapter, therefore, I focus on religious groups, without worrying how my conclusions may bear on organizations representing other comprehensive views. When I refer to "churches," I mean to include analogous units of non-Christian religions, such as synagogues and mosques.

Substantial information exists about the political activities of religious groups. As in the previous chapter, I summarize what has been and what is, before turning to what should be. In order to clarify the significance of descriptive accounts, however, I first indicate the major "should" questions that I consider. (1) When addressing their own members, should clergy and churches limit themselves to general moral ideas, or should they draw specific political conclusions? (2) Should their recommendations extend to supporting or opposing particular parties or candidates? (3) Should clergy, while strongly identified as clergy, run for public office? (4) Should clergy, churches, and other religious organizations engage in ordinary political activities, such as educational campaigns, lobbying, demonstrations, and attempts to put strong electoral pressure on officials? (5) Should they draw highly specific policy conclusions, or limit themselves to more general rec-

165

ommendations? (6) If they should act in the public arena, should they make specifically religious arguments, or nonreligious arguments, or both? As the entire book has indicated, each of these questions can be faced from *within* a religious tradition or from the standpoint of independent political theory that does not rely explicitly on theological premises.

Past and Present Political Involvement and Attitudes about It

The Past

There is a long history of religious involvement in politics in the United States, and most crucial facts are beyond dispute.[1] I speak mainly about past and present practices, but I also say something about attitudes. If we are asking how people *should* act, we need some idea how they regard actions they and others have taken.

Dean M. Kelley begins an essay on "The Rationale for the Involvement of Religion in the Body Politic" with a quote from Senator Barry Goldwater.[2] Goldwater was responding when the leader of the Moral Majority, Jerry Falwell, criticized Supreme Court nominee Sandra Day O'Connor. Accusing the Moral Majority of "undermining the basic American principles of separation of church and state by using the muscle of religion towards political ends," Goldwater said:

> I'm frankly sick and tired of the political preachers across the country telling me as a citizen that if I want to be a moral person, I must believe in "A," "B," "C," and "D." Just who do they think they are? And from where do they presume to claim the right to dictate their moral belief to me?
>
> And I'm even more angry as a legislator who must endure the threats of every religious group who thinks it has some God-granted right to control my vote on every roll call in the Senate.
>
> And the religious factions will go on imposing their will on others unless the decent people connected with them recognize that religion has no place in public policy. . . .
>
> The great decisions of Government cannot be dictated by the concerns of religious factions. . . .
>
> We have succeeded for 205 years in keeping the affairs of the state separate from the uncompromising idealism of religious groups, and we mustn't stop now!

Senator Goldwater expresses a forceful version of the position that politics should be separate from religion,[3] and his last sentence rings with a version of American history that we often hear. That version is about as inaccurate as history can be.

Churches have been involved in politics throughout the country's history. In some colonies, of course, the original government was an extension of the church; churches received state privileges and had great power even when government was separate. After full disestablishment of churches took place in states, religion continued to exercise a powerful influence. Virginia's Statute for Religious Freedom, which was drafted by Jefferson and adopted prior to the federal Constitution, was supported by pietistic dissenters as well as rationalists. Jefferson's pietistic allies "were ardent supporters of voluntarism whenever taxes for religion were at issue, but they favored Puritan laws against profanity, blasphemy, gambling, theater-going, desecration of the Sabbath and other legal attempts to maintain a Christian society."[4] After Aaron Burr killed Alexander Hamilton in a duel in 1804, ministers preached sermons denouncing dueling and urging that it be treated as a crime. Lyman Beecher, a leading minister of the day and the father of both Harriet Beecher Stowe and Henry Ward Beecher, said that citizens should refuse to vote for any duelist.[5] States responded in statutes and constitutions, and over a period of a few decades dueling disappeared. Churches were active during roughly the same period in an unsuccessful effort to prevent mail from being delivered on Sunday; these endeavors generated counterarguments that the government should not accede to "sectarian" pressures.[6] During much of the nineteenth century, churches fought against the use of lotteries to raise money.[7]

Northern churches played an important part in the antislavery movement, in some major denominations splitting from Southern churches that defended slavery. The antislavery churches, "finding petitions and pleas ineffective, turned first to colonization (of Liberia and then of Kansas) and then to civil disobedience (via the Underground Railroad), and finally to the justification of violence and warfare."[8]

Perhaps the most important aspect of religion and politics during the nineteenth century was that despite formal separation of church and state, there was "a de facto cultural establishment of Protestantism."[9] Alexis de Tocqueville found that religion in the United States was regarded as "indispensable to the maintaining of republican institutions" and that "the real authority of religion was increased by a state of things which diminished its apparent force."[10] In this period, public schools generally assumed the truth of Protestant Christianity; prayer and Bible reading in schools were common; Christianity was said to be part of the common law, and our country was called a Christian nation.

The most effective political involvement of religious groups in the country's history may have been the Prohibition crusade, which lasted about one hundred years from the early 1800s. Booth Fowler says, "[T]here is no doubt that religious leaders, churches, and concerned religious laity were the head, the heart, and the body of the movement"; in its most successful period, after 1900, the movement "formed a grand coalition of almost all Protestant churches."[11] The Prohibitionists did not try to capture a major party; instead they worked as a single-interest group. They pursued a relentless campaign of education, pushed legislation, and lobbied in legislative halls and on the campaign trail, threatening legislators "with power of the organized church at the polls."[12] They succeeded first in many states and then won national prohibition.

The Social Gospel movement, which began in the late nineteenth century, was a broader effort of clergy and other religious people to influence the world.[13] Attempts to achieve political justice were largely ineffective, because the movement lacked broad Protestant support and was informal and disorganized. In the early years of the Social Gospel, the main emphasis was on educating people to realize that Christ calls us to realize the will of God in the world, but enthusiasm for direct involvement in politics increased after 1900. In 1936, the Federal Council of Churches, the major institution created by adherents of the Social Gospel, endorsed Franklin Roosevelt for president, provoking a storm of protest. The major influence of the Social Gospel was not in accomplishing discrete political objectives but in encouraging and expanding a modest tradition of political and social liberalism among theologically liberal Protestant clergy.

The civil rights movement is a powerful modern instance of religious forces playing a vital part in political protest and change. The centrality of churches in black communities was critical, as ministers became highly active politically. "Religiously, Martin Luther King Jr. succeeded in casting the civil rights struggle as a moral and religious one, appealing to the conscience of fellow white Christians across the nation, especially in the North."[14] Although many conservative Protestant denominations and local churches felt that clergy should observe a sharp line between religion and politics, most clergy, especially of the mainstream Protestant churches, believed clergy had a right to be active politically for civil rights, including marching and protesting. Roman Catholics and Jews also provided powerful support. Church groups tried to rally a sometimes reluctant laity and "provided muscle power and the money for the endless telephone calls, marches, newsletters . . . ."[15] The considerable unity of Christianity and "elite access" in Washington of many liberal Protestant and Jewish leaders strengthened the churches' efforts.

Contemporary Practices and Attitudes

To understand contemporary involvement of religious groups in politics, we need a sense of how religion fits in our culture and of the various perspectives different religions bring to political life. The enormous pluralism of American religions, which is increasing as recent immigration policies bring us a large number of immigrants from countries where religions other than Christianity predominate, is a major factor. Contrary to theories that modernization or class conflict would bring a sharp decline in religious belief and practice, and in contrast to what has happened in other economically advanced countries, religion remains very important in the United States.[16] Roughly 95 percent of Americans believe in God, and 80 percent believe Jesus is divine; most belong to churches and go to church with some regularity.

There are different accounts of how religious activity relates to general culture in the United States. Is religion comfortably integrated with our liberal political culture, helping to shape the broader culture and reflecting it? Or does religion pose a fundamental challenge to the existing order? Or is religion a refuge from a dominant liberal order, "a refuge from (1) liberal rational skepticism and (2) liberal individualism, our peculiar, relentless, and demanding moral ideal for the human person"?[17] No doubt, there are powerful elements of integration and challenge, but Booth Fowler argues persuasively that the refuge metaphor reflects the primary relation of religion and general culture. People are attracted to religion because of its affirmation of transcendence and of an absolute, because of its aesthetic dimension, because of its social and communal aspects, and because of its emphasis on love.[18] Religion fits well with the liberal society because it softens the harshness of a skeptical, individual-centered existence.[19]

The attitudes toward politics of major religious groupings in the United States differ somewhat. Among Protestants who are liberal theologically, many are also active politically, primarily for liberal causes; clergy and central organizations tend to give political issues a much higher priority than lay members. Protestant "realists," in the tradition of Reinhold Niebuhr, are much less optimistic about human nature and social organizations and are more accepting of the necessity of political compromise, but they also fall on the liberal side of the spectrum for most political issues. There are a relatively few Protestant radicals. Some of these do not accept many traditional Christian doctrines; others, like the Sojourners, are evangelical. Conservative Protestants are often divided into evangelicals and fundamentalists; the latter tend, among other things, to be more separatist with respect to the larger culture. Until the 1920s, conservatives were an important political force, and conservative theology was sometimes linked with liberal politics, as in the case of William Jennings Bryan.[20] From that time until the 1970s, evangelicals and fundamentalists typically stressed that change can best come through individual action by people who have been transformed through the Word of God.[21] In the last two decades many conservatives have approved political activism to address "the moral decline of America" and other issues. The Roman Catholic Church continues a long tradition of involvement in public affairs; its activity in American politics has increased with greater security about the place of Catholics in American society. Jews, for the most part, have been deeply concerned with political issues, often working with other groups. Although some African American churches have withdrawn from politics, many others are among the most activist politically, and black religious leaders are often political leaders as well.

Dean Kelley well captures the outlook of many of those who support the involvement of religious groups in politics. He says that for millennia, Judaism and Christianity have "embraced the conviction that their religious duty entailed active intervention in the 'body politic.' "[22] The scriptures indicate that God cares about justice, and justice "is not a trait of individuals, but of larger systems and structures, of laws, customs and people's expectations of one another."[23] The Church's role is a prophetic one, and the pursuit of justice is "a religious obligation for all Christians."[24] In response to the suggestion that individual Christians should be left to make their own contributions to political life, Kelley answers that the "forces that affect the public policy of large communities are vast, subtle, perduring and systemic. Individuals are no match for them, unless they can be enlisted in coordinated efforts that are informed by insightful analysis that recognizes the scope and course of the opposition. For the opposition is not merely individuals but systems and institutions."[25]

Since the civil rights movement, political activity among most American religions has increased dramatically. Religious perspectives have borne intensely not only on church-state topics like prayer in public schools, but also on many other national political issues, such as abortion, pornography, equality for women, and national military policy; and religious groups have shown increasing concern about economic policy.[26] "In the United States, where official political announcements by churches traditionally have been comparatively rare, the overt linking of religious ideas with political positions has recently become much more common among almost all denominations."[27] Major religious denominations maintain permanent lobbying offices in Washington, and there are various interdenominational offices as well, most notably that of the National Council of Churches. In addition, there are organizations, such as the Moral Majority during its institutional life, that are not defined by church membership or belief but are in fact dominated by religious leaders and have a political program that fits with the religious understanding of those leaders.

Success has been mixed. It has been greatest when many religious groups agree and when lay members support the stances of their leaders. Success has been least when these factors are not present and when strong opposition has been mounted from other quarters.

The mainline Protestant denominations have taken stands on many issues. They have been effective in lobbying on domestic and foreign "hunger" issues and on foreign policy toward El Salvador and Nicaragua, but overall, their influence has been less powerful than one might expect for organizations that represent a high percentage of the American elite. According to Booth Fowler, this is partly because of skepticism that their members "can be mobilized at the polls, given notorious issue divisions and widespread and sometimes intense feelings among the laity that [political activity] is inappropriate for their churches and clergy."[28] Using a label drawn from Reinhold Niebuhr that is less than flattering, Allen Hertzke speaks of the mainline church leaders as "children of light": they "often leaven a politics of self interest with moral and religious concerns. . . . [but their] effectiveness is too often muted by a blend of naivete and sanctimony characteristic of children of light."[29] They tend to engage in a kind of "cheap prophecy" rather than "intensive parish dialogue, grassroots mobilizing, hard-headed analysis, and tireless lobbying."[30] In respect to nuclear power, liberal Protestant resolutions had less influence than the teaching of the Roman Catholic bishops through a major pastoral letter, which demonstrably shifted lay Catholic opinion on the morality of our nuclear strategy. Mainline Protestant bodies strongly opposed the Gulf War, taking a more absolute position than the "just war" approach of the Catholic Church. Some leaders made predictions about American casualties that were wildly off the mark; this caused critics to wonder where their competence for such estimates lay. In the last decade, concerns about limited effectiveness and distance from lay opinion have led a number of mainline organizations to some retrenchment of their political activities.

The Roman Catholic Church has never envisioned a sharp separation of religion from politics, but the Second Vatican Council represented a watershed in two respects. The church then accepted as fully appropriate a liberal form of government under which it has no privileged position. Prior to that time the American church had been conservative, strongly anticommunist and promilitary, and opposed to various forms of public immorality. Beginning with the Vietnam War, the church shifted to challenging our country's strategy of nuclear deterrence and its support of right-wing forces in Nicaragua and El Salvador. In the 1980s, the bishops issued a pastoral letter on the economy that sharply criticized how capitalism affects the poor and the underprivileged, and proposed programs to make economic relations more humane. On all these issues, the Catholic Church has been close to the mainline Protestant leaders; but on "moral questions," like the legality of abortion and "gay rights," its allies among the Protestants are the conservatives. In general, Catholic leaders have communicated better with lay members than their mainline Protestant counterparts, and on abortion and nuclear strategy this has undoubtedly increased their lobbying strength; on other issues, notably the economy, they also suffer the disability that legislators doubt whether they speak for the laity.

The "New Religious Right" represents a striking increase in political activity for theologically conservative Christians. The Moral Majority and other groups have cast themselves in support of families and traditional values, challenging the ban on school prayer, permissiveness about pornography, liberal abortion laws, and gay rights. They mounted sufficient opposition to the equal rights amendment to prevent its passage, and have been directly involved in electoral politics. For example, their support for Jesse Helms was important in his 1984 election. Before the 1980 and 1984 elections they issued and distributed to churchgoers "moral report cards," which ranked candidates according to their positions on moral questions. Along with the Catholic Church, the New Religious Right has been successful in sharply restricting the use of federal funds for abortions, but for the most part it has not achieved its specific political objectives nationally. Fowler attributes its comparative lack of influence to the antagonism of most of the media and political elite and to skepticism that various groups represent anything like the number of ordinary citizens that they claim.[31] Robert Wuthnow notes a lack of experience in politics among the New

Religious Right and the vigorous opposition it has faced.[32] He believes that its main effect has been in the broader public sphere, in getting issues on the public agenda about collective values. It is there, he says, that religion may be most successful, since it "is fundamentally about values, not about settling matters of public policy."[33]

Although the New Religious Right has often been perceived as not "playing by the rules" of our culture, Wuthnow suggests that it has "sought seriously to change some of the standard rules, but generally abided by the basic canons of American politics, nevertheless generating controversy because some of the rules are in flux and ambiguous."[34]

These evaluations preceded political activities surrounding the 1992 election; and it is too early to tell how more recent activities of the Christian Coalition will affect them. It and related groups have concentrated much more energy on local politics and elections than did the Moral Majority. In some areas of the country conservative Christians have organized to run their own candidates for office. In some instances at least, these candidates have not publicly revealed their religious connection before the elections, giving rise to talk of "stealth candidates." On the national scene, the New Religious Right, already associated with Presidents Reagan and Bush, developed an extraordinarily close connection with the Republican Party in 1992. It influenced the party platform on abortion, school prayer, school vouchers, and gay rights. Its two best known leaders, Pat Robertson and Jerry Falwell, were highly visible at the Republican convention. Robertson was an important speaker; Falwell sat in the vice president's box. At a conference of the Christian Coalition, Robertson declared, "We want . . . as soon as possible to see a working majority of the Republican Party in the hands of pro-family Christians by 1996."[35] Both religious leaders and party leaders continually chastised the Democrats for failing to include mention of God in their party platform. Reviewing these activities, James Wood concluded in an editorial in the *Journal of Church and State*, "While there should be no question about the right of all Americans of whatever religious faith to participate in the political process, there is something quite ominous and threatening about any religious segment of this nation aiming to dominate a political party."[36]

African American churches have remained politically active, primarily on the left, since the civil rights movement. Although secular leaders have emerged in the black community, the clergy have continued to provide major national and local political leaders, playing "such a strategic role because they command the resources of the strongest institution in black life."[37]

Major Jewish organizations have worked for liberal political causes and for support of Israel. According to Fowler, their effectiveness is aided by "the elaborate Jewish network of elite influentials . . . who have access to decision makers"[38] and by their determination to build coalitions.

Proper Involvement by Religious Groups

I now turn from this summary account of past and present practices and of some attitudes toward them to an assessment of the appropriate role of religious groups in politics. As I shall illustrate with some examples, I believe that the most one can sensibly propose in this area are provisional principles of restraint, principles that may be overridden by urgent contrary reasons. In this respect, my recommendations follow those in the last chapter.

If we try to generalize about the present views of people involved in religious activities, we are met with a kind of tension. A high percentage of church leaders and organized church bodies now take a highly activist attitude, one supporting extensive church involvement in politics. Yet, the attitude of most lay members of churches is different. According to Booth Fowler, a massive, straightforward problem is that "[t]he average church attender does not want social activism from his or her church or clergy."[39] "[T]he ethical and political ideas of a church are not very salient to people at church as a whole, [who] more than anything else . . . come to church for comfort and for social needs."[40] Robert Wuthnow says, "There is . . . a healthy suspicion in American society of preachers becoming too closely involved with politics. . . . Operationally, this is the true meaning Americans have come to associate with separation of church and state. They do object to religious specialists trying to be politicians—much in the same way they would object to them being surgeons or engineers."[41]

What should we make of the lack of enthusiasm among many lay people for the political involvement of clergy and church? A churchgoer might disapprove of involvement for many reasons. (1) She might simply be resistant to discomforting prophetic aspects of her own church's message; (2) she might reflectively believe that the center of her religion lies elsewhere and worry that the center may suffer from inattention if too much time is spent on politics; (3) she might disagree with the substance of church positions but find it easier to object to involvement than to challenge the positions head-on; (4) she might seriously believe that as a matter of religious principle such political involvement is inappropriate; (5) she might believe explicitly or implicitly as a matter of political philosophy that such involvement is not appropriate in liberal democracies or in the United States (and find no strong countervailing religious principle to justify it). I will not discuss each of these possibilities in turn, but the last option poses the most serious threat to a claim that Americans accept political involvement by churches as appropriate. That option, which I believe is realized to a significant degree, reflects a sense about the nature of our political society, not just a belief about one's own religious principles.

Preaching and Other Mainly Internal Communications

I now move to the specific questions I sketched at the beginning of the chapter. When addressing their own members, should clergy and churches limit themselves to general moral ideas or should they draw specific political conclusions? This question starts with the important assumption that preaching about morality is *undoubtedly* appropriate, even if that morality has political implications. Thus, no one can object that ministers are straying from their domain if they preach that abortion is, or is not, like homicide, or that consenting sexual acts between adult homosexuals are, or are not, sinful, or that rich people have a duty to aid poor people. What ministers may preach, so also formal church bodies may teach their members, in pastoral letters or formulated denominational positions.

Controversy begins when preaching goes beyond morality to cover specific political conclusions. Of course, no *sharp* line divides morality from politics, but there is a difference between telling people that an active homosexual life is sinful and telling them that they should support criminal sanctions for that behavior. Some have suggested that ministers and churches should limit themselves to moral pronouncements, leaving members to draw their own political conclusions. Part of the concern is that in a liberal democracy citizens should not feel that others are telling them what political conclusions they must reach. Part of the concern is that ministers and churches are not experts about all the complex factors that matter for political decision, and that they should not exceed their competence. Of course, from within any religious perspective, the propriety of political lessons will depend a good bit on what authority ministers and churches are conceived to have. From the standpoint of political theory, much rests on just *how* and *when* political conclusions are drawn. If a minister offers conclusions as her own working out of relevant moral principles, but does not suggest that all others of good faith must agree with her, she recognizes the freedom of her members and the limits of any special competence of her own. The ease of conclusions and their moral importance also matter. Sometimes political conclusions will flow in a straightforward way from moral judgments. For example, if the minister preaches that an active homosexual life is perfectly acceptable to God and not inferior to a heterosexual life, the conclusion that any criminal sanctions should be repealed follows closely. (Since many sins are not subject to criminal punishment, a belief that homosexual acts *are sinful* does not have such direct political implications.) If a political decision has great moral significance, preaching directly about it is especially appropriate. Desegregation and decisions about war or peace have this significance; so does abortion for many on both sides of the issue. In general, perhaps clergy and churches should be slow to draw specific policy conclusions; they should regard their special competence as bearing on moral truths more than complex political judgments; but no principle of liberal politics precludes their drawing out specific policy conclusions in their communications to members.

Supporting Parties or Candidates

Should the recommendations of clergy and churches to their members extend to supporting or opposing particular parties or candidates? Favoring particular laws and policies is a step beyond advocating moral positions; supporting or opposing candidates and parties is a further involvement in the political process. Most Americans probably now feel uncomfortable when religious leaders take this further step; they feel uncomfortable with the suggestion that, overall, one candidate or party is more on God's side than another. I think these feelings of discomfort are well grounded. Of course, one difficulty is that with modern methods of communication, it is hard for churches and major religious leaders to make recommendations to their members without getting involved in recommendations to the general public; but even if advice to vote for candidates or parties is limited to members, the degree of intertwining between church and potential governors is troubling. Still, at most there is a provisional moral principle against such recommendations. Some political issues are of such overriding significance that churches are warranted in opposing candidates who take positions they strongly believe are wrong. Suppose, for example, a white candidate explicitly takes the position that racial segregation should be reinstituted. In our present understanding, that position seems so blatantly immoral, so contrary to Christian values, a minister's preaching opposition to his election is proper. As this example illustrates, finding circumstances when a candidate's position would warrant opposing him is easier than concluding that all things about a candidate warrant explicit support; but in the general elections of our two-party system, opposition to one candidate often amounts to support of another.

Clergy Running for Office

Should clergy, strongly identified as clergy, run for office? In this country, clergy are not bound to the role of clergy for life. Without doubt, persons who have been ordained properly run for public office. But it is different if a minister retains a parish, continues preaching on a regular basis, and runs for office. The Supreme Court has rightly decided that any *legal* restriction on clergy occupying public office is unconstitutional,[42] but old state prohibitions of that kind evidenced a sensible worry that when practicing clergy are legislators or high executive officials, the mixing in personnel of politics and religion is too great. The general principle is that people should choose between being fully active ministers and being public officials or political candidates.

Lobbying and Other Public Political Efforts

Should clergy and churches not only speak to their own members about political issues but try to reach a larger public by educational efforts, by lobbying government officials for laws and programs and by participating in direct action such as demonstrations? Given the present amount of activity, it would certainly be unfair to expect any single religious group to eschew these activities, since so many other religious groups engage in them. The more serious question is whether over time it would be desirable for these activities to cease or diminish.

We need to narrow this question. As I have said, some pieces of legislation directly affect churches or religious practices. As affected institutions, churches should certainly be involved over legislative questions concerning aid to church schools or property tax deductions for religious property. They should also speak out when matters, such as school prayer, concern religious practices and their appropriate settings. One contemporary illustration is the Religious Freedom Restoration Act.[43] This new act is designed to overrule by statute *Employment Division v. Smith,*[44] a case that sharply curtailed free exercise rights by deciding that valid laws not aimed at religious practices could be applied against those with powerful religious objections, however great or small the government's interest in applying the laws against the religious objectors. The act restores the more protective test for free exercise claims that existed before *Smith,* one that requires the state to show a compelling interest in order to apply a law against a religious objector. Church groups were very active in promoting the legislation. They were properly involved in legislation dealing with such accommodations to the exercise of religion.

The harder question concerns broader issues of morals or social justice. As to those issues, I have said that preaching within churches about the implications of religious understanding for what our corporate life should be like is all right, and on many occasions direct endorsement of particular political objectives is proper.

The question now is whether churches and clergy should move beyond recommendations to members and participate in the political process as one might expect General Motors, or a large labor union, or the American Medical Association, to do. Such activity, as I have indicated, may seem an aspect of living out the implications of one's responsibilities to other members of society; but it carries risks of detracting from what are seen as more central aspects of religious practice and of proving ineffective, primarily because church leaders are not believed to have the support of lay membership.

From the standpoint of independent political theory there are two powerful arguments for viewing involvement as appropriate. The first is that churches should not be regarded as different from other nongovernmental organizations, and the legislative process is now replete with lobbying by such groups. The second is that churches, and larger organizations in which they are dominantly involved, often think seriously about public welfare and conscience; they are a healthy corrective to self-interested pleadings. On the negative side is the concern, already mentioned, that churches speak about matters in which they are not expert, that their involvement makes political life harsher and more divisive, and that churches might appear to control the legislative process. The consequences can include resentment against particular churches or against the arrogance of organized religion.

Is the concern about expertness well grounded? Legislators and voters must often make up their minds on matters on which they are not expert. If we take the Gulf War, for example, many people's decisions about support of the beginning of actual war against Iraq depended on at least crude estimates of casualty levels and of the length of the war. Senators were assured by military planners that the war would probably not take very long and that American deaths and injuries would be light; but given the extreme inaccuracy of military estimates about past wars, how could anyone be confident that these optimistic projections would be correct? People must often make decisions in light of competing, diametrically opposed projections by those with genuine claims to expertness. In circumstances such as these, nonexperts rely upon and argue in terms of the estimates they find most persuasive. Such assessments are made by legislators, citizens, and ordinary lobbyists all the time, so what is the problem if churches and church leaders make them too? Legislators *must* make judgments as nonexperts because their central function is to reach specific legislative decisions and discuss with each other what those should be. Ordinary lobbyists are expected to be acting out of the self-interest of the groups they represent, so everyone expects them to choose whatever estimates plausibly support the results they want. Churches are different. They are supposed to be representing a larger perspective than most other lobbyists, and they do not have to resolve which of conflicting estimates are more nearly right. For them to speak with confidence about matters on which they have no special knowledge can seem arrogant, and it can seriously detract from whatever moral force lies behind their positions. Churches should generally be highly cautious in drawing conclusions that depend on expert knowledge they do not have.

The worry about "control" is more easily met on the national level. There is such diversity of religious views, and such disagreement about political implications, that neither control nor its appearance is very likely for most issues. On some particular issues, those on which churches happen to be united or on which some group of churches exercises very great efforts, "control" may seem more of a concern. It may be a pervasive concern within some few states. I recently attended a conference at the University of Utah; in that state not much legislation gets passed over the strong opposition of the Church of Latter Day Saints. When one heard from representatives of other religions, the resentment of the Mormons' role in political life was palpable.

The wider effect of religious involvement in political life is a much more complicated problem. For some issues, like abortion, debate is more strident because religious groups have staked out powerful positions. On many other issues, religious involvement does not have such a consequence. Some studies show that persons outside churches are more accepting of opposing points of view than are church members, but *deep* religious commitment may actually promote tolerant behavior; and there is some evidence that political participation leads people to become more tolerant.[45] In any event, whatever the negative aspects of religious involvement, they must be measured against the positive values that are brought to bear not only for specific political decisions but also for the public sphere more generally. Judgments may differ, but mine is that the ordinary political activities of religious leaders and organizations are an aspect of political good health rather than ill health.

Should churches limit themselves to general recommendations or draw highly specific policy conclusions? For general educational efforts, churches may be able to concentrate on broad recommendations, but effective lobbying usually involves support for or opposition to specific proposals, and may involve formulating proposals. Just as they may appropriately recommend specific conclusions to members, churches may support those conclusions in a public arena. It is best if they concentrate on situations in which the specific conclusions flow easily from important moral judgments and on situations in which the moral stakes are high. Sometimes these conditions coincide, as in much antidiscrimination legislation and over the issue of abortion; but sometimes the moral stakes will be high, as over the Gulf War, and yet desirable policy may depend on complex factual judgments. When the churches support particular policies in such instances, they should try not to overstate the certainty of whatever factual judgments they make.

I have already suggested that churches should strongly hesitate to endorse particular candidates or parties to their own members. The mixing of religion and government is much worse if this endorsement is made to a general public and the entire citizenry is urged by church leaders to vote for particular parties and candidates.[46] That is what happened in 1992 between some prominent conservative Christian clergy and the Republican Party. Although it is not so simple to state clear principles why support of particular legislation is fairly often appropriate and support of candidates and parties is rarely so, one reason is the disturbing quality of an overall evaluation of a party or candidate as being more in tune with the religiously correct view; another reason involves the special "debt" a candidate or party may have to those who directly helped put him or it in office and whose support may also be necessary at the next election. Of course, a large part of effective lobbying is a kind of threat that a legislator may lose electoral support if he takes a contrary position, and lobbying is as important as it is in this country because politics is decentralized and individual candidates must build their own bases of support. Still, a lobbyist who has been directly instrumental in an election campaign and whose similar help may be crucial for future elections has an influence that far exceeds that of most other lobbyists. When churches play this role, they may come too close to the running of government. I am inclined to agree with James

Wood that 1992's "injection of sectarian religion in the political process is not only divisive but does not bode well for the well-being of the Republican party, a free and pluralistic society, or America's wide diversity of faiths."[47]

If churches and clergy should involve themselves in political issues, should they make specifically religious arguments, or nonreligious arguments, or both? When religious leaders and organizations are involved in the political process, perhaps they should try to develop and present reasons that will have force outside their own particular membership; but it seems evident that they need *not limit themselves* to nonreligious arguments. They have special competence to present a religious understanding, and if they are to speak at all, part of what they present should be that understanding. Thus, I suppose that insofar as religious organizations should continue to participate directly in politics, part of their contribution should be to present religiously grounded reasons. My conclusion about this depends substantially on the judgments of the previous chapter about appropriate grounds for citizens and legislators.

Conclusion

In the preceding chapters, I have rejected arguments that religious convictions, or comprehensive views, or nonaccessible grounds should be the subject of some general and rigorous exclusion in politics by conscientious actors in liberal democracies. I have suggested that such bases for political judgment may play an appropriate role in many liberal democracies, including the United States. However, I have also rejected the claim that no principles of self-restraint are apt. I have suggested that the United States now has conventions that restrict appropriate forms of discourse, not only for judges but also for other officials. I have proposed restraints for legislators and citizens; these constraints are fairly flexible and are provisional in the sense of being subject to being overridden by other considerations. I claim that for religious groups the presentation of political arguments cast in religious terms is more appropriate than it is for other quasi-public citizens or groups, or for officials. But I do suggest some provisional limits even on what such groups should do.

Throughout the book, the question has arisen what people should do if their comprehensive views lead them to judgments at variance with those indicated by models of liberal democracy. In this conclusion, I face a closely related question: What is the status of the arguments I have made? I have tried to present reasons that cut across, and would be relevant under, a great variety of comprehensive views. These are arguments of political philosophy that do not depend directly on any comprehensive view. However, readers who begin with particular comprehensive views will have to see if the analysis and proposed principles are cogent within their own views, taking into account the diversity of comprehensive views within a pluralist society. It is, of course, conceivable that one's comprehensive view will leave no room for some of the considerations I have advanced. Much more common will be a rather different phenomenon. The considerations I raise on various sides will be seen to have *some weight*, but the weight assigned will differ from that I give. For example, an evangelical Christian might acknowledge that political harmony and respect for those with different views are values of some significance, but believe that our most important task in life is to preach the true faith and that this will be most effectively done if its relevance is raised in all possible settings, including political ones. For someone who thinks conversion vastly exceeds other aspects of social life in importance, the considerations may look different than they do to me.[1]

Although I have presented my argument as if it does not depend on any particular comprehensive view, and I believe its force does cut across many such views, the argument does in fact fit with my own comprehensive view, which with some inaccuracy I may treat here as a variation of liberal Christian. (The main inaccuracy is that my view of human nature and of traditional doctrines lies closer to what is sometimes called neo-Orthodoxy than to standard liberal Christianity.) I do not claim that most of the specific recommendations I make about self-restraint are somehow derivable from premises of liberal democracy, or present American practices and attitudes, without reference to comprehensive views. I do not claim that on bases other than reference to comprehensive views, the person who disagrees with *certain* crucial aspects or assumptions of the analysis could be said to be wrong.

What force does the analysis have, then, for someone whose comprehensive view leads in a different direction? If, as I believe, the restraints (and the absence of restraints) that I suggest roughly approximate present understandings of most people who are active in the political process, a dissenter should recognize that he is not playing by the "loosely accepted" ground rules for modern political life. But one feature of liberal democracy is that it allows people peacefully to reject existing political ground rules.[2] The dissenter may claim that he has sufficient reasons for doing so. He is not to be excluded from discourse or said to be acting improperly as a citizen, since liberal democracy affords opportunities for people to challenge all existing forms of social life. However, from the perspective of those who believe that present understandings are a solid foundation for the politics of this liberal democratic society, his deviation is at odds with the practices of citizens and officials who are aware of the value of playing by the rules and try to do so. The principles I propose are ones that many people can unite behind and accept, and use as a basis for a kind of criticism of others,[3] even though the reasons for the restraints will not seem compelling to all citizens.

Notes

Chapter 1

1. Of course it *might* be said that Faith should not rely on this belief for any purpose because the belief is misguided. I am assuming that any possible error in the belief is not established by liberal political philosophy, that as far as liberal political philosophy is concerned Faith acts properly in relying on the belief as a ground for not eating meat herself and for encouraging others to do likewise.

2. Charles Larmore, *Patterns of Moral Complexity* 42–43 (New York, Cambridge Univ. Press 1987). See also John Rawls, *A Theory of Justice* (Cambridge, Mass., Harvard Univ. Press 1971); Bruce Ackerman, *Social Justice in the Liberal State* (New Haven, Conn., Yale Univ. Press 1980).

3. Larmore, supra note 2, at 44–68.

4. One could, of course, simply define everything about human action that religion covers as matters relating to the good life.

5. If one's fundamental view of life was nonreligious, but one thought that some gods had limited magical powers to help one achieve objectives, one's religious beliefs would not constitute a comprehensive view. Some people in ancient Greece and Rome had such religious beliefs.

6. I say more about the boundaries of religion in "Religion as a Concept in Constitutional Law," 72 *California Law Review* 753, 753–81 (1984).

7. *Religious Convictions and Political Choice,* chap. 5 (New York, Oxford University Press 1988).

8. See, e.g., Rawls, supra note 2; Ackerman, supra note 2.

9. See, e.g., Alasdair MacIntyre, *After Virtue* (London, Duckworth 1981); Michael Perry, *Love and Power* (New York, Oxford University Press 1991).

10. "Duties" and "obligations" may be conceived in terms of what can realistically be expected of people; "ideals" may be conceived of in terms of aspirations that no one will fully satisfy.

11. This is not to say that most people actually feel comfortable talking about religion.

Chapter 2

1. I discuss the characteristics of liberal democracy at greater length in *Religious Convictions and Political Choice*, chap. 2 (New York, Oxford University Press 1988).

Chapter 3

1. Even if an unsuccessful vote on improper grounds would not violate rights, acting to achieve an end that, if achieved, would violate moral rights is morally wrong.

2. One *could* still argue about appropriate limits as a way of explaining the implications of the ethical feelings of particular persons or some group of people, or as a way of altering their feelings. However, it is a common mistake to believe that liberalism fits especially well with a thoroughgoing skepticism about all moral choices. Such skepticism fits as well with a decision to coerce others to conform with one's feelings (more or less the Nazi philosophy, which did not in its more reflective forms purport to rest on objective bases) as with a decision to respect the subjective preferences of others.

3. The tremendous complexity of this subject is quickly revealed by the literature, including David O. Brink, *Moral Realism and the Foundations of Ethics* (Cambridge, Cambridge Univ. Press 1989); Hilary Putnam, *The Many Faces of Realism* (LaSalle, Ill., Open Court 1987); Geoffrey Sayre-McCord, ed., *Essays on Moral Realism* (Ithaca, N.Y., Cornell Univ. Press 1988).

4. The truth of a moral claim is not established by showing that it is believed by most people in society. However, if one aspect of desirable behavior toward others is satisfying their expectations, their moral beliefs may indirectly figure in how it is really right to treat them. Thus, to take a simple illustration, if the best act was one that maximized happiness, how to maximize happiness could depend on what those affected thought was morally required.

5. I believe this is more complicated than I suggest in the text. Given what I say in note 7, it might be more precise to say also that it is false that either apple or blueberry pie tastes better than the other.

6. For a treatment that I find persuasive on this point, see J. L. Mackie, *Ethics: Inventing Right and Wrong* (Harmondsworth, U.K., Penguin Books 1977). However, Jeremy Waldron asserts that many in the modern generation do not feel moral judgments are more than matters of opinion. See Waldron, "The Irrelevance of Moral Objectivity," in *Natural Law Theory* 158, 166 (Robert George ed., Oxford, Oxford University Press 1992).

7. There is a tricky question about universal, or nearly universal, tastes. If someone says, "Fresh roses smell better than rotten garbage," she may mean that physical attributes of the human sense of smell will make this true for (virtually) all human beings. That claim makes an assertion about a kind of truth and is subject to a judgment about truth or falsity. Taking Evelyn's apple claim in this way, we can say that it is in the domain of truth and falsity, and that it is false, because the taste of apples and blueberries in their pie manifestations is close *enough* in attractiveness that a judgment of better or worse is not warranted. This wrinkle shows that analysis of the status of judgments of taste is more complicated than my text acknowledges. The point of the analysis, however, is to highlight what may or may

not be sound in judgments of morality, not to provide a systematic account of what may properly be said about tastes.

8. It will also be necessary to have reasons for why the particular training (or perhaps background) is more appropriate for assesssing the truth of the claim than some alternative training that might lead to a different conclusion.

9. Putnam, supra note 3, at 45.

10. Which parts of any consensus about values are the result of unjust domination can be highly controversial. Some feminists think that virtually all prevailing values in Western societies are the product of unjust male domination. Deciding whether values are a consequence of unjust domination involves not only complicated factual inquiry but also evaluation of what "unjust domination" is. One needs a fairly comprehensive moral theory to resolve that question in some instances.

It is unjust to coerce people on the basis of values that are a product of injustice, but if the values remain widely shared, some utilitarian reasons for acting upon them may be present.

11. This judgment, of course, may itself involve controversial evaluation. The possibility of misguided practices was suggested to me by Jean Porter.

12. John Rawls, *A Theory of Justice* (Cambridge, Mass., Harvard Univ. Press 1971).

13. These entities are so devoid of human characteristics that talking about them as people is misleading.

14. J. Rawls, "Justice as Fairness: Political Not Metaphysical," 14 *Philosophy and Public Affairs*, 223, 231 (1985).

15. Perhaps even in Rawls's own more modest view, we can say that *much* of his argument is realist, because it asserts what conditions are necessary to achieve certain kinds of goods.

16. See Jürgen Habermas, "Discourse Ethics: Notes on a Program of Philosophical Justification," in *Moral Consciousness and Communicative Action* 43–115 (Christian Lenhardt and Shierry Weber Nicholsen trans., Cambridge, Mass., M.I.T. Press 1990); Habermas, "Morality and Ethical Life: Does Hegel's Critique of Kant Apply to Discourse Ethics?" 83 *Northwestern University Law Review* 38 (1989); Karl-Otto Apel, "The Problem of a Universalistic Macroethics of Co-responsibility," in *What Right Does Ethics Have?* 23–40 (S. Griffioen ed., Amsterdam, Vrije Universiteit Press 1990). A somewhat similar American view is found in Bruce Ackerman, *Social Justice in the Liberal State* (New Haven, Conn., Yale University Press 1980).

17. The claim would not *need* to be that any particular substantive values are correct; it could be the more modest assertion that whatever substantive values were selected would be correct.

18. If it were skeptical both about the correctness of moral claims and shared values, discourse ethics would be a branch of responsive ethics, which I shall shortly discuss.

19. The right may simply be *defined* as the result of the appropriate dialogic procedure, *or* dialogue may be viewed as the ideal method to learn what is independently right (*or*, perhaps, this distinction would be thought to collapse). I consider the approach to be realist in any of these events.

20. I assume here that what her superiors instruct is either the same as or consistent with what the legislature has directed. If a superior directs Olive to do something at odds with what a statute requires, determining her legal responsibility

is not so easy. Officials are not supposed to commit crimes, even when instructed to do so by superiors, but as to some other matters, it may be assumed that officials are safe in relying on a superior's instructions, and even that they should rely on what superiors tell them rather than trying to figure out what relevant statutes require.

21. These judgments *might* involve an attempt to apply the community's moral and political sense rather than the official's own.

22. See, e.g., Benjamin Nathan Cardozo, *The Nature of the Judicial Process* 102–41 (New Haven, Conn., Yale University Press 1921); H.L.A. Hart, *The Concept of Law* 121–50 (Oxford, Clarendon Press 1961).

23. See, e.g., Ronald Dworkin, *Law's Empire* (Cambridge, Mass., Harvard Belknap Press 1986).

24. I do not speak here of sufficient material welfare to make a decent life. I do think that is important.

25. As a Christian, I already believed much of this in my mind, but somehow my time with Sanja during her last illness taught me the triviality of much striving in a specially powerful form.

26. My attitude about this is different from my sense that I have duties toward my children that are personal to me. I believe that all parents in cultures with nuclear families should feel strong duties toward *their* children.

27. Probably my religious beliefs affected how I interpreted my experience. Certainly they supported my conclusions, but my conscious understanding was that I had learned the lesson at a human level that did not depend on religious convictions.

28. A more careful analysis would need to distinguish between what is good for the person and what is right and good with respect to others. I think there are powerful arguments that one should care for members of one's immediate family. What mainly is in question are one's openness to new relationships of depth and one's approach to people one knows less well.

29. However, if the issue is whether one of many uses for public funds is financing poor scholars or helping epileptics, then it may be relevant whether *some* people feel the way I do. My own experience is evidence that some others will feel similarly.

30. This is a large generalization. A fuller response would require attention to diverse functions and circumstances. Schoolteachers and youth workers may be more effective if they feel relatively free to act upon personal values. And even when a major decision is controlled by rule, there is room for an official to relate to affected persons from his or her own individuality.

31. If someone has talked with many other people who report similar experiences, and it is possible to explain why they happen, then one can offer a reasoned basis to others who have not yet had an experience why they would be likely to have it. By contrast, when one's confidence in the replicability of experience is primarily grounded internally, one has less reasoned basis to explain to others why they should be compelled to act as the experience suggests. When officials act under the law, and to a lesser extent when legislators act, it is desirable for decisions to be explained with *something more* than references to one's own deep feelings, even when the person having the experiences believes that the experiences, and the insights drawn from them, are replicable.

Chapter 4

1. I later discuss what kind of connection counts.

2. See, e.g., John Rawls, "The Domain of the Political and Overlapping Consensus," 64 *New York University Law Review* 233, 234–41 (1989). Rawls, id. at 240, distinguishes fully comprehensive doctrines, which cover "all recognized values and virtues within one rather precisely articulated scheme of thought," from partially comprehensive doctrines that comprise certain nonpolitical values and are loosely articulated.

3. I am not talking here about ethical beliefs that are connected to religious beliefs. It is at least arguable that the standard of truth for ethical beliefs is whether they yield fulfilling lives. I have in mind the differences in theological belief that divide Jews from Christians, or Mormons from traditional Protestants.

4. Of course, if truth is understood as what is practically useful, then it follows logically that the most beneficial beliefs are true. I am not assuming such a pragmatic approach to truth.

5. Such an explanation might be that these beliefs satisfy some childish psychological desire or aid people in achieving material prosperity. A different sort of explanation might be that people in a culture, even those skeptical about the religious premises, regard these lives as fulfilling mainly because they have been influenced so strongly by the religious environment.

6. I pass over the various bases for rejecting a "fruits of conviction" argument, which are likely to depend considerably on exactly how the "fruits of conviction" argument is made.

7. Someone might concede that credible historical evidence does exist, but suppose that the events described are so extremely unlikely to have happened that the evidence in their favor is outweighed by reference to other standards of knowledge. For a similar point about the persuasiveness of religious experience, see Richard Swinburne, *The Existence of God* 261–62 (Oxford, Clarendon Press 1979).

8. Mathematical and some scientific proofs might escape.

9. As I noted in chapter 1, one can imagine certain religious views that do not relate significantly to the comprehensive understandings of those who hold them.

10. Acts 9:3–6 (N.I.V.).

11. Caroline Franks Davis, in *The Evidential Force of Religious Experience* 29–65 (Oxford, Clarendon Press 1989), has a lucid account of different kinds of religious experience and the degree of their intelligibility to others. See also William James, *The Varieties of Religious Experience* (Harmondsworth, U.K., Penguin Books 1985).

12. It could also be the intercession of some devil bent on misleading Saul. I shall put aside that possibility, since not many modern skeptics about conversion and other religious experiences are inclined to attribute them to devils. However, some of those who believe their own conversion experiences lead them to truth may think conversion experiences that suggest contrary perspectives are produced by malign forces.

13. Rachel (or Saul) might think his persecution of Christians "set him up" psychologically for a guilt-induced reaction; she might further attribute the blindness to severe psychological stress, which was relieved by Ananias.

14. This challenge was strongly put in a conference entitled "The Role of Religion Arguments Regarding Public Policy in a Liberal Democracy," at the University of San Diego, Calif., April 9–11, 1992.

15. As Caroline Franks Davis, supra note 11, at 21, puts it, "Not all external percepts are 'public' in the sense that anyone fulfilling certain physical and conceptual conditions will have an experience of its seeming to them that the percept is there."

16. Thomas Nagel, in "Moral Conflict and Political Legitimacy," 16 *Philosophy and Public Affairs*, 215, 230 (1987) says about beliefs that other reasonable people can reject, "Considered as individual beliefs they may be adequately grounded, or at least not unreasonable: the standards of individual rationality are different from the standards of epistemological ethics."

17. Ronald Replogle, "Equality and Moral Uncertainty" (seminar paper for "Political Decision and Advocacy in the Liberal State," Columbia University School of Law, New York, autumn 1992), p. 21.

18. Id. at 22.

19. Id. at 23.

20. The collective force of all similar experiences might be substantial, however. It is in this sense that "religious experiences" may be taken to constitute significant evidence for the truth of some religious propositions. See Davis, supra note 11, at 66–114. In a cumulative argument for the existence of God, for example, religious experiences may count as one kind of accessible (though highly controversial) strand.

21. The incompatibility would not exist for someone who thought that other evidence (including the experiences of other people) strongly confirmed the accuracy of intuitions drawn from feelings.

22. Thomas Nagel has pointed out to me that if the issue is simply memory— I remember dessert at a dinner a year ago having been ice cream and everyone else remembers cake—it is appropriate for me to give roughly equal weight to the memory of each person involved and not to give much greater weight to my own memory. I agree. What I say in text rests on the assumption that the experiences involved are not simple memories of this kind. I have not attempted to sort through the various kinds of claims of experience on which beliefs might be grounded to divide those for which giving extra weight is appropriate from those for which giving such weight is not appropriate.

Chapter 5

1. Just how far existing materials can constrain those who in some sense are to apply and interpret the law is the subject of a wide-ranging debate in legal philosophy, one related to discussions in fields like literary theory and religious hermeneutics. My own views on that subject are in *Law and Objectivity* (New York, Oxford University Press 1992).

2. Just what is the relationship "within" the law and beyond the law of "authority reasons" and other potential reasons for decision is a complicated topic. On one view the authority reasons are exclusionary: they exclude the power of competing reasons that would otherwise be relevant for decision. See, e.g., Joseph Raz, *The Authority of Law* 16–19 (Oxford, Clarendon Press 1979); Raz, *Practical Reason and Norms* 35–49 (London, Hutchinson 1975). On another view, they always override, or almost always override, the competing reasons. See, e.g., Larry Alexander, "Law and Exclusionary Reasons," 18 *Philosophical Topics* 5 (1990).

As chapter 3 indicates, if the authoritative materials and instructions *were un-*

clear, reasons that in some sense are external to the materials might figure properly in how they should be interpreted.

3. This is a possibility explored in subsequent chapters.

4. It is *one form of coverage* for a comprehensive view to say that a subject is to be dealt with according to standards that do not depend on the distinctive comprehensive view.

5. Her position would *not necessarily be illogical if* she were less confident about her comprehensive view and its implications than about the reasons for performing her official duty. She might find herself in the position of saying something like "I think on the basis of my comprehensive view and its full application that it is 60 percent likely that it would be slightly better to violate official duty, but if I am mistaken, doing so would be a serious wrong. Therefore, I should follow the course that I am confident is not seriously wrong."

If Olive's doubt arises out of the *application* of a comprehensive view she adopts with confidence, the comprehensive view itself may take account of acting in situations of uncertain application. Then, it is possible Olive's full comprehensive view (including its recommendations for uncertainty) might approve action contrary to what she uncertainly thinks are its more direct implications for the particular situation. But suppose Olive's doubts are about the comprehensive view itself. She thinks with considerable doubt that the correct comprehensive view is utilitarianism, which weakly recommends violation of official duty that would be strongly condemned by most other comprehensive views. In this setting, it is not illogical for someone to employ a kind of probability analysis to the comprehensive view itself and act contrary to what she thinks of as the implications of the comprehensive view she finds most plausible. (One might conceive such a probability analysis as involving a kind of supracomprehensive view to deal with uncertainties about ordinary comprehensive views.)

6. Indeed, in a sense, supporting legislation with the aim to overthrow is more directly at odds with legislative responsibilities than manning the barricades, because the legislative activity engages the official role more directly.

7. I do not speak here of more complex situations in which a legislator knows that a proposed statute conflicts with a Supreme Court interpretation that he thinks is mistaken.

8. The dominant constitutional theory in the United States is that such amendments would be legal; but some scholars think that such amendments would be unconstitutional, though adopted in proper form.

9. See Kent Greenawalt, *Conflicts of Law and Morality* 62–93 (New York, Oxford University Press 1987).

10. See Oliver Wendell Holmes, "The Path of the Law," 10 *Harvard Law Review* 457, 459 (1897).

11. Unless, *perhaps,* those faiths directly promote antisocial action or preach doctrines that are highly subversive of the social order *or* of the basic premises of liberty and equality that underlie liberal democratic government.

12. School District v. Schempp, 374 U.S. 203 (1963).

13. Steven D. Smith, "The Rise and Fall of Religious Freedom in Constitutional Discourse," 140 *University of Pennsylvania Law Review* 149, 184 (1991). Professor Smith presents but does not himself endorse this position.

14. Id.

15. There is a complexity I do not explore in the text. *If* it were understood

that the government *never considered* religious reasons, then a law based on secular reasons might not "disapprove" contrary religious views. Thus, a law requiring racial integration might not "implicitly disapprove" religious segregationists' views, if all religious judgments were outside the political domain. (Still, one cannot imagine that people who think segregation is required by God would order integration for secular reasons.)

16. See Edward B. Foley, "Tillich and Camus, Talking Politics," 92 *Columbia Law Review* 954, 958–59 (1992) (review essay), who puts a similar but not identical argument.

17. Stephen L. Carter makes the closely related point that "one must distinguish between the religious motivation for a moral position that is otherwise within the power of the state to pursue and the religious motivation for a moral position that simply involves the oppression of members of other, less politically powerful faiths." *The Culture of Disbelief* 91 (New York, Basic Books 1993).

Chapter 6

1. Robert Audi, in "The Place of Religious Argument in a Free and Democratic Society," 30 *San Diego Law Review* 677, 679–83 (1993), talks of content, epistemic, and motivational criteria of religious arguments. Audi adds a historical criterion (id. at 683–85), and actually considers an antisuicide argument in discussing that. Audi apparently believes it is sufficient that the argument have a strong historical connection to religious understandings. My position is that if the argument would be understood by the speaker upon moderate self-scrutiny to rest on a religious premise, it is religious for him; similarly, if the force of the argument for a listener would upon moderate self-scrutiny rest on a religious premise, the argument would be religious for him. Presumably, under a principle of restraint, speakers should be free to advance arguments that are not religious for them even if they are religious for some listeners. For my purposes, if no one understands the force of the argument as religious, it is not a religious argument for anyone.

2. A person who grounds his entire outlook on life on the absence of any religious truth need not be *antireligious* in the sense of thinking religion is harmful or in the sense of wanting to persuade people to abandon religious beliefs. Nevertheless, such a person has an antireligious view in the sense I employ here.

My distinction between *antireligious* and *nonreligious* views raises the following problem. A *nonreligious* view does not take a stand on theological matters, but it implicitly does reject any religious claim that every nonreligious evaluation is useless. Therefore, it is "anti" some religious claims. But this view is similarly "anti" parallel antireligious claims that only atheism provides a basis for evaluation. In any event, I am taking antireligious views as ones that adopt sweeping (negative) positions on theological subjects.

3. It can be argued whether, for constitutional purposes, the government's promotion of antireligion would be an impermissible establishment of a kind of religion or a violation of free exercise of religion.

4. That is the well-developed conclusion in Edward B. Foley, "Tillich and Camus, Talking Politics," 92 *Columbia Law Review* 954 (1992) (review essay). One might believe that the threat to political life is much smaller from reliance on antireligious views (though the history of communism should give one pause); even so, the blatant discrimination of a principle that people can rely and argue on anti-

religious views but not positive religious views is too unpalatable to make such a differentiation plausible.

5. Indeed, she might find herself in the situation of knowing that religious involvement was causally important in her arriving at her present position, though she now rejects the religious premises that she accepted during the stage of that involvement.

6. See generally Foley, supra note 4, at 962. I think that Audi, see supra note 1, believes the historical connection here is sufficient to make the argument religious.

7. Robert Audi, "The Separation of Church and State and the Obligations of Citizenship," 18 *Philosophy and Public Affairs* 259 (1989); "Religion and the Ethics of Political Participation," 100 *Ethics* 386 (1990) (review essay); "The Place of Religious Argument in a Free and Democratic Society," supra note 1.

8. Audi, "The Separation of Church and State and the Obligations of Citizenship," supra note 7, at 278. In that article Audi does not address *antireligious* reasons, but the flavor of his discussion suggested to me that he thought their use was also inappropriate. He indicates that his basic principles are not themselves intended to exclude such reasons in "The Place of Religious Argument in a Free and Democratic Society," supra note 1, at 692 n.4.

9. Audi, "The Separation of Church and State and the Obligations of Citizenship," supra note 7, at 279.

10. Id. at 284 (emphasis in original).

11. In conversation, Audi has indicated that he means adequacy to depend on the actual adequacy of reasons, not a person's opinion about that. However, an individual who is told that he must rely on adequate reasons can only rely on reasons that he concludes are adequate. If a person tries hard to pay attention only to nonreligious reasons and supports a position on the basis of those reasons, it would be misleading to say that he has failed to observe a principle of restraint because his reasons turn out not to be adequate. In considering whether someone has or has not followed a principle of restraint, *his belief about the adequacy of reasons* seems to me more important than actual adequacy.

12. See Audi, "The Separation of the Church and State and the Obligations of Citizenship," supra note 7, at 286–88.

13. Id. at 280.

14. Id. at 279.

15. Audi, supra note 1, at 685–86, 696.

16. These two are close, but there is a difference between my wanting to let you know the deep roots of my concerns (communicative) and my wanting to express those directly to you (expressive).

17. Although he does not limit persuasive religious argument to this, Audi suggests, supra note 1, at 695, that *my* pointing out to you what *your* religious commitments require need not imply that the religious grounds are correct. That is true, but such arguments nevertheless may make it harder for listeners to discern what secular reasons require. Further, if I happen to share your religious views, my pointing out what your views require is hardly distinguishable in practice from my pointing out to you what "correct" views require.

18. Audi has suggested in correspondence that he has conceived the place of "persuasive" religious arguments as "restricted largely, though not entirely, to contexts in which all present share a religious perspective."

19. Audi says that "coercing a person, *S*, for reason *R*, to perform an action *A*, in circumstances *C*, is fully justified if and only if at least the following three conditions hold in *C*: (a) *S* morally ought to *A* in *C* . . . (b) if fully rational and adequately informed about the situation, *S* would . . . for reason *R* (. . . or for some essentially related reason), perform *A*, or at least tend to *A*; (c) *A* is both an 'important' kind of action . . . and one that may be reasonably believed to affect someone else." Supra note 1, at 688–89. Audi is aware that this surrogacy conception of justified coercion, which he sketches, might well exclude other bases for decisions besides religious ones. Id. at 690.

20. Foley, supra note 4.

21. William P. Marshall, "The Other Side of Religion," 44 *Hastings Law Journal* 843 (1993).

22. Foley, supra note 4, at 957.

23. Id. at 958.

24. Id. at 968.

25. Id. at 977.

26. Id. at 980–81.

27. Marshall, supra note 21, at 844.

28. In *On Liberty,* where John Stuart Mill passionately argues that people should not *condemn* others for their self-regarding acts, he also recognizes that the freedom of those who deem behavior unwholesome or abhorrent requires that *they* be able to tell the actor their opinions, to avoid his company, and to recommend that others also avoid his company.

29. The Presbyterian Church (U.S.A.), "God Alone is Lord of the Conscience: A Policy Statement Adopted by the 200th General Assembly" 48 (1989). See also National Conference of Catholic Bishops, "Economic Justice for All: Pastoral Letter on Catholic Social Teaching and the U.S. Economy" (Washington, D.C., United States Catholic Conference 1986); Martin E. Marty, *The Public Church: Mainline, Evangelical, Catholic* 98 (New York, Crossroads 1981). See generally Stephen L. Carter, *The Culture of Disbelief* (New York, BasicBooks 1993).

30. The competing values are eloquently evoked in Daniel O. Conkle, "God Loveth Adverbs," 42 *DePaul Law Review* 339, 345 (1992).

31. Audi is clear, as are other authors proposing restraints, that his principles are ones of *self*-restraint; liberty of religion for him consists partly in the freedom not to abide by such principles if one so chooses.

32. See, e.g., Steven D. Smith, "The Rise and Fall of Religious Freedom in Constitutional Discourse," 140 *University of Pennsylvania Law Review* 149, 167–80 (1991). This is not a position Smith accepts.

33. If the executive branch proposes legislation, it speaks for a part of the government in a way an individual legislator does not. Its direct use of religious grounds in formal documents proposing legislation would offend separation of church and state. How to view the situation when the president speaks "on his own" is more difficult.

34. Foley suggests that religious adherents who reject self-critical rationality will reject secular politics, supra note 4, at 972, and that adherents who accept self-critical rationality will suppose that affirmation or rejection of religious faith does not affect the substance of politics, id. at 979. Audi, supra note 1, at 697, says that "liberal democracy is or at least should be committed to the *conceptual and epistemic autonomy of ethics*." Matters seem to me more complicated. One might be self-critical and rational about one's approach to religion, and still think that one's best

religious judgment significantly affected one's political conclusions. Such a person could be a fully committed liberal democrat without thinking that ethics are autonomous from religion. In the Liberal Coalition group were persons who accepted self-critical rationality but rejected a wholly secular politics. Among the Diverse Believers were people who rejected self-critical rationality, but wanted secular politics as a protection.

35. Ruti Teitel writes, for example, "The departure from the prevailing separation model of church and state toward an acceptance of substantial religious representation in public life will ultimately threaten religious equality and pluralism." Teitel, "A Critique of Religion as Politics in the Public Sphere," 78 *Cornell Law Review* 747, 748 (1993). If, as I believe, religious factors now play a more important part in politics than Professor Teitel's idea of a "prevailing separation model" suggests, nonetheless, she could still be correct that *more* religious involvement in politics would have the harmful consequences she fears.

36. Marshall, supra note 21.

37. Id. at 852.

38. Id. at 854.

39. Id. at 858.

40. Id. at 859.

Chapter 7

1. If any use of tax money is regarded as coercing those whose money is used, then almost every action of the state coerces.

2. Thomas Nagel, "Moral Conflict and Political Legitimacy," 16 *Philosophy and Public Affairs* 215 (1987).

3. Thomas Nagel, *Equality and Partiality* 163 n.49 (New York, Oxford University Press 1991).

4. Joseph Raz, "Facing Diversity: The Case of Epistemic Abstinence," 19 *Philosophy and Public Affairs* 3, 3–4, 31–46 (1990).

5. Nagel, supra note 2, at 229.

6. In a sense, the heretic would also be treated impartially if he received appropriate retributive punishment for heinous wrongful acts or thoughts.

7. Nagel, supra note 2, at 230.

8. Id. at 230–32.

9. Id. at 223–24.

10. Id. at 227.

11. Id. at 232. Nagel makes clear that his argument does not depend on skepticism about the possible truth of conclusions arrived at by means other than common grounds of reason; it depends only on the inappropriateness of coercing others on the basis of reasons other than publicly available arguments. Id. at 223–25.

12. Id. at 233.

13. Id.

14. Id. at 234.

15. Id. at 235. David Richards reaches a similar conclusion when he writes that values internal to religious traditions are not necessarily "shared in the wider society, and are not therefore publicly accessible to all in the way that Lockean political legitimacy requires for their enforcement on the community at large." Richards, 23 *Georgia Law Review* 1189, 1197 (1989) (book review). See also Ken-

neth I. Winston, "The Religious Convictions of Public Officials," 3 *Canadian Journal of Law and Jurisprudence* 129, 132–34 (1990).

16. Raz, supra note 4. Interestingly, Nagel himself recognizes that some religious believers "might claim objective status for certain theological arguments or forms of revelation." Nagel, supra note 2, at 236.

17. Raz, supra note 4, at 41.

18. See generally Caroline Franks Davis, *The Evidential Force of Religious Experience* (Oxford, Clarendon Press 1989).

19. It would be more accurate to speak of individuals on particular subjects. People who are overmodest about the reach of reason on one subject may claim too much for reason on other subjects.

20. In his 1987 article, Nagel clearly meant to preclude political reliance on religious and other personal convictions whether or not what I have called imposition is present. In his more recent book, *Equality and Partiality,* supra note 3, at 163–68, he concentrates on acts that directly involve a lack of liberal toleration. He comments that he still believes in "the conclusion" of the earlier article though not its particular argument, at 163 n.49, but it is not quite clear how broad the conclusion is in which Nagel still believes. Thus, the book does not plainly indicate whether Nagel continues to believe that reliance on religious grounds is inappropriate in the hunting and welfare examples, and more importantly whether he thinks the *reasons* he now provides cover those examples. I am doubtful that his present reasons reach as broadly as those in the original article.

21. To be more precise, they would have to be commonly shared and be either underlying political principles or accessible to reason. Thus, if 95 percent of the population had similar religious inspirations of an intuitive kind, they could not rely upon those to coerce the other 5 percent. What grounds are accessible to reason will turn out to be somewhat dependent on deep assumptions about reason and basic values within the society.

22. John Rawls, "Kantian Constructivism in Moral Theory: The Dewey Lectures 1980," 77 *Journal of Philosophy* 515, 539 (1980).

23. Charles Larmore, *Patterns of Moral Complexity* x (New York, Cambridge University Press 1987).

24. Lawrence B. Solum, "Faith and Justice," 39 *DePaul Law Review* 1083, 1090 (1990).

25. See Bruce Ackerman, *Social Justice in the Liberal State* 10–11 (New Haven, Conn., Yale University Press 1980). I pay less attention to Ackerman's views than I otherwise would because I comment on them at some length in *Religious Convictions and Political Choice* (New York, Oxford University Press 1988).

26. Contrary to Ackerman, Solum would permit private citizens to advocate and vote on religious and similar bases. He does not say whether a legislator's relying upon the conclusions of constituents, what they think is good or right, is appropriate if the legislator avoids *endorsement* of their grounds. E.g., Leslie says: "Lacking other compelling grounds, I will vote for a restrictive abortion law because most of my constituents are Roman Catholic and favor it." From what Solum does say, I would assume this is *a* legitimate public reason for him. If it is not, a citizen's advocacy on religious grounds would be rather futile, except to help elect candidates who happen to have views about what public reason requires that fit with the citizen's religious views.

27. See Charles Larmore, "Political Liberalism," 18 *Political Theory* 339, 341–42 (1990).

A *possible* difference is that only Nagel's approach might exclude some intuitive personal convictions that are not tied to ideas of the good, but it seems unlikely that those who favor a decision that is neutral between controversial ideas of the good really mean to allow reliance on other free-floating personal intuitions; certainly the idea of "public reason" (emphasized so heavily by Rawls—see John Rawls, "The Domain of the Political and Overlapping Consensus," 64 *New York University Law Review* 233 (1989)—and drawn upon by Solum) would exclude such intuitions.

28. Rawls is clear and careful about this. His views are not the central focus in *this chapter* because his proposed principle of exclusion from politics is narrower in the subject matter it reaches.

29. The sentence in the text assumes that homosexual acts between adults should not be criminal. If a "personal life style" involves activities that are properly criminal, it is arguable whether those engaging in them deserve equal respect.

30. Relatedly, schoolteachers tend to hold up exemplars of useful lives in a manner that is hard to justify if public school representatives should be completely neutral about controversial conceptions of the good life.

31. There is an argument that funding of museums and operas is justified because, otherwise, particular forms of art might die out; but no one suggests that the government should spend a lot of money on "worthless" forms of art that might die out. The worry about extinction, thus, is insufficient to sustain aid absent any judgment about comparative value.

32. Since it is expected that *the state itself* will be neutral among religious claims even in education and subsidies, a plausible principle of neutrality among conceptions of the good may have less coverage than a plausible principle about religious conceptions.

33. Larmore, supra note 23, at 43. See also Charles Larmore, "Political Liberalism," supra note 27, at 339–60.

34. Larmore, supra note 23, at 46.

35. Id. at 44.

36. Id. at 43.

37. Larmore suggests that when full neutrality makes a decision impossible, something less is appropriate, but the aim should be to make an abridgment of neutrality as small as possible. Id. at 67–68.

38. Id. at 51. At this point, Larmore parts company with Bruce Ackerman who, he says, talks of the self-conscious value of affirmations of autonomous individuals.

39. Id. at 53.

40. Id. at 59.

41. Id. at 61. In "Political Liberalism," supra note 27, at 347, Larmore talks of "two norms of rational dialogue and equal respect" as "[t]he best justification of liberal neutrality of which I know."

42. Larmore, supra note 23, at 63–64.

43. Id. at 65.

44. Solum, supra note 24, at 1091–92.

45. Id. at 1087, 1092.

46. Id. at 1092.

47. Id. at 1093.

48. Id. at 1096.

49. I had taken the discussion in *Patterns of Moral Complexity* as an *argument*

for the principle of equal respect, but Larmore has said to me that he offered it only as *clarification*. In "Political Liberalism," supra note 27, at 357, he says that he has no "ready answer" to how to justify the principle of equal respect to those who do not already accept it. However, Larmore does not regard this concession as undermining the viability of political liberalism because the principle is accepted both by modern individualists *and* by those who assert Romantic values in criticism of individualism.

50. The latter point assumes that respect would naturally be based on exercise of the capacity *in some way* rather than mere possession of an unexercised capacity.

51. See supra note 49. Jeffrie Murphy, who finds it "very difficult—perhaps impossible—to embrace religious convictions" has suggested that "the liberal theory of rights requires a doctrine of human dignity, preciousness and sacredness that cannot be utterly detached from a belief in God or at least from a world view that would be properly called religious in some metaphysically profound sense." Murphy, "Afterword: Constitutionalism, Moral Skepticism, and Religious Belief," in Alan S. Rosenbaum, ed., *Constitutionalism: The Philosophical Dimension* 240, 248 (New York, Greenwood Press 1988).

52. Solum actually makes the argument in the context of judicial decision, including constitutional decision. In that context, his claim must face the competing argument that, in the absence of a decisive pubic reason to invalidate a statute, a court should accept the statute as valid. If a statute represses liberty, a court that favors liberty may reach a result contrary to that of a court that favors legislative choice. I disregard this special feature and consider the argument in the context of original legislative choice.

53. Solum, supra note 24, at 1102. See also Winston, supra note 15, at 134.

54. Amy Gutmann and Dennis Thompson, "Moral Conflict and Political Consensus," 101 *Ethics* 64, 68 (1990).

55. See John Rawls, *Political Liberalism* (New York, Columbia University Press 1993). I think he assumes these liberal views take no position on some basic theological questions, but that is of comparative unimportance here.

56. Similarly, one might say happiness is valued in common reason even if it is not the center of moral and political inquiry, as it is in a "greatest happiness utilitarian" comprehensive view.

Chapter 8

1. Franklin Gamwell, "Religion and Reason in American Politics," 2 *Journal of Law and Religion* 325 (1984); Gamwell, "Book Review: *Religious Convictions and Political Choice*," 8 *Journal of Law and Religion* 461 (1990).

2. Gamwell, "Religion and Reason in American Politics," supra note 1, at 340.

3. Id. at 341.

4. Id. at 339.

5. Of course, someone might hold a belief that is sound in the sense that it *could* be rationally grounded, even though the believer holds the belief for an unsound reason. Someone might believe pigs are intelligent because Wilbur was able to converse in E. B. White's *Charlotte's Web;* it may be shown on scientific grounds that pigs are highly intelligent animals.

6. I am assuming that these beliefs will be expressed and considered in realms of culture other than politics.

7. One might discern an implication that part of what we *owe to fellow citizens*

is subjecting political arguments to the measure of rationality; but Gamwell does not make such an argument explicitly.

8. Gamwell, "Religion and Reason in American Politics," supra note 1, at 338.

9. Id. at 333.

10. I pass over the possibility that if a principle of exclusion covered all comprehensive views or all controversial ideas of the good, rather than all religious views or all nonaccessible grounds for decision, some natural ethical arguments *might* be excluded or have their force diminished (in the manner described in chapter 7 that Millian arguments about human welfare might have their force diminished).

11. Michael Perry, *Love and Power* (New York, Oxford University Press 1991).

12. Id. at 17. Perry's comments here are critical of the attention I give in *Religious Convictions and Political Choice* to bases of judgment. Most theorists who urge self-restraint do not believe that coercion grounded in religiously based (or other relevant) judgments is appropriate, whether or not these judgments are offered as public justifications. So, bases of judgment matter for most theorists.

13. Perry's position in the book is that some religious arguments are appropriate in the public domain but that others are not—for example, a claimed mandate from God drawn from a biblical text. Whether officials properly *rely* on grounds that correspond to the *inappropriate* arguments is a serious question, which arises both when officials themselves believe in such grounds and when they think that citizens believe in such grounds. Further, if political *judgments* on certain grounds are proper, then, at the least, discussions within the "community of believers" of the political implications of beliefs leading to such judgments are also proper. Thus, the problem of proper bases of political judgment for citizens is directly tied to grounds for political positions that are appropriately argued within such smaller communities. One cannot escape the conclusion that reliance and argument are both important issues, and that neither is marginal.

14. Perry, supra note 11, at 14.

15. Id. at 31.

16. Id. at 35.

17. Id. at 39–40.

18. Id. at 77.

19. Id. at 73.

20. Id. at 74.

21. Id. at 92.

22. Id. at 95, 97.

23. Id. at 101. Amy Gutmann and Dennis Thompson have suggested that political dialogue in liberal democracies should be governed by principles of accommodation based on mutual respect. For them, "Mutual respect manifests a distinctively democratic kind of character—the character of individuals who are morally committed, self-reflective about their commitments, discerning of the difference between respectable and merely tolerable differences of opinion, and open to the possibility of changing their minds or modifying their positions at some time in the future if they confront unanswerable objections to their present point of view." Amy Gutmann and Dennis Thompson, "Moral Conflict and Political Consensus," 101 *Ethics* 64, 76 (1990).

24. Perry, supra note 11, at 104.

25. Id. at 106.

26. Id. at 109–10. Although they would admit some moral positions that citizens cannot decide rationally (so long as the positions are not radically implausible), Amy Gutmann and Dennis Thompson, supra note 23, at 71, argue that such appeals as to biblical infallibility "must be rejected as moral reasons [because] they close off any possibility of publicly assessing or interpreting the content of the claims put forward by the authority." Id. at 70.

27. Perry, supra note 11, at 110.

28. Id. at 120 (emphasis omitted).

29. Id. at 124.

30. Id. at 133–34.

31. Id. at 135–36.

32. This point is treated in Edward Foley, "Tillich and Camus, Talking Politics," 92 *Columbia Law Review* 954, 962–63 (1992) (review essay).

33. However, when believers make such statements, it is more difficult to know *whether* they are relying on religious premises, relying either in the sense of meaning to communicate such reliance or in the sense of feeling that the use of religious imagery and references to tradition would not be valuable unless related theological premises were true.

34. Perry, supra note 11, at 106. The relevant passage is in the text accompanying note 25, supra. It may matter how widely "one's community" is understood. Conceivably an argument about God that appeals to many theists of different religious persuasions, or a historical claim in favor of the resurrection of Jesus that appeals to many Christians of different denominations has authority beyond the confines of one's (relevant) community.

35. Id. at 109.

36. Id. at 120. I note in passing that so long as one accepts the fallibility of one's own understanding of what is true and is open to revision of that understanding, a probabilistic belief that God has communicated infallibly would not violate the fallibilism standard that Perry posits.

37. Perry criticized the suggestion that in the public forum Roman Catholics should speak in universal naturalistic language in part because that denuding of religious content would drive a wedge between internal deliberation and external deliberation. Given Perry's own fairly severe constraints of public accessibility, much that is relevant to internal deliberation of members of many religious communities will still be excised from deliberation with the broader audience.

38. Perry, supra note 11, at 45.

39. Robin Lovin, "Perry, Naturalism, and Religion in Public," 63 *Tulane Law Review* 1517, 1525 (1989).

40. Id. at 1530.

41. To illustrate the religious aim of proclamation, Lovin talks of a Mennonite farmer who declares his religious reasons for supplying fresh vegetables to soup kitchens. Id. at 1528. Since the farmer's comments do not involve advocacy on political issues, no principle of restraint for such advocacy would cast doubt on their appropriateness. When the speaker's *main aim* is religious conversion, id. at 1529–30, no principle would bar his explaining his religious perspectives for political judgments. Principles of restraint discussed in this book would bar expressed reliance on religious grounds only when the context is primarily political debate. Lovin apparently thinks that the aim of conversion is important even in that context. The third religious aim he mentions is the articulation of an idea of the human good. Id. at 1530–32. So long as explicitly religious arguments were not made, a

principle of restraint about religious grounds would not preclude one's speaking convictions that bear on this in political debates.

Chapter 9

1. David Smolin, "Regulating Religious and Cultural Conflict in a Postmodern America: A Response to Professor Perry," 76 *Iowa Law Review* 1067 (1991). See also Smolin, "The Judeo-Christian Tradition and Self-Censorship in Legal Discourse," 13 *University of Dayton Law Review* 345 (1988); Smolin, "The Enforcement of Natural Law by the State: A Response to Professor Calhoun," 16 *University of Dayton Law Review* 381 (1991).

2. Smolin, "Regulating Religious and Cultural Conflict in a Postmodern America," supra note 1, at 1079.

3. Id. at 1080.

4. Id. at 1086.

5. Id. at 1096–97.

6. Id. at 1085–86.

7. According to Smolin, the religion clauses were originally meant "to regulate competition between Christian denominations." Id. at 1069. Prominent jurists and unanimous opinions of the Supreme Court during the nineteenth century proclaimed that America is a Christian nation and that the Christian religion is part of the common law. Id. at 1070–71. (Smolin discusses Vidal v. Girard's Executors, 43 U.S. 126 (1844), and Church of the Holy Trinity v. United States, 143 U.S. 457 (1892).) Smolin writes, "Culturally, the concept of government neutrality represents a change in the self-identity of the nation, because it renders the previously dominant concept of a 'Christian America' heretical and repugnant." Id. at 1072.

8. Id. at 1103. In the course of his discussion Smolin implies that prayers at graduations of public high schools should be acceptable, see id. at 1097, 1103, and that public funding of religious schools should be deemed appropriate under a voucher plan that would enhance parental control of their children's educations. Id. at 1103. Scholars widely assume that many fewer practices would be held invalid under a coercion test than under the prevailing three-part test.

9. Id. at 1099. This passage and another that remarks on the fear of strict separationists "that America will in fact again become in substance a Christian nation," id. at 1097, led me to believe that Smolin favored a return to the nineteenth-century conception of the United States as a Christian nation, but he has told me that this conclusion was erroneous.

10. Id. at 1076–77.

11. Id. at 1077–78.

12. Id. at 1079.

13. Michael Perry, *Love and Power* 140 (New York, Oxford University Press 1992).

14. See Smolin, "Regulating Religious and Cultural Conflict in Postmodern America," supra note 1, at 1085; Smolin, "The Enforcement of Natural Law by the State," supra note 1, at 381, 410–11.

15. In a letter to me of May 5, 1994, Smolin says, "My own religious and comprehensive views, like Perry's, suggest restraints—it is just that I would not impose those restraints on others." I remain uncertain whether there are *any* restraints Smolin would think could be said to be generally applicable—such as honesty. I am also unsure how far Smolin thinks the "restraints" concerning public

grounds of argument that he draws from his religious views are genuine restraints of principle or counsels of prudence. I explore this distinction in later chapters.

16. Smolin, "Regulating Religious and Cultural Conflict in a Postmodern America," supra note 1, at 1088.

17. Id. at 1093.

18. Id. at 1102–03. Another aspect of Smolin's work is an emphasis on parental rights over education as a means of ensuring that cultural and religious groups can pass on their way of life to the next generation.

19. If one compares the vitality of religion in the United States with that in European countries with various forms of religious establishment, one will not leap to the conclusion that government support and religiosity correlate positively.

There is an argument that goes thus: "Whether or not Christianity is true, moral practices degenerate without religious backing; since Christianity is the dominant religion here, the state should support it publicly in the interests of civil morality and acceptance of the legitimacy of law." This argument, akin to what Rousseau said about civil religion in *The Social Contract*, is comprehensible and coherent; but I do not believe many people offer it seriously in this day and age, *unless* they also believe something is true or good about Christianity. Timothy Hall has suggested that modern American society largely replicates the disagreement at the time of the country's founding over the importance of religion for civic virtue. Hall, "Religion and Civic Virtue: A Justification of Free Exercise," 67 *Tulane Law Review* 87, 107 (1992). Two modern writers claiming that the connection between law an religion is critical for legitimacy are Harold Berman, "The Interaction of Law and Religion," 31 *Mercer Law Review* 405 (1980), and Dennis Lloyd, *The Idea of Law* (Baltimore, Penguin Books 1964).

20. See Samuel W. Calhoun, "Misreading the Judeo-Christian Tradition and the Law: A Response to Professor Smolin," 15 *University of Dayton Law Review* 383 (1990); Calhoun, "Conviction Without Imposition: A Response to Professor Greenawalt," 9 *Journal of Law and Religion* 289 (1992) (arguing from his own religious premises that my acceptance of people voting on the basis of their religious convictions allows too much imposition of religious positions on nonbelievers).

21. Smolin, "Regulating Religious and Cultural Conflict in a Postmodern America," supra note 1, at 1091.

22. Maimon Schwarzschild, "Religion and Public Debate in a Liberal Society: Always Oil and Water or Sometimes More Like Rum and Coca-Cola?" 30 *San Diego Law Review* 903 (1993).

23. Id. at 911.

24. Id. at 915.

25. Jeremy Waldron, "Religious Contributions in Public Deliberation," 30 *San Diego Law Review* 817, 835–39 (1993).

26. Id. at 836.

27. Id.

28. Id. at 846–48.

29. Sanford Levinson, "Religious Language and the Public Square," 105 *Harvard Law Review* 2061, 2062 (1992) (book review).

30. Id. at 2077. See also Robert M. Van Wyck, "Liberalism, Religion and Politics," 1 *Public Affairs Quarterly*, July 1987, at 59–76.

31. Daniel Conkle, "Different Religions, Different Politics: Evaluating the

Role of Competing Religious Traditions in American Politics and Law," 10 *Journal of Law and Religion* 1, 2 (1993).

32. Id.

33. Id. at 15.

34. Id. at 18.

35. Id. at 21.

36. Steven D. Smith, "Separation and the 'Secular': Reconstructing the Disestablishment Decision," 67 *Texas Law Review* 955, 1015 (1989). Compare Smolin, "Regulating Religious and Cultural Conflict in Postmodern America," supra note 1, at 1085–86.

37. See, e.g., Schwarzschild, supra note 22, at 915.

38. Larry Alexander, "Liberalism, Religion, and the Unity of Epistemology," 30 *San Diego Law Review* 763 (1993).

39. Id. at 789–90.

40. Smith, supra note 36, at 1010.

41. Stephen L. Carter, "Evolutionism, Creationism, and Treating Religion as a Hobby," 1987 *Duke Law Journal* 977. See also Stephen L. Carter, *The Culture of Disbelief* 155–82 (New York, Basic Books 1993).

42. Carter, "Evolutionism, Creationism, and Treating Religion as a Hobby," supra note 41, at 980.

43. Id. at 978.

44. Frederick Mark Gedicks, "Public Life and Hostility to Religion," 78 *Virginia Law Review* 671, 686 (1992).

45. Michael J. Perry, "Further Thoughts—And Second Thoughts—On *Love and Power*," 30 *San Diego Law Review* 702, 713–16 (1993).

46. Id. at 717–18. Perry endorses Larry Alexander's assertion of the unity of epistemology, denying that religious beliefs have an inferior epistemological status. He claims that even when religious grounds are the sole bases for state coercion, this is not invariably divisive or destabilizing, and he says that although some religious styles may improperly deny respect to fellow citizens, many do not.

47. Id. at 718–19. Perry also notes Hollenbach's recognition that " 'it is . . . neither possible nor desirable to construct an airtight barrier between politics and culture.' " Id. at 722 (quoting David Hollenbach, "Contexts of the Political Role of Religion: Civil Society and Culture," 30 *San Diego Law Review* 877, 900 (1993)).

48. Id. at 726.

49. Id. at 714.

Chapter 10

1. Rawls has increasingly focused on this subject, and his views have crystallized over time. Relying mainly on what he said in *A Theory of Justice* (Cambridge, Mass., Harvard University Press 1971), I concluded in *Religious Convictions and Political Choice* 51–54 (New York, Oxford University Press 1988), that he probably thought the relevant bases for all political decisions involving justice, and perhaps for all political decisions, should be limited to "the shared principles of justice 'and practices of common sense and science.' " By the winter of 1990, having seen his recent published work and work in progress, I understood him to believe that when issues involve constitutional essentials, "political power should be exercised 'only in ways that all citizens can reasonably be expected to endorse publicly in

the light of their own common, human reason.' " Greenawalt, "Religious Convictions and Political Choice: Some Further Thoughts," 39 *DePaul Law Review* 1019, 1038 (1990), quoting from Rawls, "The Domain of the Political and Overlapping Consensus," 64 *New York University Law Review* 233, 244 (1989). I assumed that given his own theory of justice, the constitutional essentials would include "matters relating to fair opportunity and distribution of wealth as well as basic liberties." Greenawalt, supra at 1039. Rawls's most recent work, *Political Liberalism* (New York, Columbia University Press 1993), indicates that his view of constitutional essentials is actually much narrower than all that is covered by his own basic principles of justice, which include fair equality of opportunity and the "difference principle." In presenting his views in this chapter, I concentrate on this most recent published work.

Rawls continues to think deeply about the problem of public reason, and some of his positions have shifted to a degree in work in progress. I have generally not referred to this work, because it has not yet reached a final form.

2. Rawls, *A Theory of Justice*, supra note 1. Rawls did not assert that he had arrived at *the best principles,* but he seemed to be aiming for such principles, with those he presented as the best he could do.

3. Rawls, "Justice as Fairness: Political not Metaphysical," 14 *Philosophy and Public Affairs* 223, 230 (1985).

4. See Rawls, "The Domain of the Political and Overlapping Consensus," supra note 1; Rawls, "The Idea of an Overlapping Consensus," 7 *Oxford Journal of Legal Studies* 1 (1987); Rawls, *Political Liberalism*, supra note 1, at 133–72.

5. Rawls, "The Domain of the Political and Overlapping Consensus," supra note 1, at 234; see Rawls, *Political Liberalism*, supra note 1, at 140–41.

6. Rawls lists the following social and historical conditions of modern democracies:

> (1) [T]he fact of pluralism; (2) the fact of the permanence of pluralism, given democratic institutions; (3) the fact that agreement on a single comprehensive doctrine presupposes the oppressive use of state power. . . . (4) the fact that an enduring and stable democratic regime, one not divided into contending factions and hostile classes, must be willingly and freely supported by a substantial majority of at least its politically active citizens; (5) the fact that a comprehensive doctrine, whenever widely, if not universally, shared in society, tends to become oppressive and stifling; (6) the fact that reasonably favourable conditions (administrative, economic, technological and the like), which make democracy possible, exist; and finally, (7) the fact that the political culture of a society with a democratic tradition implicitly contains certain fundamental intuitive ideas from which it is possible to work up a political conception of justice suitable for a constitutional regime.

Rawls, "The Idea of an Overlapping Consensus," supra note 4, at 4–5 n.7. See also Rawls, "The Domain of the Political and Overlapping Consensus," supra note 1, at 234–35.

7. Id. at 239.

8. Of course, if one thought that creating a theocracy was important enough, one might accept a high degree of disruption to implement it and be willing to impose it on that large part of the population opposed to it.

Many *reflective* comprehensive views do not endorse strong methods to inculcate ideals upon those subscribing to different comprehensive views.

9. "A doctrine is fully comprehensive when it covers all recognized values and virtues within one precisely rather articulated scheme of thought; whereas a doctrine is only partially comprehensive when it comprises certain (but not all) nonpolitical values and virtues and is rather loosely articulated." *Political Liberalism*, supra note 1, at 175.

10. Id. at 155.

11. Justice as fairness, Rawls's conception of justice, is thus *not the application* of any particular comprehensive moral doctrine. "The Domain of the Political and Overlapping Consensus," supra note 1, at 241–42. It is, however, a "moral conception," see Rawls, "The Idea of an Overlapping Consensus," supra note 4, at 11, not just the consequence of what happens to amount to a consensus. See also Rawls, "The Domain of the Political and Overlapping Consensus," supra note 1, at 234.

12. Rawls, *Political Liberalism*, supra note 1, at 62. See id. at 226.

13. Id. at 58.

14. See Michael Perry, *Love and Power* (New York, Oxford University Press 1991).

15. See Joseph Raz, "Facing Diversity: The Case of Epistemic Abstinence," 19 *Philosophy and Public Affairs* 3 (1990).

16. Rawls, *Political Liberalism*, supra note 1, at 213.

17. Id. at 224.

18. Id. at 243. See Rawls, "The Domain of the Political and Overlapping Consensus," supra note 1, at 243–44.

19. Rawls, *Political Liberalism*, supra note 1, at 235.

20. Id. at 215.

21. Id. at 214.

22. Id. at 226.

23. Id. at 227.

24. Fair equality of opportunity requires that people have roughly equal chances to realize their natural capacities; the difference principle permits inequalities of income and wealth only insofar as these benefit a representative person in the worst-off group in the society.

25. Rawls, *Political Liberalism*, supra note 1, at 228–29.

26. Id. at 230.

27. Rawls is thinking about decisions of legal issues. I am not sure whether he thinks Supreme Court justices, or judges more generally, are limited to public reasons in *all* the functions they perform. Rawls concentrates on the Supreme Court, but he also speaks more generally of "the judiciary." See id. at 216.

28. *Some* judicial opinions do draw implicitly or explicitly from community morality or forms of normative evaluation that reach beyond interpretations of preexisting standards. I discuss these matters in chapter 13 of this book and at greater length in *Law and Objectivity* 163–231 (New York, Oxford University Press 1992).

29. Yet, in Roe v. Wade, 410 U.S. 113 (1973), for example, the Court's opinion surveys historical attitudes toward abortion.

30. Rawls does say that the ideal of public reason "applies in official forums and so to legislators when they speak on the floor of parliament, and to the execu-

tive in its public acts and pronouncements," *Political Liberalism*, supra note 1, at 216, but this comment does not focus on the possible coverage of a requirement beyond constitutional essentials and matters of basic justice.

31. Id. at 214.

32. Id. at 228–29.

33. On page 229 of id., at n.10, he says, "Political discussions of the reasons for and against fair opportunity and the difference principle, though they are not constitutional essentials, fall under questions of basic justice and so are to be decided by the political values of public reason." Although the reader senses that the effort to decide what falls within the constitutional essentials is important for the constraints of public reason, it turns out that that effort does not really matter when a subject falls within questions of basic justice.

34. Id. at 215.

35. Id. at 235.

36. Id. at 215.

37. Id. at 215–20.

38. I take "public advocacy" as involving an expression, which others may read or hear, of the basis of one's view. One may, instead, conceive of voting as a form of advocacy, although secret voting does not reveal even one's overall conclusion and open voting (taken alone) does not indicate the basis for one's conclusion.

39. Rawls, *Political Liberalism*, supra note 1, at 217.

40. Id. at 243. See also id. at 226–27, 246.

41. This belief is based partly on correspondence with Rawls. See also id. at 241, which makes clear that a person must sincerely think his view is based on political values others can reasonably be expected to endorse. This passage does not quite cover the situation of conflicting values, but it supports the conclusion I have reached.

42. Id. at 248. However, when a society is well ordered, with a firm overlapping consensus and an absence of deep disputes, citizens will honor the ideal of public reason by appealing to the values of the shared political conception. In drafts of work since *Political Liberalism*, Rawls has approved a more extensive use of arguments that are not based on public reason.

43. Raz, supra note 15, at 30.

44. State prohibitions may reach religious practices, like snake handling, that are deemed to cause some secular harm.

45. See the discussion in chapter 9.

46. Of course, yet another logical possibility is that this view is the one a balance of public reasons would yield. I do not consider this possibility because it would eliminate (for this example) the problem I am addressing.

47. It is much more likely that a proponent of less strict separation would concede that his position deviated from a model of church-state separation than a model of religious liberty. That is, he would be more likely to concede some compromises with separation than some compromises with liberty.

48. Rawls may well regard claims that the state should promote a particular religion as in conflict with any plausible account of the constitutional essentials. He indicates that any view that would use state power "to enforce" a particular religious position is unreasonable. (The comprehensive view itself is unreasonable in that it could not fit within the overlapping consensus that might support the basic essentials of liberal democracy.) *Political Liberalism*, supra note 1, at 138. Promoting is not the same as enforcing, but an assertion that the state should pro-

mote one doctrine may be unreasonable in Rawls's special sense of not fitting with the essentials of fair social cooperation among equals.

49. See id. at 229–30.

50. Id. at 243 n.32.

51. Rawls apparently thinks it is all right for someone's *evaluation of public reasons* to be colored by one's comprehensive view, since he says that my notion that citizens might be required to "pluck out their religious convictions" does not represent his view. Id. at 244 n.33. What citizens are apparently not to do on constitutional essentials and questions of basic justice is to go against the balance of public reasons as they see them.

52. I do not have an opinion about the extent to which a conviction about abortion *should* affect one's view of fetal research and implantation. Gregory Gelfand and Toby R. Levin, "Fetal Tissue Research: Legal Regulation of Human Fetal Tissue Transplantation," 50 *Washington and Lee Law Review* 647, 649 (1993), claim that opponents of abortion have no plausible basis to oppose fetal tissue research. I present the problem here as an example of a relation between "constitutional" and "ordinary" problems that often exists. For an illuminating set of comments on the relation of religion to bioethics more generally, see Daniel Callahan and Courtney S. Campbell, eds., *Theology, Religious Traditions, and Bioethics,* Hastings Center Report, July/August 1990, Special Supplement.

53. Rawls, "The Domain of the Political and Overlapping Consensus," supra note 1, at 234.

54. See, e.g., Amy Gutmann and Dennis Thompson, "Moral Conflict and Political Consensus," 101 *Ethics* 64, 86–88 (1990). Professors Gutmann and Thompson emphasize, however, the importance of respect for diversity.

Chapter 11

1. If an authoritative text had highly detailed instructions about how to carry on one's personal life but only broad and vague generalities about political organization, the modes of interpretation might differ significantly, even for someone who thought all correct answers came down to correct interpretation of the text.

2. Since political beliefs do not have the supremacy of religious beliefs, it may be doubted if they will serve as a check on what is believable in the religious realm; but many people have a confidence about certain political beliefs that does make them hesitant to accept incompatible religious perspectives. John Rawls comments on this in "The Idea of an Overlapping Consensus," 7 *Oxford Journal of Legal Studies* 1, 19 (1987).

3. This distinction between negative and positive linkage is somewhat artificial. A positive way to put the "negative check" linkage is that we reason from our beliefs about facts and ethics to help decide what is true in religion and political philosophy.

4. In all areas of human understanding, intuitive grasp may be important to discovery; but sometimes the grasp is subject to clear interpersonal techniques of demonstration or argument; sometimes it may not be.

5. One important reason for such a belief, developed with considerable richness by John Rawls and discussed in previous chapters, is that once one accepts the basic requisites of liberal democracy, one may conclude that a theory of justice must appeal to persons with a variety of comprehensive views.

6. Rawls, citing Walter Burkert, *Greek Religion* (Cambridge, Mass., Harvard

University Press 1985), points out that when Greek moral philosophy began, the civic religion of public social practice had no particular idea of the highest good. John Rawls, *Political Liberalism* xxi–xxii (New York, Columbia University Press 1993).

7. Is this true not only for what we may call "positive" religious views that claim belief in God, ordering principles of the universe, etc., but also for "negative" views concerning religion, mainly an atheism that denies the existence of positive religious truth, and agnostic views that eschew assertion of positive or negative truth about God and other central religious subjects? An atheist or agnostic approach requires that how to lead a good life and act toward other persons must be determined independently of religious understanding (unless one's understanding of life is largely determined by despair that the universe lacks meaning). Neither atheism nor agnosticism fits well with a principle that the state should enforce or support positive religious beliefs, but each, standing alone, has less bearing on what political life should be like than do most positive religious views.

8. In actual life, things can be a bit more complicated; some people do feel sometimes that what they regard as genuine religious considerations not only give way in the face of temptation, but actually can be outweighed by other considerations.

9. I do not mean that one necessarily thinks the practices should be imposed on people who object to them.

10. Any particular substantive political principles and the techniques for arriving at them are bound to be at odds with *some* religious views.

11. As I have mentioned, a common Christian view has been that natural law (discoverable without reliance on religious premises) and revelation (resting on religious premises) yield the same conclusions.

12. Of course, Faith's reflection on freedom and consent in pluralist societies *might* lead her to think the true religion should not be supported by government even if 98 percent of the people believe it. The passage in the text is not meant to state a view about whether Faith's position is defensible; but I do think many people would find government support of religious views to be more appropriate than it would otherwise be if acceptance of a particular view were nearly universal in the society.

13. For example, someone who strongly believes in a political principle of equality between men and women may begin to feel uncomfortable about unequal status within their church; someone who accepts powerful hierarchy of religious organization may be inclined to find political hierarchy appropriate.

14. See, e.g., Michael Perry, *Love and Power* (New York, Oxford University Press 1991); Joseph Raz, "Facing Diversity: The Case of Epistemic Abstinence," 19 *Philosophy and Public Affairs* 3 (1990).

15. See generally chapter 8.

16. Of course, one might make an argument that only naturalist grounds really qualify in this way.

17. It is conceivable that particular reasons would attach to particular comprehensive views, and that a happy coincidence of quite different reasons applicable to different comprehensive views would yield mutual restraint. This *is* a logical possibility, but it seems very unlikely in fact that people would agree on mutual restraint unless there were some commonality in their reasons for doing so.

Chapter 12

1. In retrospect, I can see that some issues raised in this book might have been relevant when I worked for the federal government, as a law clerk to Justice John M. Harlan, as a special assistant in the Agency for International Development, and as deputy solicitor general; but I can recall no occasion when they mattered personally.

2. No doubt, *if* an organization had been formed to have beer parties outside the limits of (dry) Swarthmore, that organization would not have been funded. Also, the relative amounts of money given various organizations may have reflected some implicit evaluations, but the main criteria were numbers of participants and costs of programs.

3. Conceivably, if inappropriate grounds are widely enough stated, that can be a basis for someone else, typically a court, to hold the decision invalid.

4. In parliamentary systems, the executive is much more closely linked to the legislature; ordinarily, whether one political party is dominant, as in Great Britain, or a coalition of parties is in power, as in Italy, the executive "cabinet" is virtually assured that legislation it wants will be approved by Parliament.

5. Some decisions of independent administrative agencies are made by voting. However, the number of people casting votes is small (five is typical in the United States), more like a court than a legislature.

Chapter 13

1. See generally Kent Greenawalt, *Law and Objectivity* (New York, Oxford University Press 1992).

2. Some modern cases in which opinions, mainly concurring and dissenting opinions, employ religious values are cited in Scott C. Idleman, "The Role of Religious Values in Judicial Decision Making," 68 *Indiana Law Journal* 433, 475–77 (1993). Some of these opinions use the religious sources mainly to establish the truth of some moral or political position, e.g., the wrongness of homosexual behavior; others concentrate on establishing the values of our culture. For an example of what is now a highly unusual direct reliance on a religious source to establish a moral proposition of legal relevance, see the separate opinion of Justice Henderson opposing visitation rights for a lesbian mother in Chicoine v. Chicoine, 479 N.W.2d 891 (S.D. 1992). He writes, among other things, "Until . . . she can establish . . . that she is no longer a lesbian living a life of abomination (see Leviticus 18:22), she should be totally estopped from contaminating these children." Id. at 896.

3. Rochin v. California, 342 U.S. 165, 172 (1952).

4. Kent Greenawalt, *Religious Convictions and Political Choice* 239–41 (New York, Oxford University Press 1988).

5. Stephen L. Carter, "The Religiously Devout Judge," 64 *Notre Dame Law Review* 932 (1989).

6. Idleman, supra note 2.

7. Carter, supra note 5.

8. Sanford Levinson has written in depth about the confirmation of Catholic justices in "The Confrontation of Religious Faith and Civil Religion: Catholics Becoming Justices," 39 *DePaul Law Review* 1047 (1990). Justice Kennedy's remark that "it would be highly improper for a judge to allow his or her own per-

sonal or religious views to enter into a decision respecting a constitutional matter" is illustrative. Id. at 1065.

9. See also Howard J. Vogel, "The Judicial Oath and the American Creed: Comments on Sanford Levinson's 'The Confrontation of Religious Faith and Civil Religion: Catholics Becoming Justices,' " 39 *DePaul Law Review* 1107 (1990).

10. Carter, supra note 5, at 933. Carter makes a much broader claim that American politics and law trivialize religion in *The Culture of Disbelief* (New York, Basic Books 1993).

11. Carter, supra note 5, at 935.

12. Id.

13. See Kenneth D. Wald, *Religion and Politics in the United States* (New York, St. Martin's Press 1987). As I suggest below, it is not possible to be *sure* of a causal relationship *or* its direction if religious affiliations correlate with political decisions.

14. Greenawalt, supra note 1, part 3.

15. Carter, supra note 5, at 939.

16. Id.

17. I note again that some people do think their religious views can be strongly established or supported on a reasoned basis.

18. Richard Fallon, Jr., presents a powerful argument for this position in "Of Speakable Ethics and Constitutional Law," 56 *University of Chicago Law Review* 1523, 1544–52 (1989) (review essay).

19. Stephen L. Carter, "Evolutionism, Creationism, and Treating Religion as a Hobby," 1987 *Duke Law Journal* 977. He concludes, however, the decision was "correct because of the difficulty of articulating the precise secular purpose for the teaching of creationism." Carter, supra note 10, at 168–69. Gregory Gelfand concludes that the teaching of evolution, because it rejects a religious view, should be held to violate the establishment clause, in "Of Monkeys and Men—An Atheist's Heretical View of the Constitutionality of Teaching the Disproof of a Religion in the Public Schools," 16 *Journal of Law and Education* 271 (1987).

20. What I say in the text is compatible with Carter's treatment, but it oversimplifies in various respects. Insofar as creation scientists argue that evidence *fails to support* the claim that higher species evolved from primitive life forms, they use the methods of ordinary science to cast doubt on major claims about evolution. The creation science to which I refer in the text is one that closely corresponds with a literal understanding of the biblical account. Murray Gell-Mann has pointed out that creation science challenges a large portion of science. "First Word," *Omni,* February 1987, at 8. The more modest claims that a Divine Creator is ultimately responsible for life on earth and that *some* progress in life forms may not be explained by evolution are not so clearly at odds with what ordinary scientific techniques can now establish. (Indeed, the former claim is incapable of being disproved by science.) For a sharp exchange over the claims of creation science and evolution, see Phillip E. Johnson, "Evolution as Dogma: The Establishment of Naturalism," and five responses, in *First Things,* October 1990, at 15–28. (Johnson's notion of creationism is much more inclusive than the narrow biblical view to which I refer.)

21. See Fallon, supra note 18, at 1550.

22. Idleman, supra note 2, at 479.

23. Id. at 483, n.177.

24. I am doubtful that this condition is ever met.

25. One might argue that if a judge is *ever* to subvert the law, rather than

resign, he must have public reasons for doing so. Thus, a refusal to enforce the fugitive slave law might have been justified on the basis of a "public reason" that people are equal.

26. A contrary position is taken by Thomas L. Shaffer, on "Checking the Artifacts of Canaan: A Comment on Levinson's 'Confrontation,' " 39 *DePaul Law Review* 1133 (1990); he would welcome such reasoning in opinions. Fallon, supra note 18, at 1551 n.89, has expressed strong opposition to my view. He thinks judges should not rely on personal convictions but that if they do, it would be desirable to have that revealed.

Chapter 14

1. See David Hollenbach, S.J., "Contexts of the Political Role of Religion: Civil Society and Culture" 30 *San Diego Law Review* 877 (1993). See also Ruti Teitel, "A Critique of Religion as Politics in the Public Sphere," 78 *Cornell Law Review* 747, 793–94 (1993).

2. See Kenneth D. Wald, *Religion and Politics in the United States* 157 (New York, St. Martin's Press 1987).

3. Robert Booth Fowler, *Religion and Politics in America* 111 (Metuchen, N.J., American Theological Library Association and Scarecrow Press 1985).

4. Id. at 111.

5. Id. at 123.

6. Id. at 124.

7. "Praise the Lord and Pass the Loot," *Economist*, May 16, 1987, at 23. See Richard V. Pierard and Robert D. Linder, *Civil Religion and the Presidency* 274, 276–79 (Grand Rapids, Mich., Academie Books 1988). Like Reagan, Presidents Truman and Eisenhower had commonly contrasted America's "faith in God" with its godless communist opponents. See id. at 189–90. Reagan's relationship with religion and religious leaders is contrasted with that of Carter in William Ker Muir, *The Bully Pulpit: The Presidential Leadership of Ronald Reagan* 129–45 (San Francisco: Institute for Contemporary Studies Press 1972).

8. Fowler, supra note 3, at 129.

9. See Wald, supra note 2, at 160.

10. Id. at 157–59.

11. Fowler, supra note 3, at 131.

12. Id.

13. Id.

14. Id. at 133.

15. Id. at 134.

16. Mary Hanna, *Catholics and American Politics* 99 (Cambridge, Mass., Harvard University Press 1979).

17. See 137 *Congressional Record* S325–404, (daily ed. January 12, 1991). Senator Warner was the only speaker to invoke the Bible. He said, "Each of us in searching his own conscience, I am sure, has gone to the Bible. I go to Corinthians 14:8 which reads, 'For if the trumpet give an uncertain sound, who shall prepare himself to the battle.'" Id. at S392

18. The administration had adopted a rule forbidding doctors at projects receiving federal funds for family planning from mentioning possibilities for abortion to their patients. After a legal challenge to the rule had failed, Congress voted to alter it. President Bush vetoed this 1992 Family Planning Amendment Act. The

rule has been retracted during the Clinton administration. See Remarks on Signing Memorandums on Medical Research and Reproductive Health at an Exchange With Reporters, 29 Weekly Comp. Pres. Docs. 85 (Jan. 22, 1993).

19. 138 *Congressional Record* H10667–72, H10673 (statement of Rep. Dornan) (daily ed. October 2, 1992).

20. Wald, supra note 2, at 194.

21. This explicit formulation of kinds of inaccessibility was suggested to me by Vincent Blasi.

22. See especially *Religious Convictions and Political Choice* (New York, Oxford University Press 1988).

23. For what they do as quasi-public citizens, these people should probably try harder to find a *balance of public reasons* in favor of *their judgments* on positions than need ordinary citizens. In this respect, they are not so unlike legislators, whose decisions are discussed below.

24. This distinction, which now seems meaningful to me, is not one that I have drawn in my earlier work.

25. On this version, public reasons for legislators would include some deference to the opinions of citizens, even when *these* are not grounded in public reasons.

26. This roughly is the approach I am most comfortable with on the law faculty, though I do not suppose that following that approach is a general responsibility of members of the faculty.

27. Some statements of senators in the debate whether to approve the Gulf War were an interesting exception to this.

28. See, e.g., Teitel, supra note 1, at 780–92.

29. See Abner S. Greene, "The Political Balance of the Religion Clauses," 102 *Yale Law Journal* 1611, 1623 (1993).

Chapter 15

1. I draw substantially from James E. Wood, Jr., and Derek Davis, eds., *The Role of Religion in the Making of Public Policy* (Waco, Tex., J. M. Dawson Institute of Church-State Studies 1991); Robert Booth Fowler, *Religion and Politics in America* (Metuchen, N.J., American Theological Library Association and Scarecrow Press 1985); Robert Booth Fowler, *Unconventional Partners* (Grand Rapids, Mich., Wm. B. Eerdmans Publishing 1989); Kenneth D. Wald, *Religion and Politics in the United States* (New York, St. Martin's Press 1987); Allen D. Hertzke, *Representing God in Washington* (Knoxville, University of Tennessee Press 1988); A. James Reichley, *Religion in American Public Life* (Washington, D.C., Brookings Institution 1985).

2. Kelley, "The Rationale for the Involvement of Religion in the Body Politic," in Wood and Davis, supra note 1, at 159–60.

3. Lowell Weicker, Jr., when he was a senator, said more succinctly, "When you introduce religion into politics, you're playing with fire." Wald, supra note 1, at 1. At least one country, Singapore, regards the mixture of religion and politics as *so* potentially destructive that a 1990 Maintenance of Religious Harmony Act makes it a crime for a religious group or member thereof to carry "out activities to promote a political cause . . . under the guise of propagating . . . any religious belief." Such a law would, of course, be a blatant violation of the First Amendment

free exercise and free speech clauses in this country.

4. Cushing Strout, "Religion and Politics Prior to World War II," in Wood and Davis, supra note 1, at 26.

5. Kelley, supra note 2, at 163–64.

6. Id. at 164.

7. At least in northeastern states, including my own, once-forbidden lotteries have reemerged, replete with skillful advertising to prod the susceptible to invest at unpromising odds.

8. Kelley, supra note 2, at 163.

9. Strout, supra note 4, at 29.

10. James E. Wood, Jr., "Introduction," in Wood and Davis, supra note 1, at 3 (internal quotations omitted).

11. Fowler, *Religion and Politics in America,* supra note 1, at 140, 142. See also Michael E. Smith, "Religious Activism: The Historical Record," 27 *William and Mary Law Review* 1087, 1090 (1986).

12. Fowler, supra note 11, at 145.

13. Id. at 145–46.

14. Allen D. Hertzke, "An Assessment of the Mainline Churches Since 1945," in Wood and Davis, supra note 1, at 49. See also Stephen L. Carter, *The Culture of Disbelief* 227–29 (New York, BasicBooks 1993).

15. Fowler, *Religion and Politics in America,* supra note 1, at 160.

16. See generally Wald, supra note 1, at 2–10.

17. Fowler, supra note 11, at 37.

18. Id. at 38–40.

19. Professor Fowler draws this contrast as if an unrelieved liberalism is ill-suited, even intolerable, for most people. I think Fowler is right if the focus is on liberalism as a philosophy of life. If, instead, one thinks of liberalism as essentially a political theory, a philosophy of how the organized state should function, then liberalism is perfectly compatible *in theory and in practice* with other social institutions that emphasize collective and transcendent aspects of life. Religious life of most sorts fits well with liberalism as a political theory, even as it offers a refuge from a thoroughgoing liberal approach to all of life.

20. See Wald, supra note 1, at 183–84.

21. Id. at 184.

22. Kelley, supra note 2, at 168.

23. Id. at 170.

24. Id. at 171.

25. Id. at 177.

26. Wald, supra note 1, at 2.

27. Id. at 83.

28. Fowler, supra note 11, at 178.

29. Hertzke, supra note 14, at 44.

30. Id.

31. Fowler, supra note 11, at 203–26.

32. Robert Wuthnow, "The Religious Right and Symbolic Politics," in Wood and Davis, supra note 1, at 88–89.

33. Id. at 89. Wuthnow defines politics as "all the formally organized or institutionalized ways in which a society governs itself" and public policy as the "outcome of the political process with respect to specific substantive issues." Id. at 84.

He treats the "public arena," "public life," or "public sphere" as broader than politics and public policy; it is the "on-going discourse that takes place in any society about its collective values." Id. at 85.

34. Id. at 83.

35. James E. Wood, Jr., "Religion and the U.S. Presidential Election of 1992," 34 *Journal of Church and State* 726 (1992) (editorial).

36. Id.

37. Wald, supra note 1, at 250.

38. Fowler, *Religion and Politics in America,* supra note 1, at 201.

39. Id. at 171.

40. Id. at 172.

41. Wuthnow, supra note 32, at 92.

42. McDaniel v. Paty, 435 U.S. 618 (1978).

43. Religious Freedom Restoration Act of 1993, 107 Stat. 1488, codified at 42 U.S.C.A. §2000bb–2000bb–4 (Law. Co-op Supp. 1994).

44. Oregon Employment Division v. Smith, 110 S.Ct. 1595 (1990). The crucial issue in the case was whether members of the Native American Church had a free exercise right to use peyote in their religious ceremonies, despite a state ban on use of peyote.

45. Wald, supra note 1, at 273–75.

46. The Internal Revenue Code, governing exemptions of religious organizations from income tax and the deductibility of private contributions, bears on political activity. To maintain their eligibility for these benefits, churches must not intervene in political campaigns on behalf of candidates or make attempts to influence legislation a "substantial" part of their activities. These provisions have not been rigorously enforced, however, and their indirect restrictions on what churches can do are controversial. Thus, political involvements by churches are not in themselves illegal, though some might affect their tax status. See generally Derek Davis, "The Supreme Court, Public Policy, and the Advocacy Rights of Churches," in Wood and Davis, supra note 1, at 101–25.

47. Wood, supra note 35, at 728.

Conclusion

1. Of course, someone else might believe that conversion will not be served by political argument in religious terms.

2. This is a little like the opportunities that family life offers for rejecting conventional understandings of what it is to be a good parent, or child, or sibling. A parent, say, who ceases to give any financial support to a child after eighteen, on the view that this will be good for the child, could be failing in desirable and conventional responsibilities and still be acting with some sense of what it is right to do within one's role.

3. Ordinary failures would be criticized differently from deviation by conviction.

Bibliography

Books

Ackerman, Bruce. *Social Justice in the Liberal State.* New Haven, Conn.: Yale University Press, 1980.

Apel, Karl-Otto. "The Problem of a Universalistic Macroethics." In *What Right Does Ethics Have?* ed. S. Griffoen. Amsterdam: Vrije Universiteit Press, 1990.

Brink, David O. *Moral Realism and the Foundations of Ethics.* Cambridge: Cambridge University Press, 1989.

Callahan, Daniel, and Courtney S. Campbell, eds. *Theology, Religious Traditions, and Bioethics.* Hastings Center Report, July/August (1990), Special Supplement.

Cardozo, Benjamin Nathan. *The Nature of the Judicial Process.* New Haven, Conn.: Yale University Press, 1921.

Carter, Stephen L. *The Culture of Disbelief.* New York: Basic Books, 1993.

Davis, Caroline Franks. *The Evidential Force of Religious Experience.* Oxford: Clarendon Press, 1989.

Davis, Derek. "The Supreme Court, Public Policy, and the Advocacy Rights of Churches." In *The Role of Religion in the Making of Public Policy,* ed. James E. Wood, Jr., and Derek Davis. Waco, Tex.: J. M. Dawson Institute of Church-State Studies, 1991.

Dworkin, R. *Law's Empire.* Cambridge, Mass.: Harvard University Press, 1986.

Fowler, Robert Booth. *Unconventional Partners.* Grand Rapids, Mich.: Wm. B. Eerdmans Publishing, 1989.

———. *Religion and Politics in America.* Metuchen, N.J.: American Theological Library Association and Scarecrow Press, 1985.

George, Robert, ed. *Natural Law Theory.* Oxford: Oxford University Press, 1992.

Greenawalt, Kent. *Law and Objectivity.* New York: Oxford University Press, 1992.

———. *Religious Convictions and Political Choice.* New York: Oxford University Press, 1988.

———. *Conflicts of Law and Morality.* New York: Clarendon Press, 1987.

Griffoen, S., ed. *What Right Does Ethics Have?* Amsterdam: Vrije Universiteit Press, 1990.

Habermas, Jürgen. "Discourse Ethics: Notes on a Program of Philosophical Justificaton." In *Moral Consciousness and Communicative Action*, trans. Christian Lenhardt and Shierry Weber Nicholsen. Cambridge, Mass.: M.I.T. Press, 1990.

Hanna, Mary. *Catholics and American Politics*. Cambridge, Mass.: Harvard University Press, 1979.

Hart, H.L.A. *The Concept of Law*. Oxford: Clarendon Press, 1961.

Hertzke, Allan D. *Representing God in Washington*. Knoxville: University of Tennessee Press, 1988.

―――. "An Assessment of the Mainline Churches Since 1945." In *The Role of Religion in the Making of Public Policy*, ed. James E. Wood, Jr., and Derek Davis. Waco, Tex.: J. M. Dawson Institute of Church-State Studies, 1991.

James, William. *The Varieties of Religious Experience*. Harmondsworth, U.K.: Penguin Books, 1985.

Kelley, Dean M. "The Rationale for the Involvement of Religion in the Body Politic." In *The Role of Religion in the Making of Public Policy*, ed. James E. Wood, Jr., and Derek Davis. Waco, Tex.: J. M. Dawson Institute of Church-State Studies, 1991.

Larmore, Charles. *Patterns of Moral Complexity*. New York: Cambridge University Press, 1987.

Lenhardt, Christian, and Shierry Weber Nicholsen, trans. *Moral Consciousness and Communicative Action*. Cambridge, Mass.: M.I.T. Press, 1990.

Lloyd, Dennis. *The Idea of Law*. Baltimore: Penguin Books, 1964.

MacIntyre, Alasdair. *After Virtue*. London: Duckworth, 1981.

Mackie, J. L. *Ethics: Inventing Right and Wrong*. Harmondsworth, U.K.: Penguin Books, 1977.

Marty, Martin E. *The Public Church: Mainline, Evangelical, Catholic*. New York: Crossroad, 1981.

Muir, William Ker. *The Bully Pulpit: The Presidential Leadership of Ronald Reagan*. San Francisco: Institute for Contemporary Studies Press, 1972.

Murphy, Jeffrie. "Afterword: Constitutionalism, Moral Skepticism, and Religious Belief." In *Constitutionalism: The Philosophical Dimension*, ed. Alan S. Rosenbaum. New York: Greenwood Press, 1988.

Nagel, Thomas. *Equality and Partiality*. New York: Oxford University Press, 1991.

National Conference of Catholic Bishops. *Economic Justice for All: Pastoral Letter on Catholic Social Teaching and the U.S. Economy*. Washington, D.C.: United States Catholic Conference 1986.

Perry, Michael. *Love and Power*. New York: Oxford University Press, 1992.

Pierard, Richard V., and Robert D. Linder. *Civil Religion and the Presidency*. Grand Rapids, Mich.: Academie Books, 1988.

Presbyterian Church (U.S.A.). God Alone is Lord of the Conscience, A Policy Statement Adopted by the 200th General Assembly. 1989.

Putnam, Hilary. *The Many Faces of Realism*. LaSalle, Ill.: Open Court, 1985.

Rawls, John. *Political Liberalism*. New York: Columbia University Press, 1993.

―――. *A Theory of Justice*. Cambridge, Mass.: Harvard University Press, 1971.

Raz, Joseph. *The Authority of Law*. Oxford: Clarendon Press, 1979.

―――. *Practical Reason and Norms*. London: Hutchinson, 1975.

Reichley, A. James. *Religion in American Public Life.* Washington, D.C.: Brookings Institution, 1985.

Rosenbaum, Alan S., ed. *Constitutionalism: The Philosophical Dimension.* New York: Greenwood Press, 1988.

Sayre-McCord, Geoffrey, ed. *Essays on Moral Realism.* Ithaca, N.Y.: Cornell University Press, 1988.

Strout, Cushing. "Religion and Politics Prior to World War II." In *The Role of Religion in the Making of Public Policy,* ed. James E. Wood, Jr., and Derek Davis. Waco, Tex.: J. M. Dawson Institute of Church-State Studies, 1991.

Swinburne, Richard. *The Existence of God.* Oxford: Clarendon Press, 1979.

Wald, Kenneth D. *Religion and Politics in the United States.* New York: St. Martin's Press, 1987.

Waldron, Jeremy. "The Irrelevance of Moral Objectivity." In *Natural Law Theory,* ed. Robert George. Oxford: Oxford University Press, 1991.

Wood, James E., Jr., and Derek Davis, eds. *The Role of Religion in the Making of Public Policy.* Waco, Tex.: J. M. Dawson, Institute of Church-State Studies, 1991.

Wood, James E., Jr. "Introduction." In *The Role of Religion in the Making of Public Policy,* ed. James E. Wood, Jr., and Derek Davis. Waco, Tex.: J. M. Dawson Institute of Church-State Studies, 1991.

Wuthnow, Robert. "The Religious Right and Symbolic Politics." In *The Role of Religion in the Making of Public Policy,* ed. James E. Wood, Jr., and Derek Davis. Waco, Tex.: J. M. Dawson Institute of Church-State Studies, 1991.

Journals, Manuscripts

Alexander, Larry. "Liberalism, Religion, and the Unity of Epistemology." 30 *San Diego Law Review* (1993), 763.

———. "Law and Exclusionary Reasons." 18 *Philosophical Topics* (1990), 5.

Audi, Robert. "The Place of Religious Argument in a Free and Democratic Society." 30 *San Diego Law Review* (1993), 677.

———. "Religion and the Ethics of Political Participation." Review essay. 100 *Ethics* (1990), 386.

———. "The Separation of Church and State and the Obligations of Citizenship." 18 *Philosophy and Public Affairs* (1989), 259.

Berman, Harold. "The Interaction of Law and Religion. 31 *Mercer Law Review* (1980), 405.

Calhoun, Samuel W. "Conviction Without Imposition: A Response to Professor Greenawalt." 9 *Journal of Law and Religion* (1992), 289.

———. "Misreading the Judeo-Christian Tradition and the Law: A Response to Professor Smolin." 15 *University of Dayton Law Review* (1990), 383.

Carter, Stephen L. "The Religiously Devout Judge." 64 *Notre Dame Law Review* (1989), 932.

———. "Evolutionism, Creationism, and Treating Religion as a Hobby." 1987 *Duke Law Journal* (1977), 977.

Conkle, Daniel. "Different Religions, Different Politics: Evaluating the Role of Competing Religious Traditions in American Politics and Law." 10 *Journal of Law and Religion* (1993), 1.

———. "God Loveth Adverbs." 42 *DePaul Law Review* (1992), 339.

Economist. "Praise the Lord and Pass the Loot," May 16, 1987, at 23.

Fallon, Richard Jr. "Of Speakable Ethics and Constitutional Law: A Review Essay." 56 *University of Chicago Law Review* (1989), 1523.

Foley, Edward B. "Tillich and Camus, Talking Politics." Review essay. 92 *Columbia Law Review* (1992), 954.

Gamwell, Franklin. "Book Review: *Religious Convictions and Political Chioce.*" 8 *Journal of Law and Religion* (1990), 461.

———. "Religion and Reason in American Politics." 2 *Journal of Law and Religion* (1984), 325.

Gedicks, Frederick Mark. "Public Life and Hostility to Religion." 78 *Virginia Law Review* (1992), 671.

Gelfand, Gregory, and Toby R. Levin. "Fetal Tissue Research: Legal Regulation of Human Fetal Tissue Transplantation." 50 *Washington and Lee Law Review* (1993), 647.

———. "Of Monkeys and Men: An Atheist's Heretical View of the Constitutionality of Teaching the Disproof of a Religion in the Public Schools." 16 *Journal of Law and Education* (1987), 271.

Gell-Mann, Murray. "First Word." *Omni* (February 1987), 8.

Greenawalt, Kent. "Religious Convictions and Political Choice: Some Further Thoughts." 39 *DePaul Law Review* (1990), 1019.

———. "Religion as a Concept in Constitutional Law." 72 *California Law Review* (1984), 753.

Greene, Abner S. "The Political Balance of the Religion Clauses." 102 *Yale Law Journal* (1993), 1611.

Gutmann, Amy, and Dennis Thompson. "Moral Conflict and Political Consensus." 101 *Ethics* (1990), 64.

Hall, Timothy. "Religion and Civic Virtue: A Justification of Free Exercise." 67 *Tulane Law Review* (1992), 87.

Habermas, Jürgen. "Morality and Ethical Life: Does Hegel's Critique of Kant Apply to Discourse Ethics?" 83 *Northwestern University Law Review* (1989), 38.

Hollenbach, David. "Contexts of the Political Role of Religion: Civil Society and Culture." 30 *San Diego Law Review* (1993), 877.

Holmes, Oliver Wendell. "The Path of the Law." 10 *Harvard Law Review* (1897), 457.

Idleman, Scott C. "The Role of Religious Values in Judicial Decision-Making." 68 *Indiana Law Journal* (1993), 433.

Johnson, Phillip E. "Evolution as Dogma: The Establishment of Naturalism," and five responses. *First Things* (October 1990), 15.

Larmore, Charles. "Political Liberalism." 18 *Political Theory* (1990), 339.

Levinson, Sanford. "Religious Language and the Public Square." 105 *Harvard Law Review* (1992), 2061.

———. "The Confrontation of Religious Faith and Civil Religion: Catholics Becoming Justices." 39 *DePaul Law Review* (1990), 1047.

Lovin, Robin. "Perry, Naturalism, and Religion." 63 *Tulane Law Review* (1989), 1517.

Marshall, William P. "The Other Side of Religion." 44 *Hastings Law Journal* (1993), 843.

Nagel, Thomas. "Moral Conflict and Political Legitimacy." 16 *Philosophy and Public Affairs* (1987), 215.

Perry, Michael J. "Further Thoughts—And Second Thoughts—On *Love and Power.*" 30 *San Diego Law Review* (1993), 702.

Rawls, John. "The Domain of the Political and Overlapping Consensus." 64 *New York University Law Review* (1989), 233.

———. "The Idea of an Overlapping Consensus." 7 *Oxford Journal of Legal Studies* (1987), 1.

———. "Justice as Fairness: Political Not Metaphysical." 14 *Philosophy and Public Affairs* (1985), 223.

———. "Kantian Constructivism in Moral Theory: The Dewey Lectures." 77 *Journal of Philosophy* (1980), 539.

Raz, Joseph. "Facing Diversity: The Case of Epistemic Abstinence." 19 *Philosophy and Public Affairs* (1990), 3.

Replogle, Ronald. "Equality and Moral Uncertainty" (unpublished seminar paper), Columbia University School of Law, New York, Autumn 1992.

Richards, David. Book Review, 23 *Georgia Law Review* (1989), 1189.

Schwarzschild, Maimon. "Religion and Public Debate in a Liberal Society: Always Oil and Water or Sometimes More Like Rum and Coca-Cola?" 30 *San Diego Law Review* (1993), 903.

Shaffer, Thomas L. "Checking the Artifacts of Canaan: A Comment on Levinson's 'Confrontation,' " 39 *DePaul Law Review* (1990), 1133.

Smith, Steven D. "The Rise and Fall of Religious Freedom in Constitutional Discourse." 140 *University of Pennsylvania Law Review* (1991), 149.

———. "Separation and the 'Secular': Reconstructing the Disestablishment Decision." 67 *Texas Law Review* (1989), 955.

———. "Religious Activism: The Historical Record." 27 *William and Mary Law Review* (1986), 1087.

Smolin, David. "Regulating Religious and Cultural Conflict in Postmodern America: A Response to Professor Perry." 76 *Iowa Law Review* (1991), 1067.

———. "The Enforcement of Natural Law by the State: A Response to Professor Calhoun." 16 *University of Dayton Law Review* (1991), 381.

———. "The Judeo-Christian Tradition and Self-Censorship in Legal Discourse." 13 *University of Dayton Law Review* (1988), 345.

Solum, Lawrence. "Faith and Justice." 39 *DePaul Law Review* (1990), 1083.

Teitel, Ruti. "A Critique of Religion as Politics in the Public Sphere." 78 *Cornell Law Review* (1993), 747.

Van Wyck, Robert M. "Liberalism, Religion and Politics." 1 *Public Affairs Quarterly* (No. 3, 1987), 59.

Vogel, Howard J. "The Judicial Oath and the American Creed: Comments on Sanford Levinson's 'The Confrontation of Religious Faith and Civil Religion: Catholics Become Justices.' " 39 *DePaul Law Review* (1990), 1107.

Waldron, Jeremy. "Religious Contributions in Pubic Deliberation." 30 *San Diego Law Review* (1993), 817.

Winston, Kenneth I. "The Religious Convictions of Officials." 3 *Canadian Journal of Law and Jurisprudence* (1990), 129.

Wood, James E., Jr. "Religion and the U.S. Presidential Election of 1992." Editorial. 34 *Journal of Church and State* (1992), 726.

Cases

Chicoine v. Chicoine, 479 N.W.2d 891 (S.D. 1992).
McDaniel v. Paty, 435 U.S. 618 (1978).
Oregon Employment Division v. Smith, 110 S.Ct. 1595 (1990).
Rochin v. California, 342 U.S. 165 (1951).
Roe v. Wade, 410 U.S. 413 (1973).
School District v. Schempp, 374 U.S. 203 (1963).

Congressional Debates

137 *Cong. Rec.* S325–404, daily edition, January 12, 1991.
138 *Cong. Rec.* H10667-02, H10673, daily edition, October 2, 1992.

Index

Abortion, 5, 63, 65, 88, 91, 98, 112, 116–17, 154, 155, 159–60, 174, 177

Accessible beliefs, 5, 10, 23–38, 129–30, 139, 150, 157, 158; and citizen decision, 159; and comprehensive views, 44–46; and ethical views, 88; and generalizability, 34–35; and intelligibility, 40, 90; and miracles, 41; Perry's principle of, 90, 92–93; and realist reasons, 26–28; and reasonable disagreement, 77; and religious grounds, 40–43, 44; and restraint, 75–78; three reasons for exclusion of, 45–46. *See also* Nonaccessible grounds

Advocacy vs. decision, 134, 137–39, 204n. 38; and legislators and citizens, 151–64

Ackerman, Bruce, 78–79, 183n. 2, 185n. 16, 194n. 25, 194n. 26, 195n. 38

Alexander, Larry, 101, 102, 188n. 2, 201n. 38, 201n. 46

Animals: protection of, 58–59, 62, 68, 77, 146, 159

Anti-religious vs. non-religious views, 63, 70, 190n. 2

Apel, Karl-Otto, 185n. 16

Aristotelian models of public deliberation, 100

Arts funding: and political neutrality, 80, 195n. 31

Atheism and agnosticism, 206n. 7

Audi, Robert, 10, 112, 190n. 1, 191n. 7, 191n. 8, 191n. 9, 191n. 11, 191n. 12, 191n. 17, 191n. 18, 192n. 19, 192n. 34; three principles of restraint as to religious arguments, 64–69

Authority reasons, 10, 24, 31–33, 51, 52–54

Autonomy: of liberal political theory, 8, 133; liberal principle of, 66; of principles of restraint, 121–25, 131

Beecher, Lyman, 167
Bellah, Robert, 92
Biblical infallibility, 87
Burr, Aaron, 167
Bush, George, 155, 172, 209n. 18
Brink, David O., 184n. 3
Bryan, William Jennings, 169

Calhoun, Samuel W, 200n. 20
Camus, Albert, 66
Cardozo, Benjamin Nathan, 186n. 22
Carter, Jimmy, 153, 155–56, 158, 209n. 7
Carter, Stephen L., 101–2, 143–47, 149, 201n. 42, 207n. 5, 208n. 10, 208n. 19, 208n. 20
Chicoine v. Chicoine, 207n. 2
Christian belief, grounds for, 40–44
Church-state separation, 64–71, 116–17, 204n. 47
Churches: and party politics, 175; and politics in American history, 166–

219